Polar Voyages

Polar Voyages

GORDON GRAY

AMBERLEY

This book is dedicated to my wife Doreen,
who shares my love of ships, the sea and the polar regions

For speed and efficiency of travel give me Amundsen.
For scientific discovery give me Scott.
But when disaster strikes and all hope is gone,
get down on your knees and pray for Shackleton.

– Sir Raymond Priestly
Antarctic Explorer

Cover Picture. *Top image*: Author's Collection. *Bottom image*: Taken from a painting in the author's collection and with the kind permission of and thanks to the artist, Jenny Morgan, RSMA.

First published 2015

Amberley Publishing
The Hill, Stroud
Gloucestershire, GL5 4EP

www.amberleybooks.com

Copyright © Gordon Gray, 2015

The right of Gordon Gray to be identified as the Author of this work has been asserted in accordance with the Copyrights, Designs and Patents Act 1988.

All rights reserved. No part of this book may be reprinted or reproduced or utilised in any form or by any electronic, mechanical or other means, now known or hereafter invented, including photocopying and recording, or in any information storage or retrieval system, without the permission in writing from the Publishers.

British Library Cataloguing in Publication Data.
A catalogue record for this book is available from the British Library.

ISBN 978 1 4456 4748 7 (print)
ISBN 978 1 4456 4749 4 (ebook)

Typesetting and Origination by Amberley Publishing.
Printed in Great Britain.

Contents

Foreword	The Steamer	6
Chapter 1	ST *Lord Lovat* – A Trip to Icelandic Fishing Grounds	8
Chapter 2	The Royal Navy – Officer Training	44
Chapter 3	HMS *Keppel* – Midshipman's Training	59
Chapter 4	HMS *Rhyl*	72
Chapter 5	Wardroom to Fish Dock	85
Chapter 6	MV *Marco Polo* – The Antarctic	101
Chapter 7	*Professor Molchanov* – NE Greenland	124
Chapter 8	I/B *Kapitan Dranitsyn* – Franz Joseph Land	144
Chapter 9	The North Pole	175
Chapter 10	MV *Stockholm* – Spitzbergen – In Search of Polar Bears	199
Chapter 11	MV *Lofoten*	221
Chapter 12	*Fram* and Antarctica	239
Chapter 13	*Akademic Ioffe* and the Northwest Passage	260
Chapter 14	Three Key Elements – Ships, the Sea and Ice	281

FOREWORD
The Steamer

On a blustery, west highland summer's day in the early 1950s, a black-hulled, mail steamer ploughed its way northwards from Mallaig up through the sound of Sleat between the mainland of Scotland and the Isle of Skye. The spray from her bow wave flew high up her sides and dark smoke was tugged from her bright-red funnel by the wind. On the open deck, by the rails at the stern of the ship, a family group sat huddled in coats on the wooden benches while enjoying the majestic views on each side of the ship. In spite of the wind, the day was fine and the warm sun shone on the greens and purples of the heather-clad hills of Knoydart and deep into the dark entrance of Loch Hourn, while across to the west, on the Skye shoreline, the sun bathed the dazzling white lighthouse in light. A small boy, aged about two or three, wearing a green knitted top and blue dungarees, sat on the warm deck peering through the rails, his face smiling widely with excitement. The gentle roll of the wooden deck, the smoke blowing from the funnel, the sea splashing past in the wake, the seagulls wheeling overhead squawking furiously and the mixture of strange smells all filled him with excitement and enthralled him.

The boy was called back by his parents, as they were soon due to get off the steamer. They had to go down inside the steamer to a door near the waterline so they could get into an open boat that would take them ashore to the small coastal village of Glenelg.

A bright-red, clinker-built, open motor boat with just one man at the helm came out to the ship from the village, which was just a line of small, single-storeyed, white houses along the distant shore. The steamer slowed and turned across the wind then stopped to give a lee to the motor boat as it came alongside. A big, heavy, steel door near the steamer's waterline was opened and the people who had gathered by the door watched as the boat rolled and bobbed through the waves towards the steamer, with splashes of spray leaping from its bows. Mail, parcels and passengers for Glenelg were passed down to the man in the boat. The small boy was aware of being lifted out through the door in the solid steel hull, past the painted iron frames and huge rivets of the door and into the arms of the kindly, smiling man waiting below in the rocking, pitching boat. Above him, the shiny black hull seemed to stretch upwards like a cliff and a few faces peered over the railing way above him. Once everyone was on board, the red boat set off back to shore. From the boat the boy watched the steamer's black hull as the waters at its stern started to churn into white froth and it slowly turned and picked up speed heading for the Kyle Rhea narrows between Skye and the Mainland on its way to Kyle of Lochalsh. In one small boy a love of ships and the sea had been born.

MacBrayne steamer. (J&C McCutcheon Collection)

CHAPTER 1

ST *Lord Lovat* – A Trip to Icelandic Fishing Grounds

'Oh please, just let me die.' The trawler lurched again, and then dropped into another wave trough. The deck beneath me fell away, my knees slid on the deck and I hung on tighter but my arms were too weak and I slipped. The ship's bow bit into the next wave and the bathroom deck shuddered under my cold knees as I struggled to hold onto the bowl. Icy seas rattled against the outside of the bulkhead as they washed along the deck outside. 'Why won't this ship stay still? Why am I still sick when there is no more left inside me?' Seasickness has hit me for the first time in my life and I am well into the second day of it. I feel weak and totally drained. My stomach feels as though it has been turned inside out and my skin is clammy with sweat, and yet I am cold. Nothing will stay still and all I want to do is die. What on earth am I doing here? I am on board an old Hull trawler, well out into the north Atlantic, somewhere off the Faroe Islands, and heading for the Icelandic fishing grounds and we are in the middle of a Force 8 gale. This is only day three of a planned twenty-day fishing trip with no ports of call, and I am now certain that I will never survive.

How had this happened to me? How had the small boy who had been lowered out of the streamer all those years before arrived here, at the point of death in an Atlantic gale on a rusty old trawler? What was I doing here? I was a sixteen-year-old schoolboy from a normal middle-class home in Buckinghamshire, and I was hanging onto the toilet bowl of a trawler as it lurched into another wave. Why am I not at home, or out riding my bike round the pleasant leafy, sun-filled country lanes, or playing rugby with my pals on the common, even revising for my 'O' levels? Anything but this! How had I managed to get myself into this mess?

It had really started four years earlier when I was twelve, during a stay in Hull with family friends who had two sons, Peter and Michael, who were roughly the same age as me. We spent all our days out on our bikes cycling around Hull and the surrounding countryside. One day I persuaded my pals that the three of us should go down on our bikes to St Andrew's Dock, or 'Fish Dock' as it was known locally, to look at the trawlers. I had always been

Hull trawlers getting ready for another trip to the Arctic.

Hull trawler *Arctic Hunter*, H218. (J&C McCutcheon Collection)

fascinated by TV documentaries about life on Arctic trawlers and had read magazine articles about the dangers of the job and the roughness of the life but had never seen one. The romance of the names of the distant polar places that they went to excited me; Bear Island, Iceland, the White Sea, Spitzbergen and Greenland. Places from adventure books and the Viking Sagas, places from the tales of polar explorers, icebergs, polar bears and Arctic whalers.

With my two friends, Pete and Mike, I cycled down through Hull and found the way to the shopping hustle of Hessle Road and then through the Victorian streets of terraced houses and down through a dark, dank road tunnel that took us under the railway lines and up and out onto the docks. We got off our bikes and looked around. We found that we had entered a different world from the one we had left behind on Hessle Road at the other end of the tunnel.

High, flared, black bows of trawlers towered over us and dominated the immediate dockside scene. As we walked towards them we could see that the wide, open decks of the trawlers were littered with toolboxes, bundles of new nets, big round bobbins and shiny new coils of wire all to be stored away for the next trip. Some workmen were stowing some of the gear away below decks while another group worked on a big trawl winch. A tangle of masts and wires disappeared into the distance as vans and cars bustled and tooted their way over the black cobbles and through the dockside jumble of nets, pedestrians, ropes, bicycle racks, parked lorries, cyclists and huge coils of trawl warp. Looking across the dock at the ships on the far side you could immediately see their lovely lines. Their sweeping hull shape had evolved over many years of Arctic fishing; developed to deal with the worst that the weather could throw at them. Although they were only about 700 to 800 tons in size, these beautiful steel ships looked impregnable. As they lay still in the flat, calm waters of the Fish Dock it was impossible to imagine that such strong and powerful-looking ships could be tossed about in a storm, but of course they were. They all had high, flared bows to cut through the waves and throw off the icy, Arctic seas and above the bows the curved whaleback of the fo'c'sle, which gave protection and some shelter to the crew working on the open deck. From the whaleback, the high solid bulwarks then ran back past the gallows, a heavy steel arch from which the fishing gear was towed, to the low midships section, almost at water level to enable the net to be hauled over the side by hand. The midships area was dominated by the superstructure with the wheelhouse at the top. This jutted out forward from the main superstructure and stood high and fine above the deck; aloof and removed from it all. The wheelhouse windows seemed to stare out, far beyond the ship, oblivious to three schoolboys below, to the far horizons; as if they were looking for signs of more fish, or watching for a change in the weather. Immediately behind the wheelhouse was the funnel and then the low flat superstructure led smoothly aft to a rounded cruiser-style stern. Most of the trawlers were rust-streaked and had a battered, weathered look but the rust, dents and scratches could not disguise their fine lines and strength. In the sunshine those that had been freshly painted shone proudly as they lay waiting for their crew and the next tide so they could sail back to those exciting-sounding places in the far north.

To me it was all pure magic. Here were the ships that I had read about in the magazines, seen on the TV documentaries, where trawling was described as the most dangerous job in the world as well as being carried out in the stormiest, most remote and icy cold regions on the planet. Here on the dock were all the elements that went to make up a fishing trip to the Arctic: the trawler owners in their offices and all the shore support staff; the trawlermen themselves and the trawlers. I could see some of their names, fine proud names like *Stella Leonis*, *Cape Trafalgar*, *Lord Alexander*, *Westella* and *St Dominic*.

As we stood looking about and wondering what to do next (as well as making sure we did not get knocked into the dock by a passing lorry), I became aware of a gleaming black-hulled trawler that stood out from the rest as she was so clean and freshly painted. I walked towards her. On one of her lifebelts was her name, Cape Otranto, and the number H227. She had a high, white-fronted wheelhouse, which jutted out over the deck. The wheelhouse seemed to be so far above the deck that it must be like another world to be up there. As I stared, I saw an old man on board the ship. He was leaning against the bulwark by the aft accommodation. He had a weathered, wrinkled face and was smoking a pipe in the sunshine as he watched the comings and goings of the morning bustle. He wore an old blue jersey and had a scruffy flat cap on and a ragged scarf tied round his neck. I walked over and plucked up all my courage. In my southern accent I asked, 'Excuse me please, but would it be possible to see round your ship?' He seemed somewhat surprised at this, took a puff at his pipe, stood up and looked at me hard. He thought for a minute and then with a slight smile said, 'Aye, I s'pose so lad.' He took another draw on his pipe then knocked it out against the ship's side and put it in his pocket. 'Cum wi'me.' I clambered nervously over the steel bulwark and jumped down onto the main deck, calling to my two pals to follow, leaving the bikes by a bollard. I later discovered that the man was a watchman, one of many ex-trawlermen who worked as watchmen and stayed on board the trawlers when they were in dock, working twenty-four-hour shifts to keep a constant check for fires, flooding or other ship-borne problems as well as opening up locked compartments for the repair staff. He took us all round the ship.

We started in the galley. This seemed to be far too small to cater for a ship of this size. Even with the sun shining down through the skylight the galley seemed very small. It had shining steel worktops on two sides and a big black cooking range on a third as well as a number of small cupboards; but that was all. It was warm though and had a homely, warm, floury smell to it. The man told us, 'Here, when they are at sea, the cook will have to prepare and cook three meals a day for a crew of over twenty in all weathers, summer and winter. Basic food but plenty of it. If all else fails they can always eat fish!' he joked. A small wooden hatch allowed food to be passed into the bare-looking crew's mess deck while the officers ate in a separate mess with leather benches and panelled wood across the passageway. He showed us the tidy, four-man cabins down below for the crew and the single-berth officers' cabins on the main deck. The ship was warm and clean and smelt of a mixture of detergent and diesel oil and had a very secure feel about it. I remember thinking how snug the mate's cabin was, with its bunk, a little settee, a desk and its own porthole. I did not realise how little time he ever got to enjoy it. Then, the watchy took us up past the skipper's cabin, which had a day cabin and a night cabin as well as its own bathroom. Then we went up another deck and into the wheelhouse. I stepped to the front of the wheelhouse, past the big wooden steering wheel and looked out of the windows. We could see over the whole of the wide, working deck, beyond the top of the fo'c'sle and along the dock, which now seemed a long way away. I heard myself stupidly say, 'Gosh, you get a good view from up here, don't you?' The watchy, without even looking at me, just said, 'Aye, that's what it's for, lad.' And with that he shuffled out of the wheelhouse and took us back down to the deck.

On the way he explained that the *Cape Otranto* was a brand-new ship that had just returned from her maiden voyage of twenty-one days and was ready to sail again that night to the far north. She had a tonnage of 923 tons and had been built in Beverley by cook, Gemmel & Welton. She was owned by Hudson Bros, a well-established company, which named all their trawlers after capes. She was 196 feet long and was powered by diesel-electric, a new system in those days (though I did not understand what that meant then). I was entranced, and my fascination for the trawlers that sailed from the Humber to the Arctic grew ever deeper. Little did I know then that in four years time I would be back on the Fish Dock.

Why I should have such an interest in ships is a mystery. No one in the family was connected with the sea, unless you count my maternal grandfather, who was a cabinet-maker for the famous John Brown's Shipbuilders on Clydebank and had worked on both the original *Queen Mary* and the *Queen Elizabeth*. There was no sea on my father's side. There I come from a long line of grass keepers and shepherds in Sutherland in northern Scotland. However, after my tour round the *Cape Otranto* I was determined to take my interest in trawlers further and so a couple years later I wrote to the British Trawler Federation asking if it was possible to go to sea on a trawler for a trip as a schoolboy during school holidays.

They said 'Yes'. Under their 'Pleasurer' scheme, schoolboys and youths could go to sea on the trawlers as 'Pleasurers' to find out if they liked trawlers and the life and to decide if they wanted to make a career of it. They gave me the

MT *Cape Otranto* in her original Hudson Bros colours as seen by the author in 1962. Note the lovely lines of her hull and the proud look of her bridge. (Photo by kind permission of World Ship Society and Fleetwood Online Archive of Trawlers (FLOAT) http://float-trawlers.lancashire.gov.uk)

St Andrew's Dock, Hull, in 1962. The trawlers on the left are being prepared for sea.

names of some trawler owners to contact. I wrote to them all and received a letter back from a Mr Graham Hellyer, Managing Director of Hellyer Bros, one of the oldest and biggest trawler companies in Hull. He said that they were prepared to take me on a trip but I must sign an 'Insurance Indemnity Form' and be ready to go at short notice.

My parents thought I was mad. They had come from solid working-class families and spent their lives working to improve their lot and to do their best for me, private schools, and a nice home, but here I was reverting to a basic working-class environment as a holiday and treating it as a higher form of life. No wonder my mother called me an inverted snob! 'They send the ex-jailbirds out on the trawlers when they get out,' my Father told me; 'The only food on board is fish and you don't like fish'; 'Trawlers are full of thugs and layabouts'; 'You'll be seasick all the time'; 'Trawlers smell and you will come back smelling of fish'. These were just some of the many comments that were lobbed my way at home in tones of mischief and incomprehension. It only fuelled the fire. I was going to go!

One Saturday night, early in my school summer holiday, the phone rings. 'It is for you,' said my mother, 'someone called a Ship's Husband for Hellyers Brothers in Hull?' 'Hello,' I said nervously. In a gruff Yorkshire voice, the person on the other end told me to be in Hull at the offices of Hellyer Bros for nine o'clock on the Monday morning and to ask for Mr Easton as I will be sailing on the *Lord Lovat*. He also told me that I should stay at the Fisherman's Mission on the Sunday night and he would fix that for me.

Panic ensues as I rush to get my stuff ready. On the Sunday, I catch the train from King's Cross to Hull and get a taxi to the Fisherman's Mission, or 'The Mission' as everyone calls it, on Goulton Street, just off the Hessle Road. It is raining as I arrive and I am shown to my 'Cabin' by the Mission Superintendant, who is a very cheery and friendly man in a smart dark-blue suit. 'Here you are, lad, now you just settle yourself in, then come on down for your tea,' he says with a smile, then closes the door and leaves me to unpack. It is a pleasant room, with a washbasin, a radio and a big window overlooking the docks. I go downstairs. *Sing Something Simple*, a favourite Sunday night radio programme, is playing in the big mess room. We often have this on at home and a pang of homesickness hits me as I realise I won't be hearing it again for a few weeks. After a welcome supper of ham salad, a cup of tea and bread and butter, I go for a walk to see if I can still find the Fish Dock. It is now dark. I find the railway tunnel and emerge from it onto the Fish Dock. The docks look like a scene from a Sherlock Holmes film with the rain still lightly falling onto the deserted, jumbled emptiness of the docks and water drips loudly from broken gutters. My footsteps on the cobbled road echo round the tall, dark, Victorian buildings that house the trawler owner's offices and workshops as I splash through the oily, black puddles on the dockside. I try to remember the Fish Dock from my earlier visit as a twelve-year-old on that sunny summer's day as I walked along the south side. I find the *Lord Lovat*. She looks forlorn and depressingly cold as she lies dark and silent tied up outboard of the *Kingston Andalusite*. She seems so much smaller than the *Cape Otranto*. It seems a much more alien world than the one I saw on that summer's day with Mike and Pete. I seriously wonder what I have let myself in for. There is still time to change my mind.

I awake early and check out of the Mission then set off nervously by taxi to be at Hellyers offices for a quarter to nine. The morning is fine after last night's rain and the sun is breaking through the remaining clouds; everything seems brighter. The taxi takes me past the streets of Victorian back-to-back houses that cluster around the Fish Dock. These two-up two-down houses are the homes of the deep-sea trawler men of Hull. If you live there, then you are in the fishing industry. Everyone here is, or has a relation who is, a trawlerman, or who works on the Dock. The only exceptions are the skippers and owners who live in 'big posh 'ouses out of town'. Hessle Road is the heart of the Hull fishing community and the bond between the people is so strong there that it is a world on its own, separate from the rest of Hull. They support Hull FC Rugby League team and not Hull KR from East Hull. It has been home to the port's deep-sea fishing fleet since the 1850s, when the herring shoals of the North Sea were discovered and the fishermen from Devon and Cornwall moved up to the Humber to capitalise on the harvest. Now Hull is the biggest distant-water fishing port in the world and three or more full trains of fish leave Hull every morning for London and Leeds and other northern cities in addition to the many countless lorry-loads that go by road all over the country. I am about to enter that world.

I pay off the taxi on the end of the dock and stand with my bag and take in the scene. The Fish Dock is very much alive now, and a very different place from last night. I am back in the world I had last seen four years before and am excited by it all over again. I am met by all the smells of the place; fish meal, diesel oil, paint, tar and all the other scents of working docks and ships. Noises from everywhere compete with each other; tug hooters, drilling, clattering of chains, machinery being dragged over the cobblestones. Men are calling from ship to shore as the ships are repaired, stored and made ready for sea. I make my way along the south side of the dock past the trawler company offices. The office windows on the upper floors overlook and silently monitor all that happens on the dock. I walk past groups of men gathered round doorways and dockside offices awaiting their money or to sign on for the next trip. The tall wooden doors of a workshop entrance swing open and allow me a glimpse of the dark interior scenes, the blue flashes of welding torches, the scream of grinders and the banging and clanging as vital parts are machined and fabricated for the trawlers. The dock seems full of trawlers. Most of them are berthed two and three deep. They seem to be crammed in and the dock is bursting with them. The trawlers are painted with black hulls, though some have pale grey hulls and others are a yellowy buff colour. Some have white bridge fronts and a number have bridge fronts painted with a brown wood-grain effect, which matches the universal wood-grain effect of the paint on the main superstructures. This wood-grain paint effect, I learnt, is called 'scrumbling' and is common in deep-sea trawlers and smaller fishing vessels.

This is the golden era of Britain's deep-sea trawling industry. A trawler owner only has to send a trawler down the Humber with the orders to turn left at the end and head north and he is assured of a profit, providing of course, she has a good skipper. Trawlers sail from here to the distant grounds at Iceland, Greenland, the Grand Banks off Canada, Spitzbergen and the White Sea, all of which offer a rich harvest of cod, haddock and other valuable fish such as halibut, at the right times of the year. There are people, trucks, bikes, and forklift trucks everywhere. Taxis trying to get along the dock swing round piles of gear and iron mooring bollards as they fight for the clear areas of cobbled road with trucks loaded with trawl gear and nets. Smoke and steam are rising from a number of the trawlers as crews climb on board with their bags and boxes. The black oily waters of the dock are glistening in the sunshine.

Hellyer's offices are about half way along the dock and I find the Ship's Husband's Office. Mr Easton is not about so I wait, mingling with the crews. Nervousness grips my stomach again. I feel totally out of place here, a real fish out of water. After the bravado of coming up by train, now I am in the reality of Fish Dock on sailing day. The gulf between reading about trawlers in Arctic storms in magazines at home and the reality of actually being about to sail on one hits me hard. This is now reality. This is their world and I am a total stranger in it, I look it and feel it. How will they treat strangers? I am about to put myself totally in their hands for three weeks in an old trawler. The stories about ex-jailbirds being put on trawlers come back to me. Just as my imagination starts to work, Mr Easton arrives. He is a big man with a shiny bald head. It is obvious that he is a busy man. He is clearly 'Management' as he is wearing a suit. He walks briskly and has a stern and harassed look on his face. Before he gets into his office, people are asking him things and he is calling out sharp one-word answers as he goes into the office. He has a collection of papers in his hand and shouts at someone in the office to get a taxi to collect a Harry Marshal who has not shown up for the *Loch Eribol*. I must be a minor nuisance he can do without. Perhaps he won't notice me and I will miss the ship. I could slip away and be home again by tonight. Too late: he notices me. 'Gray is it? Got your indemnity form?' I nod. 'Leave your bag there then and go across to the Insurance Company and get your indemnity form signed off.' He waves an arm towards the end of the dock. 'Yes, Sir,' I stammer. I find my way there and get the form signed, then go back to the office. Mr Easton is still there. 'Now then, lad, get yourself aboard the *Lord Lovat*.' He takes the time to point me in the right direction. Smoke is now drifting up from the *Lord*

Lord Lovat at St Andrew's Fish Market on the day after she docked.

Lovat's funnel into the blue, summer sky. 'You report to the mate when you get on board, he'll sort you out.' It's now or never. I can still just walk away and half of me wants to but the other half drags me towards the unknown. I set off across the dockside chaos and clamber onto the *Kingston Andalusite* then across her deck to the *Lord Lovat*. I try to look as though I climb over trawler's high bulwarks with a kit bag every day of the week, and fail.

Once on board I find a big, fattish man with sandy hair standing watching me. 'And who are you?' This is the mate standing on the deck waiting as his crew arrives. 'Gordon Gray, I am a pleasurer for this trip. Mr Easton said to ask for the mate when I got on board.' I mention Mr Easton's name as though it will entitle me to an upgrade. Unfortunately, it doesn't. 'Well you've found him.' The mate seems a big, silent sort and just smiles in a friendly way but do I catch a slight question over my sanity in his eyes? He waves his arm towards a doorway. 'You'll be in the cook's cabin, down there, the cook is already on board.' Then he turns away as someone else climbs on board. I struggle down the steep wooden ladder to the lower deck and the smell of a mixture of detergent and diesel oil comes back to me. As I reach the bottom of the ladder I can see someone standing in a cabin. 'Excuse me, but where do I find the cook?' I ask hopefully. 'Come in, mate. I'm the cook.' He is a tall (about six feet), dark-haired guy, wearing a smart brown suit and a thin red tie. He is in his thirties and with a smiling, pleasant, open manner that immediately makes me warm to him. He actually reminds me a bit of Russ Conway. He shakes my hand, introducing himself as Dave. He is the cook for this trip and he starts asking me what trawlers I have been on before. 'None,' I reply. 'Oh Hell, we'll have to start from scratch with you then.' I am a bit puzzled. Dave carries on chatting and tells me that he is often referred to as Big Dave on board as the mate, who is also called Dave, is fatter and is known as 'Fat Dave', though never to his face, he warns. Big Dave is the regular cook in *Lord Lovat* and has done a number of trips in the ship. He has been told to expect a new galley boy for this trip as the previous one has 'gone ashore' to look for a shore job.

Just then, there is a noise from the wooden ladder and a small, thin boy in a loose, white T-shirt appears, dragging a battered old suitcase behind him. He looks round then comes into the cabin. He says he is the galley boy and is also called Dave. This is going to get very confusing! I have only met three of the crew and they are all called Dave. The cook looks relieved as he had assumed that I was the galley boy when I appeared, hence the questioning. The new Dave has already done a number of trips in another trawler so knows the job. He is a cheery sort, thin and with very fair skin and long, tousled, blond hair. I explain I am just a pleasurer and all is well. cook Big Dave then sits on the bench and fishes into his bag. He produces a bottle of rum and we all sit down on the benches alongside the bunks and he shares swigs of the rum between the three of us and all is well. I am 6 foot 4 inches and Big Dave looks at me then at the galley boy and says 'Bloody Hell, Dave, the pleasurer will make two of you, he may even eat you if the food doesn't last!' We share a laugh and they then start chatting about which ships they have been on and I look around my new home. It is a six-berth cabin with varnished wooden lockers and a sack mat floor covering. There are no scuttles as it is below the main deck level and mostly below the waterline. Dave indicates that I can have the bottom bunk of two on the port side as there will only be three of us in this cabin this trip. We are due to sail at about half past ten and other crew members have come down the ladder and found their berths while we have been sitting there. The ship gives a small jolt, the first sense of motion as it is moved by the tug off the berth and into the dock ready to sail out. My stomach lurches. Too late to get off now! I really want to be up on deck but the two Daves are chatting and having the odd swig of rum and I do not want to appear rude and walk out. I am saved by the skipper. He sends a crewman down with orders for me to go up to the wheelhouse.

The skipper is leaning against the wheelhouse front by an open window. He looks serious. 'Now then, you're Gordon, right?' 'Yes, Sir,' I reply. 'First thing, you don't call me Sir, or captain, I am just "the skipper", OK?' This is the first thing he says, as I get into the wheelhouse. 'No, Sir, er, I mean, Skipper,' I reply. He ignores my slip as I try and find somewhere to stand among the other people already in the small wheelhouse. The skipper's name is Ken. He is a quiet guy, medium height and build, with thinning hair slicked back and I guessed he must have been about forty or forty-five. 'Now then, Gordon, I never use my night cabin, especially on the fishing grounds, so shift your gear from down aft into my night cabin.' He points at a set of stairs at the back of the wheelhouse. 'You'll be better off there than down aft with that lot.' I assume he means his crew. I am feeling a bit overcome by the kindness that these people are showing me, first the cook and his rum, now the skipper and his cabin. Where are the jailbirds out to get me, the layabouts stealing my wallet? Maybe they will appear later? But for now I just enjoy the warmth of friendly, helpful people and the start of a big adventure. My earlier nervousness begins to die down a bit. The skipper's day cabin is connected directly to the bridge by a stairway and so is better for him to get to the wheelhouse quickly when he has to. He lives in his day cabin where there is a long upholstered bench settee on which he sleeps. His night cabin is off the day cabin.

The tug is let go and we clear through the lock and move out into the river Humber. Most of the crew are now on deck, some waving and calling to pals or family who have come down to see them off. I have found out from the cook that we are bound for Iceland. Five other trawlers are sailing on the same tide, three are heading for Iceland, one for the White Sea and one of them is bound for Greenland.

We make our way down the Humber in a long straggled line. After the busy and noisy chaos of sailing, everyone seems to vanish as we go down the river, doubtless back to their cabins and their own bottles. After clearing Spurn Head at the mouth of the Humber Estuary, we round our course up to north, aiming to pass off Flamborough Head and then heading for the Pentland Firth at the very top of Scotland. The sea is calm and the sky clear and sunny. The skipper tells me that on the first day out everyone not on watch turns in for the afternoon to lessen the pain of leaving home again. This includes the skipper. Radio Scarborough is playing 1960s pop music throughout the ship as she rolls gently up the Yorkshire coast with water sloshing quietly past the freeing ports.

By evening, the crew begins to reappear. George, the Radio Officer, or 'Sparks', introduces himself to me. George is an affable, laid-back guy in his late forties and has been a 'Sparks' on trawlers all his life. He spends the entire trip in the radio room, which also doubles as his cabin and, no matter what the weather, always seems to be wearing a maroon cardigan. The Radio Room is immediately behind the wheelhouse. After chatting for a while he says, 'Come, on I'll take you round.' He takes me all round the ship and shows me the layout and introduces me to the crew as we meet them. Some are still on their bunks sleeping or just lying reading. Most of the reading matter is western cowboy novels or 'wessies' or last week's Sunday papers. These are only read on the way out and then not touched until they are running for home. No newspapers are ever thrown away; all papers and paperbacks are shared and passed around the crew. George takes me up to the fo'c'sle, which has berths for up to twelve men but only six seamen are sleeping there on this trip. It is now silent as the men are still asleep, apart from about a dozen empty beer cans rolling gently across the deck. He also shows me his other domain; the cod liver oil boilers. 'When the cod are gutted, the livers are separated from the rest and put into baskets.

After the catch has all been gutted, I then take the livers aft and put them into the cod liver oil boilers,' he explains. 'If I'm not around they keep them for me to boil later.' The boilers are situated in a compartment on the starboard side aft, not far from the galley. The boilers themselves are two large vats about five feet high and with heavy lids that can be clamped shut. The boilers have steam pipe connections from the engine room so steam can be pumped through them. 'It is my job to boil the livers, which separates the good oil from the residue. This oil is then fed off into storage tanks. I am then entitled to a share of the proceeds from the cod liver oil at the end of the trip, and every penny helps, believe you me, lad!'

At 2130 every night at sea, a radio message is sent to the owners to confirm the ship's position and course. This is relayed to all the ships in the company and is sent in code so that other companies cannot find out where our trawlers are fishing. We pass a small Russian trawler drifting just outside the twelve-mile limit. She is waiting for nightfall so she can move inside and fish illegally. Nothing seems to be done about it and the Russians are definitely not regarded as comrades on the high seas. As we pass Flamborough Head and alter course for Rattray Head in Scotland, a small school of dolphins swims past heading south. They are leaping out of the sea and racing each other, clearly enjoying the evening sunshine.

I go back down to the cabin and take a look at my home for the next three weeks. The skipper's night cabin, now my cabin for the trip, is wood-panelled with the bunk running fore and aft on the inside bulkhead. On the outboard side, below a scuttle, is a locker, while a cushioned bench seat is fitted to the forward bulkhead. There is a brass ship's clock on the bulkhead and a fan which does not work. There are two scuttles, one forward looking onto the winch area in front of the superstructure and the other on the starboard side overlooking the deck. There is also a bathroom at the after end with black and white, diamond-shaped tiles and white steel bulkheads.

Lord Lovat, H148, is an oil-burning steam trawler of 713 tons and is 181 feet long and was built at Selby in 1951. In Hellyer Bros livery, she has a light-grey hull with brown scrumbling woodeffect superstructure with an ochre funnel and the company emblem of a white 'H' on a blue flag on the side. Her navigation equipment is basic: a magnetic compass, a radar set, a Decca Navigator and a Loran A radio navigation systems and an echo sounder. The days of gyro-compasses, autopilots and satellite navigation have not yet arrived. She is typical of the many distant-water trawlers built in the late 1940s and early 1950s for fishing at Iceland from Hull and Grimsby.

I sleep well that first night and awake just after seven. It is a fine, clear and sunny morning and the sun is glinting off the sea and shining through the porthole. *Lord Lovat* is rolling gently as she steams north. The crew is already out on deck setting up the trawl gear in readiness for fishing. First, they set up the fish washer. This is a large metal tank that is open at one end. It is mounted on tall legs amidships above the fish room hatch so that the open end faces aft and is a few feet forward of the fish room hatch. A hose is rigged up so that, when we are fishing, water continually flows into the tank. Then they assemble the nets. The nets are made up of a number of component parts: bellies, wings, side panels, cod end, foot ropes, head ropes, etc., and have to be built up to form the complete net. The headline with its floats and the ground rope with its big rollers or bobbins to roll over the seabed are all secured in place. These preparations carry on all morning in a happy atmosphere with the BBC Light Programme playing over the deck. Although the deck is open on all sides when we are under way it is fairly well sheltered from the wind by the high bows and whale back.

At about noon, after passing Rattray Head off the north-east tip of Aberdeenshire, not far from the fishing ports of Peterhead and Fraserburgh, we run into fog. George, the Sparks, tells me that the trawlers at Greenland are reporting that they are catching lots of fish. The *Lord Lovat* does not have the fuel capacity to get there and back and allow enough time there for a decent trip and so she is restricted to fishing at Iceland. It is a five-day steam to get to the Grand Banks and longer if they go up to Greenland and the Labrador Straits. As it is also a five-day steam home again, the skippers have to be confident of making good catches when they get there as they only have about ten days on the grounds to make a successful trip.

The skipper calls me to go and join him and George for lunch down in the officers' mess. This is a small, cosy mess, which has wood panelling on the bulkheads, very similar to the *Cape Otranto*'s and with the table taking up the whole room apart from the red leather-covered bench seats all round the side of it. Lunch is good, vegetable soup, roast beef, Yorkshire puddings, roast potatoes and cabbage. Then, there is steamed duff and custard for pudding. I had not realised that I was so hungry. My dockside nerves seem to have gone and I am feeling more confident about my time here. I haven't even felt seasick!

We are now entering the dangerous Pentland Firth; the narrow passage between Scotland and the Orkneys Islands through which the tides race; particularly at the time of the spring tides. Shipping from Europe heading for the Atlantic converges on this narrow channel with the rocky islands and skerries all around. The fog is now thicker than ever. It envelops the ship, covering everything in a heavy, wet dew, and locks us into our own tiny world, a world bounded by the wall of grey wetness about fifty yards from the ship. All sound is deadened so it feels as if we are in wet cottonwool. Entering the narrows of the Firth, an eerie feeling descends on the wheelhouse as the lookout peers out, seeing nothing but the wall of fog and the swirling waters as the tide races through the Firth. We know that we are now close to the rocky, wreck-strewn coast but we cannot see it. We can only hear a lone fog horn booming out somewhere in the fog and the plaintive hoot of our ship's fog horn warning any other ships of our presence. However, with the aid of Duncansby Head Lighthouse fog horn making fog signals of five blasts every two minutes, as well as the ship's radar, we are soon safely through. George tells me that on one of the Pentland Skerries (one of the clusters of small rocky islands in the Firth) there are the remains of an Aberdeen trawler, which was washed up in a ferocious storm in about 1965. She was not even holed and was just sitting up on the skerry.

At about seven that evening, the fog lifts and we finally see the cliffs of the Isle of Hoy to starboard and there on a parallel course and dwarfed by the cliffs is the trawler *Kingston Andalusite*, which had left the dock just behind us. As the fog goes so the wind picks up and the sea begins to sluice in through the freeing ports as she rolls along northwards.

Later that night, the wind gets up and I am woken by the change in the ship's movement. By morning the wind is up to Force 7 or 8 and the spray is being sent high over the whaleback and lashes onto the bridge windows. I do not feel good at all. I have to make a dash for the bathroom before I have properly woken up. I go back to bed and hope that this awful feeling will go away after being ill. It does not. I struggle up as I decide that I should try and keep going. Perhaps if I get up into the wheelhouse I will feel better. I lean against the bridge windows and hang on. The mate is there and looks relaxed and content with the world. He smiles at me with a knowing look. As I look out, hoping to see sunny calm seas ahead, I am hypnotised by the movement of the ship. The seas are coming from the north-east and the ship is rolling along and pitching into them with the bows swinging through 20 to 25 degrees. One moment the bow is poised high above the troughs and we were looking down on the seas, then the bow drops and sinks into the trough and the horizon is above us. Spray lashes across the windows. The skipper assures me that it will be far rougher when we are clear of the shelter of the Faeroes. I now feel even worse than I had done in my bunk and as I watch the bows once more, my stomach heaves and I make a dash below to the heads. I am experiencing my first, but by no means last, bout of seasickness.

As the day progresses and the pitching continues I feel more dreadful and think that death must be better than this. I seem to spend all day sitting on the bathroom floor. I try to keep going but whatever I do the bulkheads seem to close in on me and then a lurch of the bow as it drops into a wave sets my stomach off again. I only want one thing – to get off this thing! Nothing can convince me that I will be OK; I am definitely going to die. By nightfall I have lost a lot of strength and feel weak and terrible. I go to bed and praise the Lord that I am not expected to keep any sort of watch and so can lie and suffer my last hours in peace. I drift off into a deep sleep. The next morning, although still feeling bad I realise that I am still alive. How can that be? Perhaps the weather is improving? By the afternoon, the weather has abated and the ship is steaming along nicely. The sun is now shining again after the fog and the rough weather. By evening I am beginning to feel a little better. Somehow I have survived.

That night we arrive on the fishing grounds off south-east Iceland. After two days and eighteen hours of steaming we begin fishing. The big wooden and steel otter boards or 'Doors' are winched outboard. The doors are massive. Each is about 10 feet by 5 feet and about 3 or 4 inches thick. Made of solid baulks of timber and edged with heavy steel shoes to protect them from rocks on the seabed. A door hangs from each of the two big steel arches, or gallows, on the starboard side, one forward by the whaleback, one aft by the cod liver boiler house. The net is connected between them so that one is attached at each end of the net mouth and when the net is set the doors act like kites and 'fly' outwards in the sea keeping the net spread wide open. The net is connected to the trawl warps and the first trawl of the trip is underway. We are on Working Man's Bank, about half way between Iceland and the Faeroes. After towing the trawl net for about four hours at 4 knots the first catch is hauled and we have caught about eighty baskets of cod, a good catch to start with. A fishing vessel is losing money every minute that the nets are not on the seabed and set for catching fish. My seasickness has now begun to ease, I feel better and even manage to start thinking about food again.

We spend two days fishing in this area and catching good hauls of fish. The weather settles into a warm, sunny pattern, which cheers everyone up. When it is dull or rough the crew spends most of their time in their bunks but when it is sunny they spend any spare time on deck with a mug of tea and a cigarette and are altogether happier. By the third day the catches are not so good and the skipper makes the decision to move grounds. This is a big risk as no one knows whether better catches will be had or not. The time taken to change grounds and the cost of the fuel used will all work against the skipper if when he gets there the catches are poor. The Bosses in the office judge him only by how much he catches. We sail up nearer to Iceland and now I can see Iceland's mountains stretching along the horizon. In the days before Iceland's new fishery limits British trawlers could fish up to three miles of the coast, now we are not allowed within twelve miles of the coast. This is my first sight of the far north. Although we are still south of the Arctic Circle the sight of these snow-capped mountains is exciting. It is brilliantly clear and sunny and the mountains are sharp with every detail clear in dazzling white against the blue sky.

The skipper's knowledge of these waters is astounding. His charts have all sorts of hand-drawn alterations on them with ridges, banks, holes and fastenings all marked. He checks his chart with a big notebook that he keeps of all his trips indicating what he caught where and when and what the tides and weather conditions were. The tow is carefully plotted with the aid of electronic navigation systems such as Loran and Decca Navigator by which the skippers can calculate their position very accurately and so trawl along the edges of undersea cliffs and ridges. As the fish tend to lie in clumps feeding on the seabed, one good haul can often indicate plenty of fish in that area. When this occurs you can see the trawlers following each other round in circles as they try and fish out the area.

The VHF (a shortrange voice radio) speaker in the wheelhouse is constantly crackling away and snatches of conversations between skippers are heard all the time: 'Lord Lovat, Lord Lovat, this is *Kingston Onyx, Kingston Onyx*, are you there Ken?' The skipper of another Hull trawler, the *Kingston Onyx*, which had sailed a week earlier than us and which we had seen in the distance earlier in the day is calling up our Skipper for a chat. The two skippers know each other well. They chat away talking about the weather. 'When did you get up to the grounds?' 'How are things at home?' All this is spoken in a slow Yorkshire way with lots of pauses in the conversation and 'Ayes' followed by more pauses. Then the other skipper starts to probe Ken about catches. 'Any good where you are, Ken?' The response is cagey, 'Oh, so, so, not much to be excited over.' 'Aye ... Aye ... same here.' Ken asks if they are heading for a market yet. 'Not sure, depends on the weather' (that is interpreted as the fishing is good so they would stay unless bad weather stopped them fishing. 'Where are you abouts now?' asks Ken. 'Just having a look at Hari Kari' is the reply, i.e. trying to indicate they have just arrived on that bank. They chatted on like this for about ten or fifteen minutes with no real facts or hard information being exchanged but lots of guesswork and innuendo sent and received. The skippers are always trying to kid each other into believing there are no fish where they are when in fact there are fish; it all seems a waste of time but does keep them happy chatting. However, if one skipper can con the other skipper to move away from good catches to poorer grounds and then move onto the better grounds themselves then they will. This goes on between ships in the same company as every skipper fishes for himself. Vessels from the same company do not fish as a fleet, pooling information or calling others to good grounds; they all look after themselves but keep chatting to the others from the company and in the hope of picking up a nugget of information that the others might let slip in an unguarded moment. Every skipper is only as good as his last trip. One bad one and he can find himself out of a job as the whole industry is run on a casual labour basis.

Later in the day we steam to 'Hari Kari Bank'. It is a fine day and, as we steam north, the sun lights up the dazzling white bow wave against the deep blue of the sea. The ship rolls along free at last of the restraining net, like a hiker walking after putting down a heavy rucksack. Hari Kari Bank is so named by British trawler men because it was regarded as the last resort ground on the way home to try and save a poor trip. *Kingston Onyx* is still there and as we approach we see that she is hauling her nets. The skipper keeps *Lord Lovat* upwind of the *Onyx* so he can see her starboard side. He watches through his binoculars as they haul their net aboard; they do not seem to be getting exceptional catches after all. Maybe their skipper was telling the truth? We do not find any good catches here either so after three hauls we steam back to Working Man's Bank where our first haul is sixty baskets, not bad. The day ends with a tea of hamburgers, peas and fresh baked bread rolls and jam.

The fishing continues round the clock and the weather also continues to hold. A calm high-pressure system is giving the north Atlantic a pleasant summer and we are enjoying it. We also continue to have reasonably good catches.

I spend some time chatting in the wheelhouse to the bosun, John. He is a cheery, friendly guy in his early twenties, clearly ambitious and takes his job seriously. He always has his greased hair flicked back in a classic 'DA' style like the Rock & Roll singers of the day. He has been at sea since leaving school. Like most of the crew he rolls his own cigarettes and takes great pride in being able to roll a 'ciggy' with one hand. On first joining the fishing industry he started off as a 'Deckie Learner', which is the bottom rung of the promotion ladder. He was a deckie learner for a year and then became a 'Spare Hand'. Some deckie learners take much longer to get to spare hand. After that he gradually climbed up the ladder. He became a third hand and then after more sea time and shore exams he became a bosun. The next step for him is to become a mate before reaching the final height of skipper. There is no short cut to the rank of skipper. No college diploma, officer entry or envelope of money to the owners can make you a skipper. The only way is to start at the bottom as a deckie learner and work your way from there. As a bosun his seamanship was expected to be as good as the mate's but he needed time to understudy the mate in fishing and managing the crew. However, he is qualified to take over from the mate if needed. He would take responsibility for some of the trawls to gain experience of fishing. A good worker with determination and hard work can become a skipper in six years, although this is unusual. Normally it takes about ten years. That is a lot of time at sea. To take a mate's ticket you have to have been at sea for four years. A lot of skippers will work for about ten to fifteen years as a skipper and then retire. They earn good money if they are successful; about £8,000 to £10,000 a year at 1966 rates. However, I could not find anyone on board who actually liked the job. They all said it was too hard, boring, and too long away from home; but they could not think what else they could do or even wanted to do instead. On the grounds they are either working on deck in all weathers and seasons, or sleeping as they can often be on deck for twelve to eighteen hours at a stretch. For most this is the only working life they have ever known about. Often they are the sons of trawlermen, with cousins and uncles also in the industry. From childhood they will have seen them disappear to sea for three weeks at a time and return with good pay packets. Some of the school chums will also have gone off to sea. For those that do not have the opportunity to go on from school to university then this is the natural progression from school for those on Hessle Road. At the age of fifteen or sixteen they want to be seen as equals among their peers and to have the money to flash about that a trawlerman can have when he comes back from a trip.

There are no recreational facilities on board other than playing cards or reading their western paperbacks and old newspapers. They all buy their tobacco from the bonded store on board. They all roll their own ciggies and have their own baccy pouches and matches. Most seem to stick at the job for the money but one of the spare hands, Colin, had given it up and had gone farming with an uncle for over a year. However, he found that working out in the fields on his own did not suit him and he missed his pals and the camaraderie of mess deck life on the trawlers and he soon found that the sea was dragging him back. Also, the money was better at sea than as a farm labourer. Once someone gets so far up the promotion ladder to, say, a bosun or a mate, then they feel they are past the point of no return and are too old to start again on the shore. Also they are now earning better money than they could ashore and so they tend to carry on to the end.

The noises and calls of trawling fills the days and nights. The first call is to 'Knock out the warps.' This action releases the two towing warps from a block on the starboard side aft near the after gallows which holds the two warps together while towing and they must be freed from that to allow the net to be hauled in. The steam winch hisses as it begins heaving in another haul, the trawl warp creaking and cracking under the strain as it winds itself onto the winch drum and remorselessly pulls the big trawl net back to the surface. The ship is brought round so the wind blows onto her starboard side and she drifts away from the net and does not drift over the top of it. The yells of the men as the trawl doors, which weigh over a ton each, come up from the deep and crash and bang hard against the side of the ship, then as they clear the side they shudder as they reach the top of the gallows. They then swing and bang until the seamen get chains round them to secure them. Then the foot rope, with its spherical bobbins and rollers, clatters over the side and onto the deck. The head rope, with its floats, follows and then the rest of the trawl is hauled up and heaved over the side. The cod end floats to the surface with the air in the fish and bobs about in the sea as the gulls scream and descend onto it fighting and shrieking to tear bits of fish from the net. The mate calls for the cod end to be lifted by the derrick and swung over the deck. He ducks beneath the bulging net as the water rushes out of it and he releases the cod end knot at the end of the net which stops the fish going straight through the whole net. Fish are sticking out of every mesh. The mate grapples with the cod end knot, then with a 'whoosh', the catch empties in a slithering, silvery rush into the wooden pounds accompanied perhaps by a cheer from the men if it is a good haul.

All the while, the skipper is watching from the open wheelhouse window, eyes everywhere, to spot any danger for his crew such as a stray wire getting caught up, or a big sea rolling the ship as the crew manhandle the net over the side of the ship. He is also, of course, assessing the success or failure of the haul. Not that you would ever tell from his face. It seems to remain totally impassive regardless of the haul. The skippers know that one good haul does not guarantee another. The cod end knot is retied and the net checked for any tears, then it is manhandled back over the starboard side and shot away. The trawler then takes up another tow for three or four hours while the crew set to work and begin gutting the catch.

The fishing goes on twenty-four hours a day as long as the trawler is on the grounds. The crew carries on working regardless of the weather and the time as long as there are fish to be gutted. A series of good hauls can mean that the whole crew is on deck gutting and packing for anything up to eighteen or twenty hours at a stretch. Getting the fish below and packed on ice is all that matters.

Today is my first Sunday at sea. It is just the same as any other day, no special Sunday Service or a day off for the crew. Fishing goes on round the clock seven days a week, summer or winter, Easter or Christmas. What shore factory worker would work seven days a week for twenty-one days for just one and a half days off, all the year round? To make Sundays special at sea there is a normally a special menu on the trawlers.

The food is, so far, very good. It is also very important as it is on any ship. Food is what the crew look forward to when they are stuck out on a freezing deck gutting ice-cold wet fish for hours on end, so it has to be as good as the cook can make it with the supplies he is given. A typical day's menu might be porridge, cereals, eggs, bacon, and bread for breakfast with pots of tea. Dinner (not lunch) would be soup, a roast or sausages, or fish with vegetables, Yorkshire puddings and cake or apple pie and custard. tea could be chops and tea cakes.

While there is still fresh meat then roasts are often the main meal. It varies according to what the weather will allow the cook to make and what is left that can be eaten. The meals are at set times. Breakfast is seven to eight, dinner at twelve noon and tea at six o'clock. There are two sittings during each time of half an hour each.

On Sundays, however, breakfast is the same, bacon, eggs, beans, fried bread and fried potatoes. Lunch is a full roast dinner of roast pork, stuffing, or beef with Yorkshire puddings, carrots, peas or cabbage and a steamed duff and custard for pudding. Sunday tea is normally ham and eggs with tinned fruit salad as a pudding. For most of the crew, Sunday lunch and tea is what they look forward to all week and as in all ships a good cook and good food are essential for good crew morale. Christmas is of course a bit more homely. The company puts on board Christmas puddings and turkeys as well as extra bonded stores and liquor. Trips are normally arranged so that the ship is either steaming for home or steaming off to the grounds or in port but a large number of trawlers are always on the grounds over the Christmas period.

'Big Dave', the cook, had originally gone to sea on oil tankers and had been trained as a cook in the BP Tanker Co. so was well used to time at sea, but mostly in 50,000-ton tankers rather than 700-ton Arctic trawlers. He admitted that there was a bit of a difference between the Persian Gulf and the fishing grounds off Iceland. While life on board the tankers was good and the ships were comfortable, he found that he was away from home for too long, so he left. Tankers could be at sea for months at a time as they were often diverted mid-voyage to other ports, having set off from the Gulf bound for the UK. After he left the tankers, he did a couple of trips on timber ships that brought timber to Europe from Siberia. He told me some of his tales from those trips, of the huge Russian rivers, the poverty of Siberia and of the friendliness of the people. He explained that in summer, when the ice has receded, the timber ships steam along the north coast of Russia, along the north-east Passage, and up the big rivers of the Ob and Yenisei to load timber deep in Siberia. They can only do it in summer as the sea is frozen solid for the rest of the year, but even so the Russian icebreakers are available in case the ice closes in and the ships get stuck. A change of wind in the early part of the season can bring the ice pack back onto the coast very quickly and ships can get caught out. These sounded like fantastic trips. Eventually though, as he was a Yorkshire boy, he found that the three weeks away on the Hull trawlers was as good a deal as he was going to get so he stuck with it.

Big Dave's domain is the galley, which is situated towards the after end of the accommodation area. It is small, only eight feet by eight feet and no room for more than one person to work in it at a time; especially when Dave was trying to serve up a meal. When Dave has a full meal on the go it is as hot as the boiler room. There is no airconditioning here, just one small scuttle. The cooker is a large, black, oil-fired range, which appears to be virtually uncontrollable. Nothing that Dave does to the regulators seems to make any difference. The range has two ovens and hot plates on the top with a grid of large steel 'fiddles' over it. These 'fiddles' are movable bars that the cook can use to try and secure pots on the range in bad weather and stop them sliding right off. Dave tries to make fresh bread rolls at sea whenever he can. All the dough has to be hand-kneaded in bowls while he is kneeling on the food-store deck. The food store adjoins the galley at the after end and is slightly cooler than the galley itself. He kneels on the floor to do it as there are no worktops. The bread then has to be cooked with the oven door left slightly open, otherwise it is burned to a cinder on the outside and raw dough inside. When there are strong winds they can blow out the range fires or a sudden gust can blow back down the stove pipe which causes mayhem as the pans and hot plates are sent flying off across the galley. Every evening, when he has finished clearing up after the last meal, Dave cleans the galley deck. He does this by simply boiling a large bucket of water and, while it is still boiling, throws it across the deck and under the range. He then scrubs every inch he can and hopes that the boiling water has killed off anything nasty under the range and in the darker corners. The galley boy, Dave, whose main jobs seem to be washing up and peeling potatoes, has to squat on an upturned bucket and peel the potatoes by hand; either out on deck if it is fine or in the passage outside the galley as there is no room to do it in the galley itself. Dave reckons that he loses about 2 stone a trip because of the heat in the galley combined with the fact that he says he never feels like eating the food he has prepared. Although to me the food was good, Dave says it is poor quality when compared with the food he had been used to on the tankers. He ditched all the cabbages on day three of this trip as they were bad when they were put on board.

The crew eats their meals in the crew mess, a bare, square room immediately forward of the galley. There is a slatted wooden bench that runs round all four sides. A large, fiddled table fills the rest of the space. A tiny hatch opens through to the galley for the food to be passed through. There are no pictures on the bulkheads and just one small scuttle. The crew rarely spends much time here apart from eating their meals or having a tea break when fishing. There is always a huge pot of tea on the table and often some bread or biscuits left out by the cook.

The one thing that I cannot get used to on board is the tinned milk. The crew all seem to like it and pour loads into their big china pots of tea. I find that it has a strong taste that ruins the tea, so I drink black tea. Now, years later, just the smell of tinned milk takes me back to *Lord Lovat*.

Today, the skipper sends me down into the fish room to see what goes on down there. Here the fish are packed and stored after they have been caught, gutted and cleaned. The fish room occupies about one third of the total length of the ship and stretches right across the total breadth. When a fish has been gutted it is thrown up into the washer on the deck. This large tank is open at one end and a grill chute leads from there down to the fish room hatch. Sea water is continually pouring into the washer from a hose and as the ship rolls and pitches so the fish are washed in the tank, then they roll onto the chute, the water drains off through the grills and the fish fall into the fish room. Working in the fish room is considered to be one of the best jobs, especially in winter as it is considerably warmer there than being out on deck.

When the ship leaves on a trip the fish room is filled with crushed ice from the ice factory. The fish room is arranged into pounds by fixed vertical posts and each pound can be made up at sea to form a number of shelves, each deep enough to carry a layer of fish and ice. Prime fish, such as cod, haddock and halibut, is laid on a layer of ice and a further layer of ice is put on top of the fish, then the next shelf is set up above that and so on. The lower-quality fish, such as red fish, are packed into the pounds without shelves. These are always sold off last and often go straight to the pet food factory or the fish-meal factory.

Two of the crew are given the job of stowing the catch. Charlie and Roy, who work for the mate, are responsible for the proper stowage and condition of the catch. As I climb down the ladder into the fish room I am given an axe by Roy and told to start smashing the ice that, although it came aboard in flakes, soon freezes into a solid mass. It takes hard work with a felling axe to break it back down to flakes that can be used on the shelves. The process of breaking ice for flakes also creates room for the next row of fish shelves to be set up and so it goes on until the hold is filled. Charlie and Roy are friendly guys and are happy for me to wield the axe while they stow the fish. It is clear that stowing the fish is not that easy as the layers of ice below and above the fish have to be of a certain depth for maximum preservation without crushing the fish or wasting too much space by having the ice too deep. All the time they were under pressure to keep up with the flow of fish coming down from the washer. They also have to check that the fish are properly cleaned as if the guts are accidentally left in the fish it will rot and cause fish nearby to rot too.

Most of the crewmen seem to have been given nicknames that are less than flattering. One spare hand called Wally was known as 'Soft Wally'. The deckie learner, yet another Dave, was known as 'Daft Maggot' as he was a tubby lad and not the brightest. Dave the galley boy was called 'Midget' due to his lack of height. In spite of his small size he stood up for himself well amongst the rest of the crew. galley boys and deckie learners are prime targets for practical jokes on board and some jokes can take things a bit far. Dave the galley boy told me a story against himself when he was on his second trip the previous summer; they had gone into Akyureyri on the north coast of Iceland for repairs. It was a glorious sunny day, with sparkling, clear, blue waters. It was pretty hot for Iceland and the crew was all on deck enjoying the sunshine. They kidded Dave that he should go for a swim as the water looked really blue and inviting. He was reluctant but after some strong egging on and challenges about being a softy, he did. He dived off the ship into the harbour and by his own admission came straight back up out of the water like a torpedo. The water temperature would have been just above freezing.

On a sad note, the deckie learner, Dave, lost his life a few months later when the Hamling's-owned stern trawler *St Finbarr* was lost after an explosion and major fire off the Grand Banks on Christmas Day. A total of twelve men died that day, either due to the fire and fumes or through falling into the sea as they were being rescued. Thirteen were rescued by the stern trawler *Orsino*, which was fishing nearby and saw the flames.

After a few days on the Bill Bailey, Working Man and Hari Kari grounds we steam to Kidney Bank. There is a BBC gale warning for south-east Iceland; we could be in for more bad weather. It is the Ebor Handicap at York today and a number of the crew place bets. This is done by a telegram to their bookies at home. However, no one won any money. Like a certainty of the winners at the races, the forecast gale does not materialise either but we did have a few showers of rain.

It is an interesting day for fishing. A haul of forty baskets is deemed not too good by the skipper. He then challenges the bosun to do better and goes to his day cabin for some sleep while the bosun takes the ship on the next trawl. The bosun catches eighty baskets on his haul, much to his joy and the crew's amusement. When the skipper comes up he sets off to show that he can get a good haul too. He manages only forty baskets. He stomps off below again and leaves the mate to have a go and with orders to make sure he betters the bosun's haul. The mate then caught 120 baskets, nearly three full bags, much to everyone's amusement except the skipper's and the bosun's. It is the best haul of the trip. Three bags means that there is so much fish in the cod end that it cannot be hauled inboard in one go. With the mouth of the net safely on board, the rest of the net is left in the water full of fish; the cod end is roped off from the rest of the net then it is raised out and emptied. The cod end knot is retied then put back in the water and half of the remaining fish are brought into the cod end by hauling in on the net and the cod end filled again. This is repeated until the whole catch is emptied. Hence, three bags means three full cod ends. That night I am called out of the radio room by the mate to see the *Ross Cleveland*, which we are passing close by. She has stopped and is hauling her net on board about forty yards off our starboard beam. The crews stop working and wave to their pals on the other ship. The *Ross Cleveland* was lost with all hands, except one, in Isafjord, north-west Iceland, on 4 February 1968 after being overcome by ice in a storm and turning turtle.

The good weather continues through the trip and we are now taking this good weather for granted, with clear blue skies, calm seas and gulls around the ship. The fishing, however, is varied and we move from ground to ground in search of the 'Fish Shops' that can make a really good trip.

In the evenings I often sit in the radio room with George as I try to understand the system of 'Skeds' or 'Scheduled Broadcasts' to other trawlers and the office. George has spent most of his life on the trawlers. He explains patiently how the trawlers send their messages to the owners in Hull. If the ship is north of Wick then the ship sends a Morse message direct to Wick Radio Station in the north of Scotland. Wick then send a 'wire', a form of telegram, to the owners. If the ship is south of Wick then it uses coastal radio stations at Stonehaven, Cullercoats or Humber Radio Station.

On the grounds, one of the trawlers in the company is nominated as the 'Control Ship. It is their sparks' responsibility to contact all the company ships on the grounds and collate a 'sked' twice a day telling the company that all the trawlers are OK and where they are, what they are doing, i.e. fishing, steaming, moving grounds, dodging bad weather, etc. This is done for all the side-winders at Iceland. The trawlers at Greenland or on the Grand Banks have their own control ship and their messages are sent via Halifax, Nova Scotia or Portishead if they are in the Atlantic. The freezer trawlers have their own sked systems.

Portishead Radio Station is also used by the vessels at Greenland as it is more powerful than Wick. However, Portishead is also the 'Empire Radio Station' and handles radio traffic from ships all over the Empire so it is busier and costs more.

One evening, we are sitting chatting in the radio room and George is listening to various Morse messages that are being transmitted by Wick Radio when the bosun who was on watch calls for us to go out to see a sunset. The sun slowly sinks into the sea leaving a black sea, a warm red sky and high clouds tinged with pink against a blue sky. The sunset lingers for hours, not finally fading until after midnight. During that time we watch the *Notts Forest*, a Grimsby trawler, come up over the horizon from the south, pass us and vanish away to the north. It was a very calm, peaceful night, and the Atlantic rolls gently by. The many hundreds of stars reminded me that it was across these same waters that Eric the Red led the Vikings across the Atlantic using the same stars to set up the Iceland and later the Greenland, settlements.

The trawl deck is a dangerous place and one that the skipper would only let me onto when he deemed it was safe. The heavy steel wires, or trawl warps, that hold the net are under fantastic tension when we are fishing. If the net snags on an underwater obstacle, which happens fairly often then these warps can snap. When that happens they flick back across the deck at lightning speed as the huge tensions are released. Anyone in their way has no time to escape and men have been cut in half before they even know what is happening. Sometimes a snapped warp or wire will flick and catch a man's overall or waterproof and carry him over the side. When hauling and shooting the deck is dangerous as a number of heavy wires are being let out, or held fast, as the gear is released and set. As the ship rolls across the wind and sea to allow the men to haul the net up to the ship's side, the sea can pull the net back into the sea and if hands get caught in the net then their owner will follow them over the side. There are numerous stories of trawlermen who have been washed over the side by one wave and washed back on board and dumped unceremoniously on the deck by the next wave. There are, unfortunately, stories of those who were washed over and did not get back. However, being injured by the equipment itself is the main danger. The gallows with the huge trawl doors which have to be handled during hauling and shooting, and with the main trawl warp running through them, is a favourite place to lose a finger or hand as the ton of solid timber and steel bangs up against the steel gallows inches from thick steel wire warps under tension. When the crew are gutting, the deck is lethally slippery with fish scales, offal and seawater. The crew use razor sharp knives to gut the fish and then throw the fish up into the washer. A slip here, a trip there, a rogue wave washing aboard and you can easily find yourself being gutted. The deep-sea trawling industry has always been the most dangerous occupation, way ahead of coal mining, in terms of injuries and deaths on the job. This is something that has never been recognized in the price of fish.

Lord Lovat off Iceland in 1970, seen from HMS *Keppel* as she slowly trawls downwind.

Helping the Sparks take the baskets of cod livers down aft to the boilers, or helping chop ice down below was about as much as a pleasurer was allowed to do. It was certainly not a place to ask the crew to stop gutting and show me how to do it. They wanted to get it done as soon as possible and get back to their bunks.

We have been at sea for over twelve days now and the morning finds us towing towards the north with Iceland away on the port beam. The ragged, blue snow-topped mountains lie along the horizon. The ship is in a happy mood because of the good weather and reasonable catches.

One quiet, sunny afternoon, we are towing along and Big Dave and I were sitting in the crew mess having a pot of tea. The watch on deck is replacing a net belly after the last haul as the belly of the net was torn. It has to be replaced before the net can shot again and then the old belly is repaired. Dave is telling me about both the poor quality and small quantities of food that are put on board. Trawlers did not have deep freezers on board in those days so it was either fresh or tinned food, after the fresh ran out. He says there were only ten OXO cubes to cover twenty-one men for twenty-one days; only four tins of custard powder. By now, we have run out of potatoes, peas, carrots, and custard. There is some meat left but not enough to see us home and we are very low on flour for bread. Big Dave had ditched all the cabbages after three days and now after twelve we have run out of potatoes. We will probably be away for at least another eight days. How can we have run out of a basic item

Lord Lovat in the swell on a winter's day off Iceland.

like potatoes? This is alarming! However, it is the lack of custard powder that concerns me most. All that is left are a few poor joints of meat, tinned steak and, of course, fish. I asked Dave if there is any chance the skipper would go into Iceland for more food and he replies without hesitation 'No chance, but they might sack me at the end'. He tells me that Hellyers has a reputation for poor food and that no fresh fruit is ever put on board except on Christmas trips. He also tells me that he has been sacked four times from trawlers for running out of food. Is that a good thing to know I wonder?

Some of the crew wander in and sit down for a pot of tea. Colin, the Spare Hand, who had been farming and is the vocal one amongst the crew, rolls himself a ciggy and starts to quiz me as to why I am there. 'What does a posh southerner like you want to be doing on this rust bucket?' This is a logical question, but one that I suddenly find very difficult to answer. Saying 'because I wanted to see what it was like' seemed very weak. I burble about always having liked trawlers and wanting to go to the Arctic. They stare at me incomprehensively. To them there has never been any thought as to going to sea in trawlers. It is the world in which they have been brought up. It was expected of them and it is what they expected to do. Equally, they cannot comprehend someone from such a different environment and background even wanting to see what it is like. They have probably never given any thought to seeing the Arctic as a romantic, faraway place of famous explorers or of getting excited by the look of trawler's fine lines. To them it is just a job and, apart from the money, not a very good one. Why would anyone from outside the industry ever want to spend three weeks on a trawler unless they were totally mad? I am sure that this is what they think but they are decent enough not to actually say it. They change tack and ask about my school, home and whether or not I have a girlfriend. Why did I want to leave her for three weeks to come here? I could see their point. Maybe I am mad?

I keep occupied by doing odd jobs about the ship such as painting the steering box in the wheelhouse as it was badly scratched and looked scruffy against the big, varnished, wooden-spoked wheel. I polish all the bridge brass work again, which has become my main role on board. I also try and help out a bit in the galley, with Big Dave.

We are now drawing near to the end of the trip. Colin calls me aside on deck and says 'You spend a lot of time in the wheelhouse, has the skipper said anything about heading for home yet?' 'No, not a word'. Most of the crew recognise when the end of a trip is approaching by the amount of fish we are catching and a good estimate of the ships endurance. No one says anything and the skipper certainly never gives a clue to anyone. He keeps all his options open until the very end. If for example his last haul is a bumper one he may stay and fish out the 'Fish Shop' before setting off. However, I did hear the skipper and the mate, discussing which market they thought they should aim at. This is the critical issue, as to land on the same day as a lot of other trawlers means low fish prices on the market while to be the only ship landing can lead to bumper prices, especially near the weekend. Again, guesswork and intelligence combine to give a best guess. Which ships sailed in the days before us and where they are fishing; what time is high water in Hull and what day of the week will our catch be marketed? These are factors that all go into the intelligence pot. Today is Saturday and they were discussing Thursday or Friday markets. To catch Friday's market would mean docking on the Thursday morning tide as the evening tide would not give the bobbers enough time to land the catch.

The next afternoon we are towing peacefully along. Fat Dave is on watch, the skipper is turned in and most of the crew are below as the last haul has all been gutted. The cricket test match is playing on the radio in the radio room. Suddenly, the ship gives a jolt. 'We have come fast!' calls Dave. 'Go and tell the skipper.' I turn and jump towards the ladder down to his cabin, but by the time I get to the top of the ladder, the skipper is already halfway up it. 'Stop Engines, Hard a starboard', he yells. 'Already there, Skipper', calls Dave. 'Knock out the warps!' yells the skipper into the intercom down to the crew's mess as the watch on deck emerge from the mess after feeling the jolt. The ship stops with the warps pointing straight out to starboard. 'Release the winch brakes', the skipper yells out of the window as the bosun runs forward. Slowly the ship eases round on to her track and then gently retraces them. The term 'Coming Fast' means that the net has snagged on an underwater object. It could be a

Lord Lovat from the fo'c'sle.

protruding rock or a piece of wreckage. It could certainly destroy the whole net as well as lose whatever catch is in it. In bad weather, coming fast can endanger the whole ship if the net is either not cut away from the ship quickly or the ship can release the net herself. This is always the preferred action but it is not always possible. The cost of losing a complete net, trawl warps and the doors is very high and one that would need a lot of explaining back in the office. The plan is to slowly turn the ship round then tow the net backwards off the fastening, or obstruction, from the direction she towed onto it. This will certainly result in losing all of the fish already in the net but, hopefully will prevent further tearing of the net. Most of the time, it works. The loss of one haul is small compared to the cost of a complete net and ground gear. On this occasion we are lucky. The weather is calm and the net has not got itself too entangled with the obstruction. The net is hauled back in. Luckily it is not too badly damaged and the crew get it repaired and back in the water in a short time. The skipper heaves a big sigh of relief then spends some time studying the charts and marking the position of the fastening so he can avoid it next time. Then he leaves the mate to it and goes back down to finish his sleep.

A couple of days later, we are enjoying a fine and sunny morning after a good breakfast of eggs and bacon and the ship is towing along in a calm blue sea. The crew is now getting restless to know when we might stop fishing and head for home and the tension is beginning to mount. They are certain that the skipper has made up his mind but just won't tell them. As the pleasurer, I am quizzed almost hourly as to what the skipper might have said. They do not seem to believe me when I say he has told me nothing. The rumour is that we will be heading for home tonight. At about seven o'clock that evening I am in the wheelhouse with the skipper and we have just had a good haul of sixty baskets. He turns to me and says with a smile on his face 'Should we have one more tow?' 'You are the skipper, but why not, one more for luck?' I reply. He nods, still smiling. At half past ten that night we haul in a catch of fifty baskets and the skipper seems satisfied. The skipper leans out of the bridge window and yells down 'Take in the Doors.' A cheer goes up, as that is the sign that we have now finished fishing and heading for home. The big trawl boards are hoisted inboard and secured and the nets are stowed against the bulwark. The last catch of the trip is being gutted as the telegraph rings down 'Full Ahead' and we set off on a course of south-south-east. The ship gently vibrates as the propeller bites into the cold Atlantic and starts to push us towards home at full power. We do not have a full hold but the skipper has worked out that, if we catch the right market, the catch we have might fetch a good price. A holiday atmosphere descends. We have been at sea for fifteen days and now are heading for home. I spend the late evening in the wheelhouse watching the sea slide by. The skipper has turned in and begins to try and catch up on his many hours of lost sleep.

I wake at seven the next morning. It seems quiet with no winch noises or calls of the watch on deck gutting. I hear the sound of the sea rushing past as the ship rolls along, the cabin and bunk are gently vibrating and far away I can hear the deep throb of the engines. As I go up into the wheelhouse I look out and see that the south-eastern horizon ahead is dominated by a wall of rocky cliffs capped by dark mountains and cloud. 'Faeroes', said Roy who is on watch, 'They are about 60 miles away.' What a fantastic sight they are. The apparent closeness is caused by an optical illusion often seen in the Arctic that allows you to see objects much further away than you can at lower latitudes. I watch these towering cliffs through the binoculars. It is not possible to see the foot of the cliffs but the cracks and gullies on the cliff faces are plainly visible.

After breakfast, the crew begins to break down and stow the nets. The bobbins and head ropes are detached. The washer is taken down and stowed. The sun breaks through and it turns into a fine sunny day, even so the clouds hang low over the giant cliffs of the Faeroes all day and make it seem a forbidding and dangerous place. This is not an area to be caught without power on a lee shore! The cliffs are about 1,000-feet high and drop vertically down into the sea. There is no sign of any habitation and no sign of any form of shore, just sheer cliffs straight down into the Atlantic.

At about four o'clock we pass the *Kingston Sapphire*, outward bound for

A Hull trawler fishing off Iceland, winter 1970, with ice forming on deck. Believed to be *St Gerontius* owned by T. Hamlings.

Iceland. She is also owned by Hellyers and we all cheer each other from the bridge. The noise brings others up from below.

By evening, the Faeroes are dropping astern and cloud still tops the mountains but the cliffs are now looking a little softer as they glow a deep red colour in the evening sun. A long north-east swell is running and seems to be giving the *Lord Lovat* an extra shove for home with each wave that rolls under her. I take the helm for an hour or so. I had had a couple of goes on the way up to Iceland but not with the stern sea. It is tricky getting the hang of it with the quartering sea lifting and turning the ship in spite of my efforts to keep her straight and not to 'Chase the lubber line'. This is easily done when you are a novice and you try and steer the compass point towards the ship rather than the ship towards the compass point. I struggle and at one point Roy calls out 'Bloody hell, Gordon will have us back at Iceland next.' 'Go the other way.' I get the hang of it after a bit more practice. Several kittiwakes sit motionless on the whaleback watching the seas go by. Others hang motionless in the air alongside the bridge, letting the wind off the ship give them all the lift they need. It is very unusual for birds to sit on ships for long periods of time as they can and do get seasick.

By now, the food situation has got worse and fish has become the main food item. A few people are starting to moan. Today we have fish again but without chips, as the potatoes have all gone. We had a stew yesterday that Big Dave concocted from whatever tins he could find in the cupboards. The flour has all gone too so there will be no more fresh bread.

In spite of this, the work continues. The mate supervises everyone, including me, to get the ship tidied up and scrubbed clean for docking. Drums of detergent are brought up from the stores and we all set to scrubbing the passageways and bathrooms, clearing out old newspapers from the mess so that the ship will be as clean and tidy as possible.

As it had been foggy on the way out I want to see the Pentland Firth on the way home so I get up at three in the morning to see it. On the starboard side we can see the street lights of Thurso as we get into the Firth. The skipper points out the various lights of Stroma, Dunnet, and Hoy, etc. Dunnet Head light, with its whitewashed cottages, looks very peaceful and clean. A small cargo ship looms up coming towards us. We can hear her engines throbbing as she heads out into the Atlantic but we can see no sign of life on board.

Dawn is breaking as we round the sheer cliffs of Duncansby Head and come back into the North Sea. We feel as if we are almost home! I see the trawler that George had told me about, the one that had been washed ashore on Stroma, which I missed seeing on the way out. It is just a rusty hull now but clearly a trawler sitting high and dry on the flat rocks. As we sail down the Scottish coast, past Kinnaird Head, Rattray Head, Fraserburgh, and Aberdeen, the work goes on of cleaning and stowing everything and getting the decks and storage racks properly squared away and making the ship spotless for entering port. All the bathrooms and heads are scrubbed out and the smell of industrial strength detergent fills the ship. I ask if the ships are ever checked when we get in and am told yes as one of the managers from the office always goes round them and if they were not properly clean the mate gets it in the neck.

That evening we find ourselves looking at about forty radar contacts dead ahead. This turns out to be a large German fishing fleet moving north. It is a very impressive sight. The Germans are regarded as good professionals in the deep-sea trawling game. Their new big freezer trawlers are bigger and, so the crew tells me, better equipped with better accommodation and better run than ours. Later that night we see the red looms of the lights of Newcastle and Sunderland over the western horizon. I wonder what people in those places are doing as we steam down the coast. Is anyone watching our lights and wondering what ship we are? I somehow doubt it. At sea you are out of sight and out of mind for those ashore.

Today is the last morning at sea. I awake early and see Spurn Point Light out of the porthole. We are almost home and about to enter the river Humber. The water is mud brown from the Estuary and flat calm as *Lord Lovat* turns into the Humber past Spurn Head Lighthouse and we slide up the wide, brown river. A light summer haze lies along the fields and it seems strange to see hedges and fields again as I watch a small brown van driving along a lane by the water. The sun shines brightly as we pass Grimsby and Immingham and finally we sail by the city of Hull itself. The light mist on the land lifts to leave a fine morning and the spires of the city are standing proud of the rest of this maritime city and its history. How many ship's crews over the centuries have returned from the Arctic to see this scene? I think of all the whalers and the trawlermen that had sailed up this river at the end of long and punishing trips to the Arctic and looked at this scene. It feels good to be back again.

We drop anchor at Killingholm in No. 1 anchorage to wait for high tide, which is due at quarter past ten. We will be the first trawler to dock. An hour later, the *Portia*, a new diesel-electric powered trawler and also owned by Hellyers, arrives and drops her anchor astern of us. I say thank you to the skipper and George, and thank the skipper for the use of his bunk. He smiles and says it has been fine on the couch. He tells me to jump ashore with the crew at the dock Head and to get on my way. After packing my few belongings I go back on deck. As the *Lord Lovat* heaves in her anchor and steams slowly towards the lock head the rest of the crew start to emerge on deck carrying their bags but I do not recognise any of them. They have all spent the morning showering, shaving and cleaning. They have changed into their smart, going-ashore suits and shining, winkle-picker shoes, and have washed and combed their hair for the first time all trip. The strong scent of after shave lotions envelops the deck. They are all chattering excitedly about going ashore and being home again; even though in two days time they will be sailing again.

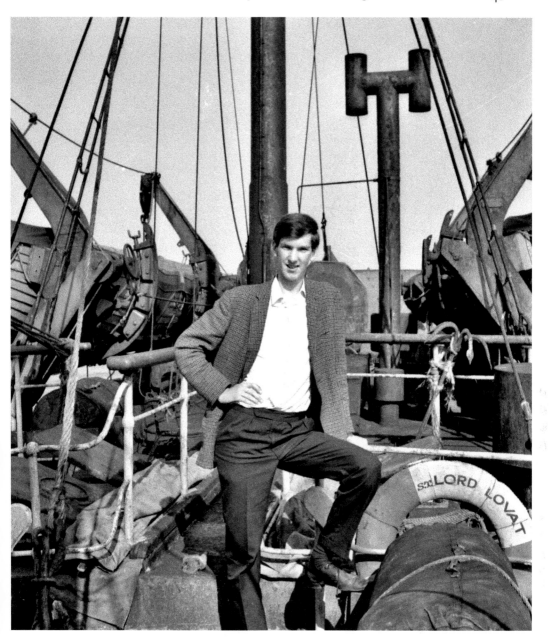

The author on board *Lord Lovat*, dressed up in his 'going ashore rig' just before we docked.

At 10.30 a.m. we come alongside the pier by the dock Head. The Customs man jumps aboard. Colin shouts across the deck to him 'Watch him, mate, he's a Pleasurer and has thousands of fags in 'is bag.' The crew laugh. The Customs man looks at me, then smiles, seeing the joke. 'Ave a good trip, lad?' 'Anything else to declare, lad, other than the fags?' 'No.' 'OK, off you go.' With that I jump ashore with the others as the tug comes out of the dock and makes fast to the stern of *Lord Lovat*. The only ones left on board are those needed to help get the ship towed into the dock and up to the berth on the Market. I stand on the quayside watching as *Lord Lovat* is towed stern first through the lock and up the St Andrews Fish Dock to her berth on the market. I watch her until she disappears behind the gantry of the road bridge and the other trawlers in the dock and feel a little sad that it is now all over.

The catch will be unloaded by the bobbers during the night so it will be fresh and ready for the market which opens at seven o'clock in the morning. The crew will come down to the office at about ten o'clock to collect their pay, which depends totally on the value of the catch. Crew pay is calculated on a sliding scale applied to the whole crew from the skipper down to the deckie learner and the galley boy. As a pleasurer I was not due to get anything.

Big Dave is chatting with his taxi driver. Every trawlererman seems to have his own taxi driver who automatically comes to the dock to meet him and take him home. Big Dave gives me a lift in his taxi. He drops me off at the Mission before heading for his home up on the Yorkshire coast.

The next day I go down onto the dock and see a few of the crew by the office. They have got their 'Settlings'. Not a bad trip, but not the best, seemed to be their verdict. I say my final farewells to them as they then head off to the Subway Club on Subway Street for a few beers. I walk on up the dock looking at the trawlers getting ready to sail and reflect on the trip. It has been an eye-opener to life at sea. Whatever I do I cannot really see myself becoming a trawlerman. That, I think, is something that you are born to and is not really a career choice. In spite of that my fascination for Arctic trawlers and the life they entail is deeper than ever. I have found enough in what I have seen and learnt to know that I certainly want to do something connected with the sea and ships. Time alone will tell me what. The memories of this trip will stay with me and will never be forgotten.

I reach the end of the dock. *Lord Lovat* is still berthed on the market quay. Now everyone has gone, the fish has been landed and sold and she lies on the berth, forgotten, silent, empty and dead. However, later today she will be towed down the dock where she will be refueled, fresh ice will be loaded, new and replacement nets will be put aboard, and fresh food stores stowed. Then tomorrow night the crew will return, her boilers will be fired up, generators will hum into life, lights will go on and she will come back to life. At high tide she will sail north for the Arctic again. I wonder whether I will ever return to

Hull Fish Dock and the world that revolves around it. I take a last look at *Lord Lovat*, listen to the bustle of the dock then turn and head for Hull Station. In fact, I was to return to Fish Dock and work for Hellyer Bros. But that is another story.

CHAPTER 2

The Royal Navy – Officer Training

With the innocence of youth and the blindness of inexperience, I set out on a route that would pitch me head first into the life of a Nelsonian seaman where I was to become the subject of a Royal Naval board of Enquiry on my very first day at sea. I had been struggling to decide which career path to take. In spite of my love for travel and the sea, vocational tests pointed to architecture as the best career for me. As I had some doubts, before embarking on a seven-year college course I went to work in an architect's office in London as an 'architectural assistant', which was basically, an office boy. The work consisted of learning to draw different scale plans of drainage systems under supervision from one of the partners, as well as making the coffees, getting rid of unwanted sales reps, and visiting the local printers two or three times a day. Unfortunately, after working in there for nine months and seeing first-hand what the daily nine to five life of the qualified architects consisted of, I was convinced that this was not really the career for me.

Having spent so many hours staring aimlessly out of windows dreaming of ships and the sea, I had seen an advert for the Royal Navy and decided to try and see if I could get in on a five-year Short Service Commission. I would then, hopefully, be able to say that I had done something of note that was recognized in civilian life and might even help me on in the world afterwards. So, one lunch time, I walked down to Whitehall and up the grand steps into Old Admiralty Building. I was met by a slightly surprised civil servant and I asked him, 'Excuse me but how do I join the Navy?' He did not seem sure, not an encouraging start, but he went away and returned with a form for me to take home and fill in. This was duly sent off. Some weeks later and after having decided that my application had been rejected, I was stunned to get a letter inviting me to the Admiralty Interview board in HMS *Sultan*, a naval shore establishment in Gosport.

The Admiralty Interview Board

This was three days of non-stop activity. The boards were run throughout the year with each board selecting two or three candidates for the next term's entry. In our batch of applicants there were about twelve to fifteen of us, all competing for two or three places at the Britannia Royal Naval College at Dartmouth, where if we were successful, we would be trained to be naval officers. Most of the activity took place in a red brick, two-storey building where we slept in a dormitory, ate in a mess room and did our written tests in the classrooms, and the oral phases of the interview process took place in a large board room on the ground floor.

The first day was spent doing written tests. These essentially were testing us for basic literacy and included mathematics and geometry, essay writing and tests on the use of English. We also did a number of psychometric tests that looked at our abilities, personality traits and attitudes. After dinner on the first night one of the officers came in and said 'You do not have to stay here all evening you know. Why don't you go to the pub for a drink? It's just down the road' 'How friendly the Navy is', we all thought. So off we all trooped down to the pub. It was not too crowded. There was a mixed group of people at one table and a couple of men on their own playing darts. Most of the men seemed to have naval haircuts, but then in Gosport so did everyone as nearly everyone was Navy. Once we had got our beers, I found myself chatting to Nick, a guy about my own age who also wanted to do a Short Service Commission and had been on a trip on the *Malcolm Miller*, though not a full Tall Ships Race. After a couple of beers, Nick and I decided to go back to the mess but a group of the others who were beginning to enjoy themselves stayed on 'just for one more beer'.

In the brief that was sent to us before we came to the board we were asked to bring swimming trunks and plimsolls. The next day we found out why. At breakfast we were all given a set of navy overalls and told to wear them over our swimming trunks. As we were being mustered by the POs, Nick nudged me in the ribs. 'Aren't they the two guys who were playing darts at the pub last night?' I looked across. They were! It was now clear that they had been in the pub, appearing to be normal pub goers, but were in fact watching us and our behavior once we were clear of HMS *Sultan*. I wondered whether those that had stayed on for another beer or three had spotted them too!

We spent the day undergoing physical leadership tests, which took place in a converted warehouse about a quarter of a mile away. For these tests we were divided into teams of six and each team had to complete a series of six timed tasks. One person in the team was nominated by the examiners as the leader for each task, but the other members were expected to contribute ideas as the task went on. Each series of tasks involved arranging a given set of equipment such as planks of wood, wooden poles, large oil drums, lengths of rope, and heavy

Britannia Royal Naval College sitting high above the town of Dartmouth.

ropes that were suspended from the roof. The team then had to design and build a route across or around an 'obstacle'. They then had to take an 'object of high value', in most cases an old ammunition box; across the imaginary obstacle in a set amount of time. For most tests there was only one way to do it and at first glance there never seemed to be enough equipment to complete the task. The nominated team leader had to work out how to rig the available equipment and then brief and lead the team in its construction. Then he had to get the 'object' and all his team over it in the time allowed.

For some tests the obstacle was a 12-foot wide by 5-foot deep tank of cold water, for others just the floor, but a floor that was deemed to be a bottomless ravine and anyone or anything that was dropped was immediately deemed to be out of the game. My swimming trunks were put to good use when I lost my balance and fell into the water tank on the second test. I was then wet and cold for the rest of the morning. On the test for which I was nominated to lead the team, we had to build a rope and plank bridge across a bottomless ravine. All the time an examining officer was yelling 'You should have finished planning it by now!' 'How much more chatting are you lot going to do?' 'You should have your bridge built by now!' 'You only have ten minutes left' Get a move on! Are you sure you have done that right?' and other such motivational shouts. I managed not to panic, and we persevered; but when we ran out of time we had not even completed the bridge, let alone got anyone across it! We were told that we had made a mistake at the beginning by misjudging the width of the gap and the length of the planks so were really doomed before we started. However, we did not lose any men down the ravine and I thought that perhaps I had shown signs of leading from the front, but even so I did not feel very optimistic about my chances of selection.

After we were allowed to dry off and change, the rest of the day was taken up with one-to-one interviews with a psychologist who probed us about our views, family, background and our personal prejudices. There was then a further group interview. In this, a team of six of us sat before the main board and were given a written brief of the problem to be solved. In our case it was set in Antarctica where a member of a small naval survey party had been badly injured in a fall down a crevasse up on a glacier. We had to decide how to get the injured man back to base. However, there were all sorts of limitations placed on us such as the helicopter's fuel, bad weather and other higher priority tasks for the helicopter. This was a free-thinking session with no nominated leader but designed, I think, to find out who in the group could or would take a lead and, with help from the team, think the problem out and persuade the others that this was the right solution. Our group seemed to deal with the problem rationally and each step was worked out and agreed and we got close to some form of a solution when the captain stopped us by saying, 'OK you seem to have a fairly good handle on this. Let's look at what you missed.'

On the last day we met the board individually and were quizzed about our reasons for being there as well as our background and future aspirations. This was perhaps the most daunting part as the board. I was sent in and found myself in a large and otherwise empty room. The board members, six officers led the captain, sat on a low stage behind a long table. In the middle of the room, and placed on its own facing the board, was an upright chair for the candidate. I was directed to sit down on the chair. I was reminded of the painting by William Yeames of the small son of a Royalist being questioned by a group of Roundhead soldiers and titled 'And when did you last see your father?' The proceedings began with a general background session and then my CV was investigated. Misleading or erroneous statements in CVs were quickly discovered and no mercy was shown if anyone tried to bull their way through. A little earlier one candidate came out almost in tears after his CV was found to contain some fiction and he was left in no doubt what the board thought about it. I was then asked to point to the correct parts of a blank map of the UK when asked where certain places were located. The same test was then done on a blank world map. The Chairman asked 'What have you done in your life that makes you feel that you are qualified to join the Royal Navy?' I recounted my trips to sea on the *Lord Lovat*, the *Silvana* and the *Sir Winston Churchill* in the Tall Ships Race. Most of the board seemed to accept that as an OK thing to do. One of the officers however did not. 'Why on earth would you want to do that?' 'A Hull trawler for goodness sake!' The implication being that a naval officer would never do such a thing. At the time I thought this was strange as surely a naval officer would and should know what life on a trawler was like but this was all part of the interview technique and was done to try and make us lose our cool. I bit my tongue and said nothing. What could I say?

The questions resumed. 'If you were to join the Royal Navy what type of ship would you like to serve in and why?' Prior to going to the interview I had no idea about the different types of naval ship. They were all just warships to me and I had not thought too much about it. However, the previous day I had noticed a large model in the main hallway of an RN County Class destroyer, (whatever that was?) and an engraved plate describing the ship and all the gunnery systems, missile and special systems with which it was fitted. When I was asked the question I tried to remember what I had read on this plaque and caused a few smiles along the board when I said in a confident voice that 'I want to serve in a County Class Destroyer because it has stabilisers, Sir.'

After three days we were sent on our way, exhausted and confused. The board gave us absolutely no indication of how we had fared and each of us was sure we had failed to get into the Royal Navy. What would I do now? Perhaps I should now try the Merchant Navy? All they said was that if in the next week to ten days we were invited for an MOD medical examination this would mean that we had passed the board and would be selected for the Royal Navy, provided that we passed the medical tests. A week or more went by with no word, but then I received a phone call from the MOD telling me that I was invited to the Services Medical Centre in London for a full medical and dental check. Following an afternoon in Empress State Building near Earl's Court of being endlessly prodded, poked, asked to cough, 'now stand against that freezing cold X-ray machine', told to put out my tongue, cough, touch my toes, and being hit with a hammer I was allowed to get dressed. 'Right, that's all here, now just your dental check up!' Was joining the Navy really worth all this? Finally I was allowed to go! Happily, a couple of days later a letter arrived saying that barring a couple of fillings, I was fit enough for the Royal Navy!

BRNC

The Britannia Royal Naval College at Dartmouth stands proudly behind the town, overlooking the river Dart and out to sea. A few weeks later I found myself, along with over 200 others, standing on the parade ground in the front of the college. We had been brought into the college by bus from Newton Abbot Station. As I got off the bus a petty officer yelled at me 'Name and initial?' 'Gray, G.' He consulted a list, 'Right, stand over there by the green flag. Next!' Why was everyone yelling? For a naval cadet on day one it was an imposing and very intimidating scene. As we waited for everyone to be sorted I looked about my new home. I felt sure that the architect, Aston Webb, had deliberately designed the facade of the college so that all the windows and tall white towers glared critically down on us. It was as if the college was already looking for our failings and weaknesses and was keeping a logbook with all the reasons why we were are not fit to follow the great naval heroes who had trod this parade ground before us.

To our left, the gleaming white figurehead of Britannia herself, complete with her Triton, stared past us and out to sea as if we did not exist. Later we would learn that one of the biggest mistakes we could make in any written work at the college was to misspell her name. This instantly earned us the yell from the lecturer of 'Britannia with ONE "T" and TWO "N"s'. Report to Britannia, salute her and repeat 'One "T" and two "N"s twenty times!' You then had to double from the classroom to the figurehead, and stand there, alone on the parade ground, saluting and calling out 'Britannia with one "T" and two "N"s'. All the time the rest of the college watched you from the glowering windows. You only ever misspelt her name once! At the river end of the parade ground the captain of the college's house stood in its privileged and dominant position and glared suspiciously at us all. It represented somewhere we should aspire to live one day, but really without much hope as we were mere cadets and to live in the captain's house was something from another world.

A young, tall and pale sub-lieutenant, called 'SIR' to us, took charge of about forty of us and marched us to Drake Division. Nervously, we looked about us at the long corridors with polished wood floors, the endless rows of framed photos of groups of cadets who had gone before, or of naval heroes from the past, all wrapped in the smell of wood wax polish. We went across the grand double-storied quarter deck and past the library, then up endless stairs until we were told to stop in another long, dark, wooden-floored corridor. This was the part of the college that would be our home for the next year. We were a little encouraged as the sub-lieutenant not only looked younger than some of us but seemed more nervous than we did too. I was lucky to find I was in a two-berth cabin which I was to share with a friendly Londoner called Geoff Luker. He was a friendly, easy-going guy and he and I shared the cabin for six months, becoming good friends. In spite of all the rigours and constant demands of naval training, I cannot remember Geoff and I ever losing our tempers or falling out with each. He seemed to be able to take everything with a shrug and a smile and it helped me no end, as I tended to take things, perhaps, a bit too seriously. Unlike some cadets who had fathers in the Navy, or some form of naval family background, Geoff and I had none at all so we were able to help each other along as we unraveled the seemingly endless mysteries of naval life, its customs and language.

Once I had settled in, one of the first things I did was to look up an old acquaintance. At school the Combined cadet Force had a Royal Naval section as well as the army and RAF sections. After a compulsory term in the army section we were given the chance to apply to join one of the others if we wanted to. The most popular was the naval section and I applied to join. The master in charge of the naval section was a teacher called Derek who was not only my physics teacher who I knew well, but also the school swimming coach, and I was part of the school swimming team. I felt that as he was a good, fair man I had a chance, but sadly my application was rejected so I had to stay in the army section and while my pals in the naval section went off for days at sea on MFVs and visited HMS *Victory* and modern warships in Portsmouth; my army pals and I learnt how to clean rifles and crawl through hedges and wet ditches keeping our bottoms down. A few years later Derek left the school to take up a senior science lecturer's position at BRNC, Dartmouth. A couple of years after that, as a new cadet, I had great delight in knocking on his study door at Dartmouth. He opened it and the look of surprise on his face was a picture. 'Crickey, Gray! What are you doing here?' 'I live here now Sir', I replied, he looked at me a little mystified. 'But you weren't in the naval section at School!' 'No Sir, you may have rejected me, but the Queen didn't.' He smiled and invited me in for some tea.

There then followed twelve months of rigorous naval shore training. Discipline was strict and the minor punishment for failure to follow College rules was normally an early morning run at 0600. The worst crime was being late. Or 'Adrift' as the Navy called it. 'Always be there five minute early' – Unless you want an 0600 run! As the divisional chief petty officer said 'Thems' wots keen gets fell in previous!' The training was thorough and covered everything from personal fitness to navigation, from parade-ground marching drills, to rifle shooting and swimming tests. We were taken on special fire-fighting training courses and taught how to deal with major shipboard fires and oil fires in all conditions, including the dark. We experienced CS gas for riot-control training and were taught to row and sail down on the river Dart. The subject list seemed endless and the classroom subjects included mechanical and electrical marine engineering, meteorology, naval supply, administration and management, communications and the principles of Action Information Organisation, or Command and Control as it is now known, and the theory of radar, radio and sonar. We learned seamanship from the three volumes of Admiralty books, including anchor-handling using fantastic working models of a battleship fo'c'sle with all the anchor cables, windlasses and slips. We learned coastal navigation and struggled to grasp the principles of circular geometry that applied to astro-navigation. On top of that they found time to send us out onto Dartmoor for expeditions that involved rigging timber A-frames to get across rivers, camping out and navigating ourselves across the moor. We were sent up the river Dart in 30-foot motor whalers on night exercises. These were a form of treasure hunt in the dark; where the clues were hidden at various land-based locations near the river. Each crew had its own leader who determined which clues to pursue and then the rest of the crew were dispatched ashore to find the clues, then work out the correct answers that would lead on to the next location. In the process, we had to avoid the many mud banks and shallows that lurk beneath the tidal Dart just waiting to catch a cadet on a falling tide. The night rang out with the calls of cadets who had lost their boat or a crew trying to drag someone back on board from the river, as well as calls for assistance or a tow from those who had run aground.

Sleep was a treasured commodity at Dartmouth. For the first six weeks we were not allowed out of the college at all; so we had to wait until we could savour the delights of Dartmouth town. Our days started at 0630 with physical exercise of some sort, PT or a run. There were also regular early morning Morse code reading sessions using a signal lantern. Then it was breakfast, where kindly ladies provided all the food that you could eat. One lady, trying to ensure her charges did not fade away from under nourishment, told a cadet 'Now you be sure to drink all your milk, young man!' 'That's what I tell my three-year-old son' growled the twenty-three-year-old ex-rating who was now an officer cadet. The mornings were filled with classroom studies while the afternoons tended to be for boat training on the river or sport. Further classroom studies took place in the evenings. The classroom studies and homework were important as at the end of the year we all had to pass our final exams to enable us to 'Pass Out' of the college. The lecturers were either civilians, like Derek, or naval officers and all were helpful and competent. As most had been through Dartmouth themselves, they knew the struggle we were facing and were eager to help us all they could. At 1600, it was rugby training or maybe a home match. And so it continued through to dinner. After dinner you had to get the cabin ready for rounds by the duty sub-lieutenant at 1930. This meant your beds had to be correctly made, clothes had to be folded and stowed correctly, shoes clean, parade boots bulled and no dust anywhere; even on top of the door or under the bunks. If any was found or there were other faults, maybe your parade boots were not up to standard, you were given a 'Rescrub' at 2100. As long as the cabin had passed rounds homework could be fitted in after that.

In addition to the new cadets there were also a similar number of sub-lieutenants on their third year courses at the college. These were officers who had just completed their midshipman's year at sea and had returned to college for further naval training and higher education courses. They provided the college staff with an extra set of monitors to hound and chase the worthless cadets. As cadets we had to run, or double, everywhere in the college. Run to meals, run between classes, etc. This was all part of getting us fit. The fun side of this was that in our smooth-soled shoes or hob-nailed parade boots you could slide enormous distances on the wood block floors! If any sub-lieutenant caught you not running, or indeed doing anything that you should not be doing (being caught with your hands in your pocket was always a favourite), then they could and often did, impose punishments then and there. The yell of 'Double that cadet' was often heard echoing round the red brick walls and the sound lives on in the heads of all those who were its target.

One of these allowed punishments was 'Quick Changes'. The sub-lieutenant would order you to attend his cabin at say 2100 in your daily battle dress rig and parade boots and then he would tell you to report back in three minutes wearing your gym kit. Then when you got there he would say 'Right, now be back here in three minutes in full mess undress.' Panic would set in (this rig was a real bummer as you had to have your bowtie tied correctly as well!). All the while the sub-lieutenant would be standing with his watch in his hand. Then he would order you to appear in, say, your sailing rig complete with seaman's knife, clean shoes, etc. Each new rig change was designed to ensure maximum clothing being removed and maximum chaos caused in the cabin. This would go on for as long as the sub-lieutenant wanted but often for at least half an hour. By this time, and given the number of different sets of clothing you had, your cabin looked like a Chinese laundry after a typhoon had hit it. The sub-lieutenant would then say 'That's all, don't do it again. Oh, by the way, I will do rounds on your cabin in ten minutes.' Even greater panic! Failure to have all your gear re-stowed and in the correct locations could result in another Rescrub thirty minutes later when all you really wanted to do was go to bed. With any luck your cabin mate would have been there all the time helping get the right rig and putting others away as you tore them off. In hindsight, it was all great fun and mattered little in the great scheme of life, but at the time it seemed that your whole life depended on it.

Sport was a big part of college life and I was fortunate enough to get into the rugby 1st XV, which gave me a lot of extra physical training most days as well as two matches a week. It also allowed us to get out of the college to play away matches against local colleges, such as Millfield College, and local rugby clubs such as Exeter. These away games normally involved a stop for fish and chips or beer on the way back. I also discovered that being in the 1st XV enabled you to escape duty parades, like rounds, if there was a college match on. Representing the college at a major sport also counted highly in your final assessments. Bit by bit I was learning how to survive and enjoy life in a navy blue suit.

HMS *Tenby* – Sea Training

Following two terms at Dartmouth we were sent to join our first ship, HMS *Tenby*, which was one of the ships in the Dartmouth Training Squadron. This squadron consisted of three frigates each converted to take a large mess deck full of cadets. The other two ships were HMS *Scarborough* and HMS *Torquay*.

HMS *Tenby* was a Whitby-Class, or a Type 12, frigate. She had been built at Cammell Laird in 1953 and commissioned in 1955. She was 360-feet-long, was

HMS *Tenby*, a Whitby-Class frigate and part of the Dartmouth training squadron in 1970. (J&C McCutcheon Collection)

2,600 tons and had twin screws. This class of ship was designed to be a fast escort with an ASW (Anti-Submarine-Warfare) capability. A feature of the class was the hull design, which gave the ships a high fo'c'sle with a sharp, flared bow to throw the seas up and away from the ship and to enable it to continue at high speed in bad weather. It was also designed to minimise the amount of water getting onto the deck that could then freeze and cause icing problems in the Arctic.

Life in the mess deck was not a great deal of fun, but then it was not meant to be. As they say in the Navy, 'If you can't take a joke, you shouldn't have joined.' There were no portholes or natural light and no air conditioning. As in the days of Nelson and HMS *Victory*, we slept, ate, read, got dressed, did our studying, and wrote letters home; all in the small same cramped space as fifty other cadets. We slept in hammocks slung directly above the fixed mess tables and benches. Each hammock touched the ones next to it with four or five to a row. The rope lashings at each end overlapped the lashings of the next row so that your head was only a couple of feet away from the feet of the guy in the next row. We each were allocated a steel locker, roughly 1 metre by ½ metre by 1 metre high, which was exactly the same as those used by the ratings, in which we had to keep everything we possessed. From our best uniform and working rigs, sports clothes, parade boots and working shoes to our civilian clothes, training books and midshipman's journal, as well as any personal items we might have.

There was a leading seaman living in the mess with us to oversee us and make sure we did things properly, especially cleaning and washing up the mess tins after meals. The first thing he showed us was how to rig and then stow our hammocks. If done properly they were as safe as houses. If not, then you could crash down in the night onto the mess table below. I had found hammocks to be good for sleeping in when I was on the *Sir Winston Churchill*, and found the same in HMS *Tenby*. Once you had mastered rigging the hammock and getting into it and sleeping on your back, they were very comfortable. Most nights the non-stop routine of cadet life in HMS *Tenby* was such that we fell asleep instantly as soon as we were in our hammocks. My immediate hammock neighbour was Graeme. Graeme and I had become friends over the months at the college and, once we were allowed to have shore leave, Graeme and I were often to be found testing the different whiskies in the Dartmouth hostelries. Graeme was a quiet guy, but bright and cheery with a very dry sense of humour. He was from Worcester Park in Surrey and had joined the Navy straight from school as a career, or general list, officer.

We all kept watches throughout the twenty-fout hours so we had to learn where everyone else slept so you could give anyone a shake in the night for their watch. It was not a popular move to wake the wrong guy. If you did and the right guy did not get his shake it was still his fault if he was late on watch.

On board we formed a part of the ship's crew and carried out the duties that the junior rates, who we replaced, would have done as well as having to carry out our practical officer's training. We were treated, as the lowest of the low. We were junior to the most junior seaman on board and regularly reminded of it.

Mortar Bombs

We sailed from Devonport for our training Cruise to the Baltic. We were all fairly excited to be at sea as naval officers, albeit very junior ones, on our way out into the big wide world and our minds were full of gorgeous Swedish blondes that we were bound to meet! On the very first full day at sea we were all sent to our action stations while the ship carried out ASW (Anti Submarine Warfare) exercises off the South coast.

My action station was in the Port Mortar Handling Room and I shared this with Bas, a fellow cadet. This was a compartment where the ASW mortars were stowed. These were large torpedo shaped items about 5 foot long and 19 inches in diameter. They were fired in a pattern of three from launchers up on the deck so that they landed in a triangular pattern round the enemy submarine and exploded to cause maximum damage. They were all painted to a colour code; some mortars were red, some green and some black, depending upon their usage. They were stored in horizontal racks that ran fore and aft along the compartment in such a way that they could be rolled onto the special lift at the after end that took them up to the Mortar Launcher compartment. The TAS (Torpedo & Anti Submarine) Petty Officer (PO) had briefed us that three of the mortars, also painted black, were set aside on the lower of two racks by the hoist. These mortars contained special calibration, test and tuning systems and they were inserted into the launch barrels and used to test and tune all the firing circuitry of the system but were never actually fired.

The job Bas and I had was to load onto the lift whatever mortars the petty officer up in the Handling Room called for. The PO simply called down the chute from the mortar bay itself, telling us which ones he wanted for the next shoot and to send them up on the lift. We were using 'Black Inert' or practice mortars on this exercise and all went well as both Bas and I were, by now, highly trained naval officers and could tell black from green and red.

After about an hour or so, and having sent up all the black ones allocated for the exercise on the main rack, the call came down the chute from the PO to 'Send up the other three'. Bas and I looked at each other. 'Which three is that?' Bas called back as we did not have any more of the black inert ones ready to send up. 'The three on the other rack' called the PO. We sent them up and heard them successfully fired in to the sea. After the exercise was concluded the PO called down for the Test Mortars to be sent up. 'Which ones are those?' we called back, both of us a little puzzled. 'The black ones on the bottom rack' he called. Bas and I looked at each other again as alarm began to strike home. Bas called back 'But we have already sent them up when you asked for them last time!' Bas has not finished his sentence when the PO burst into the Handling Room. He was, I must say, very good about it and apart from some understandable naval swearing he did not chew us out too badly. He was more concerned about going to see the Torpedo Officer to report that the only test mortars the ship had, and which were worth a considerable sum, were now on the seabed.

The torpedo officer was not so good about it. He was called Charles and was in fact the same Charles who had been the stand-offish watch officer on Sir Winston Churchill. Bas and I were summoned to the ops room. In front of the captain and a full ops room he openly accused Bas and I of lying and demanded that we be severely dealt with. The captain maintained a calm exterior and sent us away. A board of Enquiry was called on board ship that afternoon and both Bas and I spent the rest of our first full day at sea in the RN as subjects of the enquiry and explaining to the first lieutenant and the Engineer Officer exactly what had happened. Our stories tallied and the petty officer was good enough to admit to us and the Enquiry that perhaps we could have been confused and that his instructions could perhaps have been clearer. In the end he got the blame for not supervising us more closely as how could we, on the first visit to the mortar room, be expected to tell the difference between a black inert and a black test mortar let alone to question a direct order 'to send up the three on the other rack' from the petty officer torpedoes.

Our relationship with 'Charles' never recovered but we learned later that no one got on with him anyway, but our relations with the petty officer torpedoes did and we got on well with him for the rest of the three months we were on board and stationed down in his mortar handling room. Bas incidentally did very well, as he was a bright lad, becoming a full captain (air engineer).

Foreign Expedition

The training Squadron that term went to the Baltic, stopping at such places as Stockholm, Copenhagen and Kotka, in Finland. As part of our training we were expected to go on expeds (expeditions) during the ship's periods in port. These were just really camping trips aimed at sharpening up our initiative skills and get us out of the ship for a while. Graeme and I had planned to do one but Graeme went down with a bad sinus infection so a fellow cadet, Keith, and I decided that we would go camping in Denmark's sunny pastoral landscape for two nights during the ship's stay in Copenhagen. We submitted our proposal, which was accepted, got all the camping gear loaned to us from the ship's stores and set off with a map and wise words from our divisional officer, 'OK, off you go, you have the ship's phone number to ring if you need help don't you?' 'Yes, Sir' we replied. This was unlikely as we had no intention of going any further than the nearest half decent cheap hotel and enjoying a proper bath and a proper bed for two nights after putting up with the mess deck and hammocks for over two months. We soon found a pleasant small hotel in a back street near Copenhagen's old harbour. The hotel was very clean and friendly and we were shown to a bright, sunlit, twin-bedded room. It was ideal. We celebrated our freedom with a steak meal and probably more than a few lagers. We considered that we were not skiving, but actually on an 'Escape and Evasion' exercise as we certainly did not want to bump into any of the ship's officers over the next couple of days! On the second morning Keith had gone out for an early walk along the quay and I went along the corridor to the bathroom for a bath. As I tried to open the room door to get back in I realised with horror that I had left the key by the bed. I then spent a damp and chilly fifteen minutes in the Hotel Reception, standing patiently in a queue of guests who were checking out while dripping water all over the polished floor, and clutching a small, wet towel round my waist, so I could ask for a spare key. There was much Danish chuckling going on.

Once back on board we sat down together and wrote our reports of how friendly the farmer was to let us sleep in his field and how attractive his sheep were (well, we had been at sea for a while).

Seaboats

'Pull! Pull! damn you. Pull! you lazy shower!' These friendly words still haunt me. Every day at sea at 1600 we had Seaboat Pulling drills. The sea boat was a heavy 27-foot Monatague whaler; this was a wooden boat that took a crew of five oarsmen, a coxswain and a bowman to propel it. It was secured fore and aft to the ship's davits by two heavy manila ropes, called falls, which needed a good team of men on each one to lower and raise the boat with any degree of control. There were no winches, hydraulics or electric motors here. The exercise commenced with one part of the watch manning the boat and the other part manning the falls. The gunnery officer was in charge. He would stand one deck above us and became a fierce and friendless demon who clearly hated each and every one of us and who we all hated back with a vengeance. The falls were released from their cleats and lowering began. Each team on each fall had to lower away and make sure that the boat was lowered evenly or else they risked tipping the boat's crew twenty feet into the sea. Any mistakes by any individual resulted in the instant command 'That cadet, twenty press ups, now!' Then, as the sea boat reached the water, ideally as the top of a wave lifted the boat, the coxswain yelled 'Slip' and one of the boat's crew pulled the slip that released the falls from the boat. If the coxswain got the timing wrong and we missed the top of the wave, then the boat dropped a number of feet and hit the water with a crash that inspired the gunnery officer to even more inventive use of the English language. It also gave cadets in the boat very bruised backsides and rattled a few teeth; but no one ever seemed to worry about that. The boat swung out away from the ship's side and the boat rope was released by the bowman. The boat rope, that was attached to the sea boat's bow, was secured on board the ship well forward of the sea boat. It ensured that the sea boat moved off at the same speed as the ship, when it hit the water. At the same time, the ships engines were stopped then run slowly astern. We now had to get the oars out smartly and row round the ship, which towered above us and was still going faster than we were able to pull. All the time the ship was slowly, slowing down and as we rowed for the bow we just hoped that they had enough astern power running so that we did not get cut in two by the ship as we went round the bow. The grey, sharp-edged bows loomed over us as the coxswain tried to judge the turn. It was always a finely judged manoeuvre; either to give the bow a wide berth and use up precious time by pulling further, or try and save time and then risk getting the oars tangled up in the bow. That only brought on a tirade of abuse from above about scratching the ships paintwork; so it was best avoided. As we rowed our little hearts out the gunnery officer was following us round the fo'c'sle giving us lots of encouragement from high above. 'Pull you lazy lot! My four-year-old daughter could pull better than that' 'I bet she can, just to get away from you!' muttered the bowman! Many other such motivating words of advice were offered down to us from on high. Once safely round the bow we had to race down the other side. We all tried to pull together and look professional but we never quite seemed to succeed. By now though, the ship could even be going astern giving us further to row. In all sorts of seas we struggled through this daily hell. Hands and fingers aching as we hung onto the heavy wooden oars, backs sore, crabs being caught as we missed the water with the oar and much muttered cursing in the boat about the gunnery officer's parents and other general fun filled our late afternoons. Once round the stern it was back to the falls and the task of getting the oars in, not hitting the ship and hooking up to the falls. Each fall had a large, heavy, wooden block at the end. In the boat were two metal releasing mechanisms called the 'Robinson's Disengaging Gear'. As we approached, the two great wooden blocks swung menacingly at head level challenging us to catch them. We had to grab these things, drag them into the boat and hook each one onto the hooks on the releasing gear in the boat. Then we had to wait while the other part of the watch started to haul us and the boat back up to the top of the falls. Once we were back at the top and all was secure the gunnery officer told us how long we had taken and what a useless shower of girls we were and reassured us that we would never get a job on the Gosport Ferry. Then it was someone else's go! Every day we gleefully looked forward to this wonderful form of sado-masochism, which undoubtedly made men of us. Electric or hydraulic davits indeed! How soft are sailors today? 'Come on lads; time for a brew of tea on the mess deck'.

The Tot

Officers were not entitled to a daily rum ration, or the tot, as it was known. However, as officers under training we were required to witness the issue of rum that took place on board every RN ship every day at noon. This tradition ended in July 1970 after being a central part of RN life for nearly 300 years.

CHAPTER 3

HMS *Keppel* – Midshipman's Training

After our year at Dartmouth and successfully passing the final exams, we graduated or 'Passed Out' of the college at Lord High Admiral's Divisions. This major ceremony is held annually and was normally attended by HM The Queen. This is followed, the next day, by the summer ball. It is a huge affair with bands, pop groups and discos playing in different areas all over the college. Sumptuous buffet dinners for all and every Dartmouth hotel and guest house full of parents, girlfriends and close relations. Later in the evening some of us went down into the old town and looked back up at the college. Now that we had overcome the challenges that we had been set, the college's wide imperial facade of red brick and Portland stone with its central clock tower did not seem so intimidating. It looked magnificent under the floodlights and seemed to float majestically above the surrounding trees high, up on its hill overlooking the town. The warm, soothing sounds of a Caribbean steel band playing outside on the parade ground drifted down over the town, making Dartmouth a Caribbean hot spot for the night.

We were now promoted to midshipmen and sent off for a year's solid sea training in the Fleet. Here, we would live in the wardroom with the other officers and be treated as colleagues. After the trials and indignities of life as mere cadets, we left the college excited and eager to see what being an officer at sea in the Royal Navy really meant. This next period of sea training was to cover all aspects of operating a fighting ship from learning to be the officer of the watch to working in the boiler room, understanding the practicalities of stores management and catering to learning about gunnery and anti submarine warfare as well as trying to gain our qualifications for bridge watch keeping and ocean navigation. We were also expected to learn how to become a valued member of the wardroom. Oh yes, and how to clean the bilges underneath the main boilers! This year was to put all the theory we had learnt at Dartmouth into practical application. We also had to complete task books that formed a vital part of the final Midshipman's Board exam that we had to take at the end of the year at sea.

HMS *Keppel*, a Type 14 Blackwood-class ASW frigate, turns at speed in a calm sea. With thanks to David Page at www.navyphotos.co.uk. Also thanks to Peter Swarbrick at peter@swarbrick.com.

I was fortunate in that, purely by chance, I was paired up with my good friend from Dartmouth, Graeme, for our first spell as midshipmen. We were both sent to HMS *Keppel* for the first half of our midshipman's year of training at sea.

HMS *Keppel* was a Type 14 frigate, one of the 12 Blackwood Class of second rate ASW (Anti-Submarine Warfare) frigates built for the RN in the early/mid-1950s and all named after famous RN captains. They were of 1,456 tons displacement and 94 metres long with a beam of just 10 metres. They were designed to be single role, anti-submarine ships and built to help address the growing Soviet submarine threat in the north Atlantic. They were smaller and cheaper than the Type 12 frigates, such as Tenby. They had a single screw and were powered by a steam turbine. They were armed with two Limbo ASW Mortars mounted aft. Although they were essentially good sea boats, they had a terrible reputation for rolling in any sort of a seaway. Her CO was Cdr Richard Onslow.

In the 1950s, 1960s and 1970s, Britain's main fishing efforts were in the Arctic, especially round Iceland and the Barents Sea off northern Norway. One of HMS *Keppel*'s main roles was fishery protection in the Arctic. Graeme and I joined her in her home port of Rosyth in Scotland.

We arrived on board, feeling nervous and excited but looking forward to life at sea as a 'proper' naval officer. However, we were greeted on board by a strangely subdued and reticent atmosphere in the wardroom. No one seemed keen to talk to us or make us very welcome. The steward showed us where our cabins were and left us to it. Later in the day we were called down to meet the first lieutenant. Without preamble he began 'You are here for training. When not on duty you are expected to be studying in your cabin and not sitting around drinking coffee in the wardroom. The wardroom is for meals and that is all. You will address every officer on board, including the sub-lieutenants, as "Sir" and will not fraternize with the senior rates. I will inspect your Task Books every week and failure to meet the required standard is totally unacceptable due to the disgrace it would bring to the ship.' This friendly greeting took us by surprise, as this was totally contrary to what we had been led to believe that life in the fleet would be like. Everyone at Dartmouth had said how much better life as a middy would be after the strict regime of the college. We believed that we would be part of the wardroom and treated as equals (well almost equal) by our fellow officers so we could learn from them.

It was also accepted that you could call sub-lieutenants and lieutenants by their Christian names. Lieutenant commanders and above were 'Sir' to everyone below them anyway. Being told not to fraternise with senior rates was also strange as we had been told that the senior rates were the guys who could help us the most in learning about the ship and completing out task books. This was not a good start. Graeme and I found ourselves on our first day aboard sitting in my cabin wondering whether we had all been told a load of rubbish at Dartmouth.

It took us a few days to find out what was happening. The correspondence officer, or Corro, was a sub-lieutenant called Simon who was one of the good guys. He took pity on us and one afternoon called us down to his office when the first lieutenant was ashore. 'The two previous midshipmen here both badly failed their boards,' he said. 'It was obvious to everyone that they would, as they had not done any work on board and had spent most of their time loafing in the wardroom or senior rates mess. The previous first lieutenant did not chase them up at all and they failed so badly that the ship has been warned by the Admiralty to buck up. The Captain took it personally and 1st Lt got a roasting for being too lax with them'. Graeme and I were now reaping the rewards of their efforts. 'I am afraid that you two will have a tough time here as the CO and Jimmy will be onto you if they think you are not doing well enough, hence this nonsense about not being seen in the wardroom.' He added, 'Personally I think it is wrong. You have just arrived from Dartmouth and should be treated as midshipmen should be and not punished for the failings of others.' The First Lieutenant, Dave Marsh, was actually a pretty good bloke but could not show us he was.

We accepted the situation as we had no choice and were effectively excluded from the wardroom. The only officers who tried to show us some companionship were Simon, and the Torpedo Officer, Tom. At first I thought Tom was a bit stand-offish as he was very much in the image of a smooth and proper naval officer, complete with white silk handkerchief in his breast pocket. However, he was also kind and helpful as well as professional. In the meantime, Graeme and I just ate our meals and went to our cabins if we were at sea; or ashore if we were alongside and not on duty. In fact, poor Graeme did not even have a cabin. We were told that accommodation was scarce in *Keppel* and while I was allocated the last spare cabin, Graeme was told he could stow his gear in my cabin but was to sleep in the sickbay.

Luckily, Graeme had a pal in the Navy who was a couple of years senior to us and who had been based in Rosyth until just recently and he knew a group of girls in Edinburgh. They were mostly physiotherapists and nurses, and he kindly introduced us to them. Therefore Graeme and I went ashore to the 'Burg' by bus most free evenings to enjoy the company of these ladies and the comforts of their Edinburgh flat and the nearby pubs; rather than the emptiness of the cabin. The girls introduced us to others in Edinburgh and our circle of friends grew. We all went out in a group to pubs or to dinners and dances in Edinburgh. Although no romantic relationships grew from these friendships, the girls' kindness provided us with a warm and reassuringly normal base whenever *Keppel* was back in Rosyth and both Graeme and I were most grateful to Maggie, Debbie and Barbara for all their kindness.

HMS *Cavalier* – Gunnery Training

As part of our midshipman's training we had to complete the section on gunnery. Keppel did not have a big gun, well not one that would count in the gunnery exam, so we were sent off to the famous Second World War destroyer HMS Cavalier which was doing a gunnery work up in Portland. HMS Cavalier is a fine looking, open-bridged destroyer and was still one of the fastest ships in the Navy. She also evoked a strong feeling of the last war and memories of the black and white movies about the war at sea. I always expected Kenneth More in a duffle coat to come round the corner at any moment.

She was, by our standards, a big ship too, having 2 x 4.5-inch gun turrets forward and one 4.5-inch turret aft. Our gunnery training proceeded well alongside the ships own gunnery exercises and we seemed to do OK. During the firing exercises we spent time in all the main compartments including the magazines, the gun turrets, the ops room and even the gunnery radar dome at the very top of the mast. It seems strange now to remember that the computers used for gunnery predictions were mechanical systems dating from the last war and full of cogs, rods and gears grinding round under a big, glass-topped table rather than the Laptop/PC type of systems that ships have today.

HMS *Cavalier*, in dock at Chatham, a true warship and a fine-looking ship. She was also one of the fastest ships in the Royal Navy. (Photo with thanks to David Page at www.navyphotos.co.uk and Peter Swarbrick at peter@swarbrick.com)

In between the gunnery exercises it was a great thrill to be on the open bridge with the ship going at speed. The open bridge was designed so that most of the wind was swept up and over the bridge rather than allowed to blow through it so it was not as windy a place as you might think. I loved to be on watch and lean over the front of the bridge, look down onto the two gun turrets and the finely-pointed bows as they sliced through the Channel throwing the seas aside in disdain. The nearest comparison I can make is that it is the difference between being in a car and on a motorbike. With an open bridge you are part of the seascape, at one with all that is out there and aware of any changes. You can hear and see things more easily, without reflections on glass windows or bulkheads getting in the way. In a closed bridge, while it may be warmer and dry, you are removed from the real world outside and isolated from the weather and other ships. However, I am not sure I would be saying that if we had been in Cavalier in the Arctic winter as we were in *Keppel*!

Graeme and I were made welcome in Cavalier, being treated well by the captain and the officers in the wardroom and even getting an invitation down to the chief's mess when the training was over. We both came away feeling proud to have spent time on such a famous old ship and even better for feeling that, at least in some ships, midshipmen were treated as fellow officers. HMS Cavalier is now preserved in Historic Chatham Dockyard and is well worth a visit.

North Sea Storm

Back in *Keppel*, life went on. We sailed from the Forth on a fine day but with the weather forecast to be bad with a storm on its way. We were off to take part in an exercise with aircraft and submarines well out in the northern areas of the North Sea. The exercise commenced and we midshipmen were expected to witness most of the activity in the ops room. This was always difficult as the officers directly concerned in the exercise spent their time leaning across the plotting table and so it was normally impossible to see anything except their backsides and they never had time to stop and turn round to tell you what was happening so it was all a bit of a waste of time! After we had been chasing around the sea for a couple of days the weather deteriorated rapidly and seasickness took its firm hold. The sickbay attendant gave me Marzine tablets to counter it. They were supposed to dull the brain's senses to movement. They did that OK, and they also made me very, very sleepy. I spent most of the next couple of days doing nothing more than trying to stay awake. I had no idea what was going on in the exercise and cared even less. At one point I woke up to find myself standing up and literally hanging by one hand onto an overhead pipe in the ops room. I could not have been asleep for long but I had definitely been asleep on my feet. We were also tormented by the RAF Shackleton Maritime Patrol aircraft that flew low over us during their searches for signs of submarines. As we bucked and rolled in the rough seas below, they turned round at the end of their time on task and flew back to their base, for a pleasant afternoon tea with scones and jam by the fire in the mess at RAF Turnhouse. In the meantime, the weather continued to deteriorate. We were now well out in the middle of the North Sea and well clear of any shelter that the land might have offered. The winds blew down from the Arctic with nothing to break their blast and increased beyond Force 8 and were soon well into a Force 9 from the north-west and the seas quickly building up.

Early in the storm they had been lumpy and confused, as if the waves themselves were not sure which way they should be going. These would hit the ship with a loud bang on the bows that shook the ship, and knocked her out of her rhythm as she tried to make her course. The smashed wave disintegrated into a mass of spray that rose high above the bows, was caught by the wind and sent smashing against the bridge windows blocking all vision for three or four seconds before it drained off. The ship would judder as if we had hit a submerged object, and we grabbed for a hand hold as we did not know which way the ship would fall away from the wave. The sound of breaking crockery from somewhere down in the ship, often followed by a muffled curse or a yell often, accompanied the sea's attack. We could sometimes see these lumpy rogue waves coming, sometimes not, but they always seemed to catch us unawares; forcing us to grab any handhold available or risk being sent flying across the

A North Sea storm sends the seas over the bows of HMS *Keppel*.

ship into any sharp projection that always seemed to be where you landed. Finally, the exercise coordinators ashore wisely decided to cancel the exercise as it was now a full Force 9 or even Storm Force 10 at times and impossible to do anything except try and stay afloat.

'May Day May Day May Day' crackled faintly from the bridge VHF loudspeaker. Instantly everyone on the bridge was silent and alert. We strained to make out the details but could not. We called the Wireless Room to pick up the call and reply if the other ship could hear us. We passed the details to the coastguard. The call came from a Scottish fishing vessel, which was in serious difficulties somewhere well to the north. We, therefore, headed off in that direction to try and see if we could help in the search. Other ships were nearer but we still responded. This was almost into the wind and sea, which were coming from the northwest. Once the wind had been blowing at Force 9 for a length of time, down the length of the Norwegian Sea and the North Sea, the waves settled into a more regular rhythm and pattern but they also grew in height. We watched from the bridge as the next wave rolled towards us, its crest level with the bridge. As the ship slipped through the trough the bows dipped under the waters of the next wave, the sea rolling gently over the bows, trying to push her down. The ship then fought back as her buoyancy caught and threw off the water on her bows sending a mass of water rushing back along the fo'c'sle to smash against the front of the superstructure. She rose strongly, lifting us up to the top of the wave. The sky was an opaque mist and the horizon a mass of white spray where the crests had been blown off the wave tops and swept horizontally across the top of the sea. The wind had become a screaming, vicious roar as it tore past the ship. So the weather continued for at least another two days. Somehow we hung on. Watches were changed and we got what sleep we could, wedged hard in our bunks, knees against one side and backside against the other. Luckily, the bunks were deep-sided and we had proper bunk boards that fitted onto the front edge so we did not fall out. The galley was closed for all normal meals and we were reduced to eating ships biscuits and the occasional 'pot mess'.

We rode the seas by steering a course at about 30 degrees off from the wind. In this way we lessened the physical impact of the waves and the motion of the ship as the 30- and 40-foot-high waves rolled by. The bridge was asking the engines for 14 knots of speed but the ship could only make good 4 or 5 knots due to the seas and weather. There was nothing we could do but keep going as by this stage turning round across the huge seas would have been very dangerous.

As the days went on there was still no positive news on the fishing boat and a search was continuing up north. Our ship gradually took more and more damage. One of the emergency sound powered telephones rang on the bridge. I picked it up. 'Bridge.' 'Sir this is Leading Seaman Jones down aft, in the after seamans mess. The Forth Bridge has been knocked off its mounting and we cannot get forward.' 'Stay in the mess while we check it out,' I replied. The chief shipwright went to have a look. 'They are right. It is unsafe to use as it could go over the side at any time. We cannot do anything about it in this weather, as if I put a man out there we will lose him,' he reported. There were two sailors' mess decks situated right down aft. Normally, the sailors could get to the main forward area of the ship, where the galley and bridge areas were, via the open deck. In this weather that was impossible as the decks were constantly being swept by the seas as they rolled by. The alternative route, which they had been using was for them to go up onto the deckhouse roofs and come past the funnel and across a metal girder bridge, called the Forth bridge, that linked the after deckhouses to the forward part of the ship. However, the seas had smashed the securing points for the bridge and it had been shifted off its mountings and lay tilted at a crazy angle so there was no way for the seamen to get forward. So the sailors down aft were ordered to stay there for the time being. In fact they were there for about forty-eight hours surviving on whatever food they had in their mess.

The damage inflicted elsewhere on the ship was heavy. The seas broke open welded joints between the open weather deck and the vertical boiler room casing. Water flooded into the boiler room which needed constant pumping until the seas eased. The anti-submarine mortar launchers, which were normally stowed vertically, were smashed down flat, damaging their gearing in the process. The metal screens around the mortar mounts themselves were smashed and bent out of shape or broken. Then, water started to break through an emergency escape hatch on the fo'c'sle. This was at the forward end of the main passageway, at the top of an escape ladder. There was no way anyone could get out onto the fo'c'sle deck to secure it so we tried to secure it from below with rope lashings and tackles to try and keep it as tightly shut as possible. If that hatch had gone then we could have been in deep trouble as, with the ship burying her bows into the waves, she would quickly have flooded. The ship's wireless aerials were ripped off, some of the liferafts on the port side were torn off and both of the ships wooden motor boats were badly smashed up on their davits and unusable. The full power of the sea was demonstrated by the effect it had on the paintwork. Right round the forward part of the engine room casing along the main deck, where the seas had rushed and channeled themselves when they rolled aboard, all the paint had been rubbed off by the seas constantly smashing their way along the deck. Whole areas of the bulkhead, many square feet in size, were stripped back to bare metal and left shining like silver.

People used to gather outside the ops room by an aft facing door out onto the upper deck one deck above the main weather deck. From there you could not only get some fresh air into the ship, as the normal ventilation system had been shut down, but you could stand in safety and watch as the seas roared round the side of the superstructure and pounded aboard, raging across the open weather deck and smashing all in their path.

The search for the fishing vessel was finally called off and *Keppel* was told by the coast guard that she was no longer needed in the search so once the seas allowed we gingerly turned and made our way back to Rosyth. I think the captain, Richard Onslow, had spent at least forty-eight hours on the bridge through the worst of it all. It was only then as we entered the shelter of the Forth that we were able to get out on deck and view the damage. Engineers were trying to plug the broken welds and signalers were rigging temporary aerials. When we got back to Rosyth, the ship spent three weeks in dock for the damage to be repaired and a number of other alterations done to try and prevent it happening again. This was October and the ship's next two missions over the winter were to Iceland and the Norwegian Arctic.

The Arctic

Arctic Fishery Protection is one of the oldest duties that the RN is called upon to perform. Its history can be traced back to 1586. Lord Nelson himself was a midshipman on HMS *Carcass* on fishery protection duties in the Arctic in 1773 and later he was captain of HMS *Albermarle* when she was engaged on fishery protection duties. Nelson has a great deal in common with me as I also learned how to sail on the Norfolk Broads, as did he, and we were both midshipmen in the Fishery Protection Squadron. But that, I am afraid, is where the similarity

HMS *Keppel* running down sea off Iceland.

ends. In the early seventies, Arctic Fishery Protection was still a major activity not least because of the outcry that had sprung up after the loss of three Hull trawlers within one week in January and February 1968. Two were lost off north-west Iceland and one in the Norwegian Sea.

That week, during exceptionally bad gales, blinding snow storms and heavy icy conditions in the area, two trawlers, the *Kingston Peridot* and the *Ross Cleveland* were seeking the shelter of Isafjord, a long fjord on the north-west tip of Iceland, as excessive ice built up on their masts and rigging. Even with all hands smashing at the ice with picks and hammers it was impossible to clear such huge amounts of solid ice. Sadly, both ships were overcome by the ice to the point where they became top heavy and capsized. That same week, a third trawler, the *St Romanus*, disappeared without trace somewhere in the Norwegian Sea. There was only one survivor from all three ships. His name was Harry Edom and he was the mate of the *Ross Cleveland*. A fourth ship, the *Notts County* from Grimsby, nearly suffered the same fate but managed to run herself aground on a beach in Iceland and all but one of her nineteen crew were rescued by the Icelandic coastguard ship *Odinn*. That week a total of fifty-seven Hull fishermen were lost, including a fifteen-year-old boy, Michael Barnes, who was on his first trip as a galley boy. This series of disasters caused a lot of questions to be asked and provisions were made to prevent it happening

MT *Portia* in Isafjord in north-west Iceland. Isafjord was the scene of a double tragedy in the winter of 1967/68 when two Hull trawlers were lost due to heavy ice.

again. Protest groups were set up by the wives of the trawlermen. They simply wanted all fishing in the Arctic to be banned in winter. It was an understandable position to take, but it was never going to happen in spite of all the protesters' strong feelings about the safety of the trawlers, the dock head protests and TV coverage. That same winter week, over 120 men still set sail in trawlers from Hull for the Arctic in search of fish and a good payday.

Keppel's role was to provide support where we could, carry out checks of fishing gear on all ships in the area, not just British, and to monitor the activities of the Icelandic Coast Guard vessels. Two Ministry of Agriculture & Fisheries fishery inspectors sailed with us and we had a naval doctor on board for the trip. To accommodate these extra officers I was turned out of my cabin and sent to join Graeme in the sickbay. This was a small compartment with two bunks, and its own tiny bathroom with a ¾-length bath. This bath had a rickety temporary bunk rigged over the top of it. As one bunk had to be kept free at all times for any emergency, I took one of the two bunks and Graeme decided to take the bath bunk as he was much shorter than me. As we sailed further north, it became clear that the bathroom had no heating in it at all. This was fine in the North Sea but, once we got north, poor Graeme came out in the morning absolutely blue with cold. We tried tying the door open, extra blankets, etc., but none of them worked and Graeme spent the winter freezing.

In late November off northern Iceland there are twenty-four hours of darkness; a slight lightening of the southern sky told us it was about noon, but apart from that it was dark all the time. The inspectors spent time crossing to trawlers by rubber boat to check their nets and the ships' engineers occasionally went off to assist with repairs if needed. On one occasion the diving team went off to help the *Northern Gem* free a net that they had got badly tangled round their propeller. This turned out to be a much bigger job that they anticipated and took most of the day. However, a grateful crew did send them back with a boat full of fresh cod. Fresh fish and chips for tea tonight boys!

We were patrolling the Denmark Strait and a large stationary object was reported on the radar about 20 miles away. We set off to investigate. We came up to the edge of the pack ice and could see a large iceberg frozen into the pack ice. For most of us on board it was a first. It was a dark, cloudy and gloomy day and the iceberg sat about a mile away trapped in the pack ice which itself stretched off as far as we could see.

In January, we were sent to northern Norway. As we went north we saw the fantastic beauty of the Lofoten Islands in all their winter glory. Beautiful snow-covered, pointed mountains bathed in sunshine and contrasting with the black, deep, cold waters of the fjords. We stopped in the fishing port of Harstad. It was here that I managed to get myself into trouble again. I was the Officer Of the Day (OOD) so I was not able to go ashore. That evening a cocktail party had been arranged on board for local dignitaries. After the official party, an informal one developed in the wardroom. Graeme and I were grudgingly allowed to attend these functions, but only under sufferance. One of the party guests was a rather nice young lady and I wanted to escort her home. Graeme agreed to take over the duty and the young lady and I left by taxi. I saw her back to her parent's home just out of the town. They lived in a beautiful, wooden house, which was wrapped in the folds of the deep forest snow and lit by candles in the windows. After a pleasant 'coffee and chat' we agreed to meet again the next day when she would show me around Harstad.

When I arrived back on board, it was well after midnight and the quartermaster told me that the first lieutenant wanted to see me in his cabin immediately I got back on board. This could only mean trouble but I could not think of anything that I had done! Dave was sitting at his desk reading. Without looking up he said 'And where are the OOD keys?' A jolt ran through me and my day collapsed. I realised instantly that they were still in my pocket. These were the keys to the main keyboard on the ship. They are always kept by the OOD and are never, ever to leave the ship. I had forgotten to hand them over to Graeme in my hurry to get ashore. 'Oh hell,' I said 'I am sorry, Sir, I forgot to hand them over.' That cost me three days stoppage of leave and killed stone dead any possibility of a budding romance with the young lady. The moral here 'Don't let your heart rule your head!'

The next day Simon called Graeme and I down to his office. 'The Admiralty have written to the ship telling you your next ships for the last six months of your Mids year. Gordon, you are going to HMS *Puncheston*.' 'A sweeper!

Great! But where is it based?' Simon checked some papers. 'I am pretty sure she is based in Bahrain', he said. 'Bahrain! Oh Lord, that is the last place I wanted to go. The Arctic to the Gulf; who says the RN does not have a sense of humour?' Graeme was going to a minesweeper, HMS *Wooton*, based in HMS *Lochinvar*, just across the Forth from Rosyth, so he would be able to continue with the friendships we had developed in Edinburgh and would be much nearer Edinburgh too. 'You jammy-wot-not Graeme!'

CHAPTER 4

HMS *Rhyl*

To equip me to be a junior lieutenant in HMS *Rhyl*, a frigate, I was sent on various specialist courses. One was a Flight Deck Officers Course, which was great fun, and I spent an enjoyable few weeks, with other trainee flight deck officers, at the Royal Naval air station at Portland learning about helicopters and their operation and how to marshal them over a pitching deck and bring them down safely. A lot of this course involved spending sunny days out on a barge that had been converted into a dummy frigate's flight deck and was anchored out in the middle of Portland harbour. An endless series of helicopters then flew out and practiced landing on the barge under our inexpert guidance as each of us took turns to wave ping-pong-bat-shaped batons at the helicopters trying to get them to do what we wanted them to do and trying to talk to them on the radio.

I also attended the divisional officer's course. In the Royal Navy, an officer will have a number of senior and junior ratings in his 'Division'. The DO is responsible for giving the rating regular formal appraisals and writing his official report when he or the DO leave the ship. He also ensures that the ratings are put forward for the appropriate training courses so they get the right qualifications and experience to go before promotion boards. Equally important, the DO is the rating's point of contact for getting help or advice of any kind; be it professional or personal. As a lot of ratings are newly married with very young families, the separation that being at sea brings can cause tensions and problems both at home and at sea. The DO is there to help the rating and his family when these and other problems occur. For a young, single officer this brings its own challenges as to how to understand and handle some of the marital problems that can arise! The DO also represents the rating if he gets into trouble and is responsible for knowing each rating well enough to be able to speak on his behalf at the captain's disciplinary hearings on board or indeed at civil courts ashore if need be.

Joining HMS *Rhyl*

To join HMS *Rhyl* I was flown out by the RAF in a VC10 to Singapore, where the ship was undergoing a short maintenance period during a Far East deployment. HMS *Rhyl*'s new Flight Commander, Tim, and I went out together to join the ship. Oddly enough, both our fiancées were Wrens and both were serving in the Admiralty in London and knew each other. The two-day flight out was a long one as we went via Cyprus, Bahrain, and Gan, a tiny coral island Indian Ocean. Gan is a British RAF base on a tiny island and a few even smaller islands. The runway is short. When you are landing you think you will touch down in the sea but, just when you are reaching for your life jacket, the wheels thump down hard onto the tarmac and immediately starts to brake hard. When the plane has stopped it's very rapid braking and turns slowly round at the other end of the runway you are again looking straight down into the blue waters of the Indian Ocean, but on the other side of the island. It has been a staging post for flights going out to the Far East for many years but is always an interesting landing for passengers. We were allowed off the aircraft and went into a pleasant transit lounge for a while as they refueled the aircraft. Our short stop in Gan reminded me of a story that I had heard about Admiral Le Fanu when he was First Sea Lord in the 1960s. He was one of the most popular Admirals of his day and had the 'Nelson Touch' in terms of how well he treated others. He came to speak to us at Dartmouth and started his talk by telling us. 'I have a carved wooden sign on my desk in Whitehall that reads "There they go and I must follow them for I am their leader".' He said it reminded him to keep up with what we were all doing out in the real Navy.

HMS *Rhyl*, a Rothesay-Class type 12 ASW frigate shown here before her refit in 1972 when a hangar and flight deck were added. (J&C McCutcheon Collection)

A story is told that on one occasion he had an urgent need to get out to the Far East quickly and sought the help of the Fleet Air Arm. They happened to be about to fly two Buccaneer aircraft out to Singapore so the Admiral, as an aviator, 'cadged a lift' flying in the observer's rear seat of one of the aircraft. On arrival in Gan, the flight was met by the base CO who took the two pilots off to the officer's mess and instructed a flight sergeant to take care of the No. 2s. In the RAF, the observer would normally be a flight sergeant rather than an officer, let alone a full Admiral. Admiral Lefanu, all done up in his flying overalls and with no real badges or rank epaulettes showing, was taken to the Sergeant's mess for a cup of tea. A few hours later they were told that the aircraft were ready so went back out and flew on to Singapore. A week or so later, the CO of RAF Gan received a letter thanking him for the hospitality of his sergeant's mess during the stop over and signed by the First Sea Lord. Oh, to have seen his face!

We finally arrived in Singapore about mid-morning on a hot and steamy Singapore day and went on board HMS *Rhyl*, We were hot, tired, grubby, jet-lagged and dispirited after the marathon flight. As we got to the top of the gangway, a lieutenant commander in tropical white shorts was standing by the rail talking to a chief petty officer. He was a large man but had a friendly open face and from the way he was watching everything that was going on I thought he must be the first lieutenant. He watched Tim and I struggle up the gangway with our bags and came over and introduced himself to us. 'I am Mike, the first lieutenant', he said, extending his hand. 'You two must be our new joining officers?' We put down our bags and shook his hand. 'The bad news, I am afraid, is that, as part of the maintenance work, the ship's water main is down today so there is no air conditioning and no water in the ship today. The good news is the engineers hope to have it back on tonight. That's why I am up here in the tropical sun as it is cooler than being inside the ship. Welcome to *Rhyl*!' 'Thanks', was all either of us could say! The ship was like a sauna inside and it was certainly hotter than the outside air but we just had to bear it and sweat it out until late in the evening when normal water and air conditioning were resumed. Having flown out together and both of us with Wrens as fiancées, as well as both being 'New Boys' on board; Tim and I became good pals.

HMS *Rhyl* was an anti-submarine frigate of the Rothesay Class; commonly called the Type 12. She was 370 feet long and weighed about 2,500 tons. A twin-screw ship with a top speed of 30 knot, she had a long, thin hull that sliced beautifully through the water. She carried a crew of 235 including about sixteen officers. HMS *Rhyl* had been built in the Naval Dockyard at Portsmouth and launched in 1959. She was equipped with ASW Mortars, a twin 4.5-inch gun and an ASW Wasp helicopter. She lived a long life before finally being sunk as a torpedo target ship in 1985. The Type 12 was replaced by the highly successful and, in my view, one of the most attractive ships the Navy ever built, the Leander-class frigate.

HMS Rhyl

HMS *Rhyl* post 1972 refit. She now carries a Wasp helicopter. She was decommissioned in 1985 and sadly sunk as a torpedo target.

The CO was Commander John Hall. He was an aviator, in fact an observer as had been the CO in HMS *Nurton*. On first meeting him he struck me as a slightly shy man but he tried to be friendly. However, as most of his welcoming words were what he did not expect his officers to do, I decided that he was a bit of a stickler for things being done his way and this proved to be the case over the coming months (I suppose that as he was the captain this was to be expected). After the formal introduction and his pep talk, he told me what my responsibilities would be on board. 'Now Gordon, you are one of my sixteen officers on board and I expect the best. As you know, you will be one of my bridge officers of the watch at sea as well as an officer of the day in port. You have passed your FDO Course so you will be an FDO. I also want you to be the "Top Part of Ship" officer and the boats officer'. The Top part of ship was the main midships section of the ship's upper deck and it was here that the boats were stowed. This meant that all upper-deck maintenance and painting schedules were my responsibility along with the top part of ship petty officer. HMS *Rhyl* had two boats, both wooden motorboats, which were expected to be ready to be launched at any time and whose maintenance and appearance was now in my hands. 'In addition you will be the divisional officer for all the operations room senior and junior ratings and I want you to be the wardroom mess treasurer'. This last task involved keeping a check on all the officers' food and bar bills, laundry bills and other expenses that they built up each month and issuing them with their mess bills, collecting their money and keeping the books straight. 'Any questions?' 'Err, No, Sir', I managed. 'Good. Carry on.' I left his cabin thinking 'Where the hell do I start with this lot?'

As I left the captain's cabin, my head spinning, a voice called out 'Hi Gord! How's tricks?' It was Dave Askham. He was also one of the other lieutenants on board and we had been at Dartmouth together. He had been here for a few months already and was the 'Baby Guns' or Deputy gunnery officer, to give him his proper title. 'I think need a drink' I said. 'No problem, it's on me.' 'Thanks Dave.' After a large horse's neck (brandy and ginger ale) in the wardroom to recover I tried to remember what I had been told.

Hong Kong

About a week later the last dockyard worker left the ship and our Maintenance period was over. We cast off and sailed for Hong Kong and a deployment that would mean endless days at sea on defence watches, doing six hours on, six hours off on the bridge or the flight deck. I soon found my way around and got into the routine of life on a 'big' ship. In between the continual two- and three-week-long exercises we had just two or three days break in various ports around the region.

We were working with HMS *Tiger*, a helicopter cruiser, and HMS *Dreadnought*, the RN's first nuclear-powered submarine as well as other RN frigates in the region and an RFA that kept us fuelled and fed. Mostly, we carried out anti-submarine exercises, but there were replenishments at sea (RAS) every other day, OOW exercises and damage control exercises. No one was ever going to be bored in *Rhyl*.

We arrived in Hong Kong and berthed at the RN Base, HMS *Tamar*, right in the middle of the harbour front on Hong Kong Island. Hong Kong, with all the bustle of the harbour, the junks and sampans, lighters loading cargoes into the moored freighters out in the harbour; was exactly as I had imagined it to be. The Star Ferries constantly thrashed their way across the harbour to Kowloon. In fact, there are only two places in the world that were exactly as I had imagined them before I went there. One was Hong Kong and the other was New York.

On the first day that I was clear to go ashore, Peter, the navigator, and I went over to Kowloon one Saturday morning. Peter had been here before. 'If you have never been here then you have to go on the Star Ferry!', he said. We travelled First Class, on the upper deck, for 20 cents and watched as the harbour carried on its daily business around us and the green and white double ended ferry *Evening Star* ploughed its way between the tugs and barges over to Kowloon. In Kowloon, the main street, Nathan Road, led all the way to the border with Communist China but, at its Kowloon end, its fascinating side streets were a series of Aladdin's caves crammed full of electronics, stereos, cameras, clothing and watches. 'Buy here Jonny, I give you good price!' 'Heh, Mister! You want watch!' 'No mister you come back here, I give another 20 per cent discount!' It was a fantastic place. Peter and I explored as much as we could but after a while, the noise, the dust, the heat and the humidity pressed down on us until we had to get out of it all. Peter led the way. Just off Nathan Road, on Canton Road, we entered the Hong Kong Hotel through heavy glass doors. The air conditioning hit us like a cooling shower. Its lobby was a haven of peace, civilization and culture, instantly shutting out the noisy chaos and heat of the street. I followed Peter straight into The Gun Bar, just off the lobby, which offered chilled, draught San Miguel beer and soft easy chairs. 'Two pints of San Miguel please'. 'Yes Sir,' replied the immaculately smart barman, his red jacket matching the red décor. The soft, cool atmosphere of the bar wrapped us in its luxury. He returned with two brimming, pint-glass tankards of chilled beer sitting on a white-napkin-covered tray. We salivated while he carefully laid out the paper coasters, then the beer, the condensation already forming on the glass. Finally, he moved away with a genuine 'Enjoy your beers Sirs'. We did. Oh the joy as the iced liquid slid over our dry throats and cooled us as it went down.

We were berthed near the Wanchai area, so in the late evenings we used to make our way down to the world of Susie Wong. Wanchai covered a few blocks of narrow streets by the waterfront, but here were streets full of food stalls, bars, restaurants and local food shops. Just above our heads, hundreds of dazzling, coloured, neon signs were directing us down to see bigger, better, barer girls in the dim, dark, girlie bars. 'Heh, Gringo, you want lady? I fix for you lady, very good price!' 'I am not a gringo!' I growled back. The noise of people filled the air, stall owners chanting their wares, club hostesses calling to sailors, cyclist ringing their bells and pop music blaring our from some of the street-front bars. There always seemed to be wall to wall people; mostly they seemed to be those who lived and worked here, carrying boxes or pushing loaded hand carts, but also American sailors on R&R from Vietnam and some, just like us, tourists. We drank in the heady atmosphere of the place and its non-stop vibrancy. Exploring the bars, (a San Mig' beer here, a San Mig' beer there) and then sitting at the food stalls eating all sorts and watching the local ladies was something new and exciting for most of us. The tourist sights could wait until tomorrow!

Before we docked in Hong Kong, Tim flew the helicopter ashore to the RAF station at Kai Tak as he could not fly it off from the ship when the ship was alongside the main naval base at HMS *Tamar*. One day at breakfast Tim took me aside. 'Can you get off for today? I am taking the helicopter up for a training flight over the harbour and up into the New Territories. Do you want to come for the ride?' 'You bet I do.' I quickly cleared it with the first lieutenant and we flew from Kai Tak out low over Hong Kong Harbour, past the ship berthed at *Tamar* and we hovered over the wreck of the old Cunard liner, RMS *Queen Elizabeth*. She had been sold by Cunard to CY Tung, a famous

Hong Kong ship-owner who had nearly finished converting her into a floating university, to be called *Seawise University*. Unfortunately a fire broke out on board and she was destroyed. She was lying on her starboard side with half of her rusted and blackened hull and superstructure sticking out of the water and looking anything but the fine ocean liner that she had been. She was a really sad sight. She was eventually broken up where she lay, which was close to the main channel into the container berths. We carried on our flight almost up to the Chinese border, then back to Kai Tak.

During our second stop in Hong Kong a couple of months later there was a Typhoon warning and we were ordered to sail at once and head to the south to avoid the projected route of the typhoon which took it right over Hong Kong. Thirty-six hours later, the typhoon had passed and had missed Hong Kong so we were told we could return to port. We were planning to arrive at the entrance to the main harbour at 7 a.m. I was on the midnight to 4 a.m. watch (or 'The Middle') that night when a signal arrived from Hong Kong HQ telling us to re-plan our ETA for 0730. I handed over the message to the navigator when he came on watch at 0400. I was asleep in my cabin after my watch when at a quarter to seven the captain called me to the bridge. 'Why did you not call me when this signal came in?' 'Well, Sir, it was only a thirty minute delay and I did not think it was important enough to call you. I gave the signal to the navigator when he came on watch at 0400.' The captain disagreed. 'I will be told of all signals concerning our programme when they come in. Your shore leave is stopped for the next three days. Now, carry on.' 'Yes Sir.' Three days stoppage of leave over the last three days in Hong Kong before we headed for home. 'Great! No chance to buy any presents now!' I muttered to myself and vowed to return one day.

In the course of the next few months, as breaks between these exercises, we visited some super tropical places such as Rabaul and Manaus, both down in jungles of New Guinea; Guam: and the huge American base at Subic Bay in the Philippines, where the American insisted on buying us whisky whether or not we drank it, as well as Mauritius and Simonstown in South Africa.

South African Waters

South Africa was as lovely as I remembered it from our stay there in *Puncheston*. Unfortunately, we were not able to stay as long this time and after a couple of days we were off again, back out to chase submarines. During our time in South African waters we did a number of exercises with the South African Navy. During one of these two things occurred that helped to convince me that I was probably not cut out to be an Admiral. As a bridge watch-keeping officer in the RN you are totally responsible for the safety of the ship and her crew. While you are always under the captain's orders, the actual handling of the ship and collision avoidance and safe navigation during your watch are your responsibility. As a young twenty-two- or twenty-three-year-old this is a massive responsibility as you have, in HMS *Rhyl* for example, over 200 officers and men sleeping below decks in a ship with a wafer thin hull, who are totally dependent upon you for their safety. The following two events reflect the seriousness of the job and show how easy it is for major mistakes to take place.

Near Misses

Collision avoidance is probably the most important aspect of the bridge watch-keeping and 100 per cent pass mark is demanded in all exams during training. This covers all the different lights, shapes and sounds that every type of ship undertaking every possible activity will display or make at different times and from different angles, day and night and in fog. It is therefore something that becomes second nature as you spend at least eight hours a day on the bridge. However, there are times when things go awry.

On the first occasion one of my fellow watch keepers and pal from Dartmouth days, Dave, came down to the wardroom from the bridge at midnight where he had been officer of the watch since eight o'clock. I was having a late coffee when he came in. He was white and shaking. I asked him what was wrong. When he had got a brandy in his hand he told me. There was yet another submarine exercise going on and *Rhyl* was working with two South African frigates to try and locate and 'catch' the submarine. Dave explained that he had been concerned during the watch that the captain and ops officer down in the ops room were not totally aware of where the other ships were in relation to ours as we had all been maneuvering at high speed all over the place and a certain amount of competitiveness between ships of different nations creeps into these exercises. However, there was nothing he could do but drive *Rhyl* exactly where the CO ordered him to via the intercom. Quite often this was at speeds of up to 28 knots. During these exercises all the participating warships were in a state of 'Darkened Ship'. This meant that they had all their navigation and upper deck lights switched off and all the deadlights down over the scuttles to prevent visual detection from the submarine's periscope. The only exceptions were the helicopters, which always had all their lights on including their flashing orange strobe lights. Dave had been driving the ship all over the ocean with big and frequent course and speed changes all night. When suddenly, a dim, round, light, low down near the sea level, appeared out of the night and moved rapidly down the starboard side of our ship and very close to us. So close, in fact that Dave lost sight of it as it passed below the level of the bridge window. After a second he realised that it had been a single scuttle of another ship. He called the ops room to report it and mayhem broke out as they had no idea that we were anywhere near another ship. In fact, it was one of the South African frigates, also darkened down. Someone had forgotten to drop the deadlight on a single scuttle near the stern. We had passed her within 50 feet at about 25 knots and had not even known there was a ship nearby. If we had hit her, both ships could have ended up in half.

A few nights later, on another similar exercise, on a dark and cloudy night, a similar thing happened to me but in a different way. Again, all ships were darkened, except the helicopters. I was OOW and spent the watch holding the ops room/bridge intercom microphone in one hand and listening to and responding to orders from the CO in the ops room; and the wheelhouse intercom microphone in the other hand to pass on those orders to the wheelhouse team. At the same time I was hanging onto the compass stand, or pelorus, by my arm as the ship heeled over during another tight turn. In this exercise HMS *Tiger* was the ship we were protecting and we had been deployed as a screen to detect submarines out in front of her. During these exercises it is accepted that the OOW never has time to go to the back of the bridge to check the bridge radar screen or to go to the bridge wings for a visual check outside as the orders come up in a constant flow from the ops room below and you have to remain fixed to the conning position. As the ops room had all the relevant radar and sonar information they knew where all the other ships in the exercise were. During this exercise, the ops room team was desperately trying to keep track of a submarine contact on the sonar.

As we were altering course at 24 knots and steadying up on a new course I looked out ahead and was glad to see that there were no merchant ship's lights down the course we were now on. Then, dead ahead, out in the blackness, a red light came on. It was one small, steady, red light. In the dark it was impossible to gauge its distance from us but as it was quite high up it must be quite close or, something very big. However, it still looked like a small light and not really like a ship's red port light, which have a faded glow about them; this was a sharp crisp light. I stared at it hard through the bridge window to try and work out what I was looking at. 'Ops bridge, can you identify any contacts dead ahead. I have a single red light on our current heading?' I never got a response. My brain was racing. Was it a red flare of some sort? This one red light could not be a merchantman as there were no other masthead lights or deck lights. It was most unlikely to be one of the warships in the exercise as they were all fully darkened and the light was too high up to be from any of the ships with which we were working. In the absence of any guidance or information from the ops room and, as we were doing 24 knots directly towards this light, which was now getting ever nearer; I decided that I needed to act. 'Starboard 20, Revolution 120', at the same time I switched on all our navigation lights. We came round 40 degrees off our original course and reduced speed to 15 knots. I put the lights on so that whatever this red light was, it would be able to see us while I worked out what was going on.

'What the hell are you doing officer of the watch? You have messed up the attack on the submarine!' The CO had appeared behind me in a wild rage having rushed up from the ops room one deck below. 'Sir, can you tell me what that single red light is? I asked him. 'What light? The light was now out on the port beam but still there. I pointed it out to him. He looked at it, said nothing then dashed off below to the ops room to try and find out what it was.

In a couple of minutes it became clear what it was. HMS *Tiger* had a very high flight deck, about twice as high as other warships. One of her Sea King helicopters had started to switch on its engines as I steadied onto a collision course with her. Apparently, when Sea King helicopters start to switch on their engines the first thing that comes on in the start sequence is their navigation lights. This happens before the normal yellow strobe lights. We therefore had been steaming at 24 knots directly towards a ship about four times bigger than us and apparently no one in our ops room knew she was even there. If the helo had not started up at that moment we would probably have hit *Tiger* full on. I always had an impression that the submarine was actually hiding underneath *Tiger* hence our attack course directly at *Tiger*! However, I was not impressed by the CO's reaction as my sole responsibility as OOW was ship's safety. For doing my job I got a bollocking as his game of chasing a submarine had been spoiled.

Unfortunately, later, during the same series of exercises, two South African Hawker Hunter jets collided in mid-air while flying together in thick cloud over the sea and we had to search for wreckage and the bodies of the two dead pilots for two days until they were found.

We finally made it back to Plymouth and half the ship's company were sent off on early Christmas leave. I volunteered to stay on board until Christmas Eve and take the later leave period. I got back home at about five o'clock on Christmas Eve and Doreen was there to meet me on the station. We hugged for several seconds. I had last seen her nearly ten months ago at Brize Norton and I can still remember how good that hug felt.

North Again

It was a cold, still, clear January night off the north Cape of Norway. We were steaming north at a gentle 12 knots and I was on watch on the bridge for the middle watch (midnight to 4 a.m.). We have been sent north on Arctic fishery protection duty. I was working on the chart table when I was suddenly aware that there was a bright light coming into the bridge from outside. I turned round to find that the night had turned into day. The northern sky had a bright, milky white curtain spread across it with an arm of light stretching up into the heavens. This spread, slowly at first, then more quickly until it formed a giant arch, like a very bright Milky Way, up across the sky and over our heads and beyond. It flickered and grew, then slowly shrunk and faded. Then, a few minutes later it started again, this time more strongly with green washes of colour in the milky whites and in a wider arc with definite shapes and folds. I hurried out onto the bridge wing with the duty rating and we stood open-mouthed staring up at the skies. It looked as if the Viking gods were gently shaking successive rows of giant, sheer silk curtains of shimmering light as they drifted across the sky. We could see the stars through these curtains and the trawlers that were around us all lay illuminated by the bright Aurora light. As the lights danced so they changed colour, the milky whites had now given way totally to pale greens, then to stronger, brighter greens and then to bright emerald greens as the bottoms of the shot silk curtains rippled and shimmered over our heads in a cosmic breeze. Sometimes, showers of colour seemed to fall from the curtains as if shaken loose while the lights continued to move and dance. We felt dwarfed by the magnitude and magnificence of this spectacle as it enveloped us totally. It continued to ebb and flow over many minutes. As it reached its peak, soft pinks and deep reds fused into the edges of the greens and whites and the lights stretched almost completely across the whole dome of the sky. Only the southern and eastern skies were unaffected. As suddenly as it came it began to fade and shrink back to the northern skies, back to pale greens, then to milky whites then just a white glow in the north. It went completely and darkness returned. I do not know how long it lasted but well over twenty minutes. Later in the watch smaller displays revealed themselves but by four o'clock it was all over. It was the most fantastic display of the Aurora Borealis (Northern Lights) that I have ever seen.

Perisher

In the spring we were sent to the Clyde to take part in the 'Perisher Course'. This is the final course for submarine officers to qualify for command of a submarine. All of the candidates, or students, are experienced submarine officers and have been selected to come on the course. It is referred to as 'The Perisher' because if the officer fails he will 'perish' as a submariner. If at any point the examiner, or 'teacher' as he is known, decides that a candidate does not have what it takes to be a submarine CO he is put ashore that night and is never appointed to submarines again. The teacher is always a senior and experienced submarine CO who is always very well respected by the 'students'. The final two weeks of the course consists of the candidates taking turns at various manoeuvres and attacks while the surface ships do what is requested by the teacher to provide a good examination. As the course progresses these become more involved with two and finally three frigates acting as targets. For the submariner these are fraught times. They are listening to sonar reports, looking through the periscope when they have to so they can look at the frigates to calculate the rates of bearing change, the courses and speeds of the different frigates and then trying to get the submarine into a torpedo firing position and at the same time not getting hit themselves. It requires, cool, mental agility and at least three stopwatches to be able to do all the mental calculations in a career threatening practical exam situation with the examiner standing right behind you. By the end of the course the frigate officer of the watch has instructions from his CO that when he sees a periscope ahead, he is to charge it at top speed. This is great fun if you are the OOW of the frigate. It is not so much fun if you are the submariner candidate and have not seen the frigate coming. On a number of occasions I stood on the bridge steering for the periscope and willing it to go down as I lost sight of it under the bows of the ship. We never did hit one, though a few must have been very near misses. We were assured that 'teacher' always had things under control and could always 'Flood Q' if he had to. Q was the biggest ballast tank in the submarine that when flooded, it filled so fast that the submarine went down like a lift. Every evening, after the exercises were complete, the submarine would go into Arran and one or more failed submariners would be put ashore.

I am afraid to say that on those runs we often went far too close to some of the local fishing boats, which were trying to earn an honest living. We must have scared them half to death as a 3,000-ton frigate rocketed past a 50-ton fishing boat about 50 feet away at 28 knots.

After our time in the Clyde we went into Liverpool for an official visit. I was the quarterdeck officer at this stage and responsible for managing the crew working at the very stern of the ship as we docked. As we approached the lock entrance, a tug was positioning itself at the stern and waiting for a line to be thrown to it. For some reason the lads were not at their best and three heaving lines all fell well short of the tug. All the time the ship was moving slowly towards the Lock entrance. 'Come on lads, concentrate and get the throw right', I shouted. Another two lines fell short, then one landed on the tug but bounced off. I was getting exasperated but there was little I could do. Throwing a heaving line needs to be done properly and cannot be hurried so hounding the lads was counterproductive. The ship's PA from the bridge then burst into life and the first lieutenant's voice boomed out over the deck. 'Quarterdeck Officer! How much longer are you going be getting a line on the tug?'

In my frustration at the lads, and at the stupid question that had just been asked, I picked up the microphone and replied in as calm a voice as I could muster 'One minute, seventeen seconds, Sir'. There was silence, apart from the lads on the quarterdeck giggling. Ian, the WEO, who was on the bridge at the time said the place fell apart with laughter, even the captain smiled! The first lieutenant never mentioned it again. Well, it was a stupid question.

After such exciting games, my naval career drew to an end as I had done my time as a short service officer. The Navy had offered me a full-time career, but they could not offer me any Arctic fishery protection ships, or a job as a specialist Torpedo and Anti-Submarine Officer (TASO) a subject in which I had become quite interested. I tried to see if I stood any chance of serving in the ice patrol ship, HMS *Endurance*. My appointer informed me he could not put a short service officer forward to serve in HMS *Endurance* as, ideally, I needed to be a career officer, probably a specialist hydrographer and a preferably a 'high flyer' as well. I was certainly not a hydrographer and I had the feeling that 'high flyer' was not a term that the Navy applied to me; so that solved that problem.

The Navy could however, offer me a career that entailed another twelve years of continuous sea jobs in the ops room as a warfare/operations officer before I could expect a job ashore. I did not really fancy that for twelve years so I decided to move on, said thank you very much and a little sadly, left the RN. While the Navy was not to be my career I am still extremely proud of the RN and my short time serving in it. The naval training and discipline undoubtedly did me some good and stood me in good stead for my future. The experiences and responsibility I had, even as a junior officer, were beyond the comprehension of many of my school pals who had gone on to university. When you join the Navy you become suspicious of the intensity of the training and the dogmatic manner in which it is carried out. There is a tendency to see it as brain washing. While you are in the Navy you do not see, or really appreciate, the benefits and the quality of the training you have had. Not just technical and academic training but the need for honesty, integrity, self discipline, self pride in your appearance and team work. When you are living and working day and night in very close proximity with your shipmates, you have to get on with people and ensure you do not antagonise them. In the close environment of a warship any personal failings such as dishonesty or laziness are very soon found out. Giving 'Service' for others quickly becomes second nature and runs deep in the naval blood. It was only when I left the Navy and witnessed the attitudes and lack of professionalism of some people in the civilian and commercial worlds that I realised how lucky I had been to have had the training and experience I had in the Navy. Again, there is a Navy truism for it – 'Once Navy, Always Navy'.

CHAPTER 5

Wardroom to Fish Dock

'You will never get a job ashore. All you're qualified to do is stand on the bridge'. Such was the encouragement from Kevin, the bumptious Deputy Weapons Electrical Officer (DWEO) on *Rhyl*. 'Maybe, but we will see'. I said in bravado, but quietly thinking 'Well, he has a point!'

A few weeks later, in a large wood-panelled office overlooking the Hull Fish Dock, Mr Hellyer looked over his specs at me and said 'Well, the job is yours if you want it. Just let me know in a few days.' For about six months before the end of my time in the Royal Navy I had been looking for a job outside the Service and, at the same time, Doreen and I were planning to get married. For work I had targeted the fishing industry due to my previous interest in it and love of trawlers. One of the companies that I wrote to was Hellyer Bros of Hull who had taken me to sea as a sixteen-year-old on the *Lord Lovat*. Hellyer Bros were now part of a huge trawling company called British Untied Trawlers (BUT), which was the biggest trawling company in Europe at the time. Graham Hellyer was the managing Director and offered me the job of Electronics Manager for BUT at a meeting in his office during my Easter leave period. It was Graham himself who had agreed to let me sail in the *Lord Lovat* those years before. He was a tall, slim gentleman, fairly quiet and probably shy, unless angered. He drove a beautiful, old, grey Bentley, always seemed to wear soft green tweed suits and I always found him to be polite and interested in what I had to say, a complete gentleman. But then I was never in the same position as one of his skippers after a poor trip.

Doreen and I got married in her local church in Stirlingshire and set up home in Beverley, a wonderful Yorkshire market town a few miles north of Hull.

So here I was working on 'fish dock.' I had gone from life in an RN wardroom to 'Ull Fish Dock'. This really was 'From the Sublime to the Cor' Blimey'. At the time, the trawling industry was going through an electronics revolution; new types of echo sounders, sonars, net monitors and fish finders were coming into the industry, as well as new radio technology such as single side-band radios and new navigation systems such as Loran C and even satellite navigation were appearing; so the trawler companies needed to be able to keep up to speed on these issues so they fitted the right and best equipment to their ships. The plan was that this was to be my role.

Hellyer Bros was now part of British United Trawlers, or BUT, and Graham Hellyer was its MD. He was a legend in Hull. His grandfather had started the company, Hellyers Bros, in the south-west of England with his brother in the nineteenth century and the family had moved up to Hull when the North Sea herring were discovered in the 'Silver Pits.' After his father retired, Graham and his brother Mark ran the business, continuing to expand and grow the fleet and to send trawlers to the Arctic and return with a profit. They ruled with rods of iron. Hellyers', by the early 1960s, had become the biggest trawler company in Hull and probably the country at that time. Any skipper was only ever as good as his last trip and a couple of bad trips could see him out of a ship and a job for a long time.

The formation of BUT created the biggest deep-sea trawling company in Europe. It now included many of the old trawling companies that had grown up independently over the years. The BUT group operated trawlers out of five UK ports, Hull, Grimsby, Fleetwood, Aberdeen and Granton. In total, BUT owned and operated over 130 side trawlers (freshers) and a fleet of about fourteen of the latest and most sophisticated factory freezer stern trawlers (freezers) in the world, each of about 1,000 to 1,500 tons.

The Job

In spite of the fine title of electronic manager and an office overlooking the dock, as the new boy on the dock I still had to learn the ropes and I started each day at seven o'clock on the fish market. The catches from the ships that had docked the day before were all laid out overnight and sorted by fish type and date of catching ready for the market. The market was a wet and noisy place; water from melting ice was always running everywhere, the rattling aluminium kits of fish being slid across the wet concrete market, the yelling of fish merchants making their bids and the constant calls of salesman running the auction. The filleters, who worked for the fish merchants, were setting up their stands to start their day's work of standing out in all weathers, filleting ice cold fish in ice cold water. Added to all this was all the other apparent chaos of people milling round the fish on an often cold, wet and windy market.

For all matters concerning the fresh fish side trawlers and the morning side trawler inspections at the market, I reported to Fresh Fish Trawler Manager George Hartley, who had been on the fish dock since he left school. George had a wealth of knowledge and was very highly respected. He was a small bull of a man with a shiny, bald head. He was always smartly dressed and mostly a cheery soul. He was very firm and very fair, always asked the right questions, (especially when you did not want him to) and was someone you would not want to cross. He reported directly to Graham Hellyer, or Mr Graham, as he was known to everyone on the dock.

Every morning I got into my overalls and boots and went aboard all the company trawlers that had landed and checked that all the fishing gear had been properly stowed away, that the ropes, wires and bobbins were all properly stowed, etc. These checks also included making sure that the insides of the cod-liver boilers had been thoroughly cleaned. I also checked the accommodation, the galley, the bathrooms, messes, etc., to ensure that they were all clean and tidy and ready for the next trip, which would probably sail the following night. I always went up to the bridge and radio room to read any notes left for me and the radio repair companies by the RO. I then reported back to George that all was well, or not. In general, however, the ships were always clean, safe and tidy.

What made these early morning starts more pleasurable was that after the market had finished (normally by about half past eight or nine o'clock) those of us from the office that had been on the market changed out of our market overalls and into our office suits, then sat down to a proper Yorkshire breakfast of eggs and bacon, toast and marmalade and tea in the directors' dining room, which overlooked the Humber and often, a warming sunrise coming up over the river. Breakfast in the directors' dining room was a welcome time to recoup after the fun of the market and before the day's real work began and to catch up on dockside gossip.

By about eleven o' clock 'the Trip was in'. This meant that the office had worked out the total sales from the catches and deducted the running costs of the ships for the trip and then calculated the pay for each crewman on board. So, by eleven, the MD knew exactly how much money each trip had made. It was a very neat commercial exercise.

Ship to Shore Communications

When I joined BUT the system used for the daily radio position reports from the fleet was under severe scrutiny following the loss of the BUT freezer trawler *Gaul* in early 1974. She had disappeared with all hands in the Barents Sea in atrocious weather. There was astonishment in Hull that a new ship equipped with the latest communications systems could just disappear. The Official board of Trade Enquiry into the loss of the *Gaul* opened in Hull on the same day that I started work for the Company. Late that same afternoon Graham Hellyer returned from the inquiry and called me down to his office. It had emerged at the Inquiry that it was over forty-eight hours after the ship was last seen before anyone in the Hull office realised that something was wrong.

He ordered me to investigate, as a matter of urgency, the whole radio reporting system and the procedures currently used and to devise a better and more foolproof method of monitoring the ships when they were at sea. Every trawler in the company was supposed to make contact with the office, either directly or indirectly, at least once every twenty-four hours. The old Morse radio systems on board the older ships did not always make this easy and quite often trawlers simply could not make contact with the UK shore radio stations. This could be due to lack of transmitter power, atmospherics, bad weather, or just the sheer distance from the UK. I had to sort this out and create a foolproof, disciplined system that would ensure every trawler at sea was accounted for by the office at least twice a day. To achieve this I would need the help of the radio operators and to spend time at sea in the Arctic seeing first-hand what went on.

In the winter of 1974 there had been a large number of trawlers that had missed their scheduled office calls, or 'Skeds' as they were known; for all sorts of reasons and had then called in a day or so later saying all was well. It was this element of doubt that had to be removed so that the duty manager in the office could be confident that all was well, or if not, start a full search at the earliest opportunity. After a few weeks work, and after trips to sea and many discussions with the ROs, I put forward a new system that overlaid the existing system so that if a ship did not respond to a timed sked call a procedure was set in place to find her. One of the trawlers on the ground had to take on the role of control ship and was responsible for all the skeds of the other company ships while it was the control ship. When it left the grounds another ship would take over control. The new system was documented and published in a little red book that was inspected and approved for use by the Trawler's Mutual Insurance Company. Every skipper and every RO was issued with a copy. The books were accompanied by a note from Mr Graham telling the ships to use it – or else! On fish dock an 'or else' from Graham Hellyer meant 'Do it if it kills you because if it doesn't, I will.' In the following winter of 1975, with the new procedures in force, there were no incidents of any trawlers missing their skeds so the new system seemed to work.

Cassio – Trip to the Barents Sea

To properly understand the needs and issues of the radio operators and resolve the daily reporting issues I needed to spend time at sea on board the ships and see how what daily life as a trawler RO was all about. My first trip away nearly started out as a fiasco. I was due to sail on the *Cassio*, a freezer trawler bound for the Barents Sea. The RO was 'Jesse' James. Jesse was a great guy who took his job seriously and we had had many chats in the office where he was happy to explain to me about the issues he and other ROs had in terms of keeping the 'Skeds', contacting shore stations and repairing equipment.

The stern trawler *Cassio* in Hull Fish Dock. Like many Hellyer Bros trawlers, she was named after a Shakespearean character. Her handsome superstructure is a prominent feature. (Photo with approval from and thanks to the *Hull Daily Mail*)

The *Cassio* was due to sail on a Saturday morning. 'What time do you want me down on the dock tomorrow?', I asked Ben, the Ship's Husband. 'Ten o'clock', he said. At ten to ten, Doreen drove me onto the dock. 'Oh look,' I said, 'one of the other freezers is sailing too', as I saw the white superstructure moving slowly above the other trawlers, out through the lock and into the river. Then it hit me. I had missed the ship! It was the *Cassio*! The ship's husband had meant that the ship would sail from the dock at ten (or even earlier), not for me to arrive at ten. I was immediately terrified of the idea of going into the office on Monday morning and having to say I missed the ship. I thought rapidly 'How can I catch up with her?' 'Doreen, quick, drive me down to Corporation Pier.' Doreen drove me down to the Corporation Pier, which was a mile or so downstream from the fish dock, where a duty Pilot Boat was often berthed. My luck was in and a pilot cutter was alongside the Pier. I rushed down the pontoon and onto the cutter. 'Look, I am sorry but I have missed the *Cassio* in the dock, Can you please take me out to her as she goes past?' 'Oh yeah, and who the 'ell are you?' was the friendly response! I explained. My luck held and they smiled at each other and agreed. We could already see the *Cassio* as she moved out into the main stream and started to pick up speed. She came down the river towards us and her dove grey hull towered over the pilot boat as she approached. The pilot had called the skipper over the VHF radio 'We have got late crewman trying to join the ship. Can you please stop the ship skipper?' *Cassio* slowed, a rope ladder was dropped down the side and I scrambled on board. I made my way sheepishly up to the bridge for a roasting from the skipper for holding up his ship and messing everyone about. However, I was met by a beaming face of the skipper Alfie Myers, and Jesse, who both thought the whole thing was a big joke with lots of comments about 'Management time keeping', and 'Managers always have a long lie-in on Saturdays'. All was well and the trip had finally got off to a good start.

Cassio was built by Yarrows on the Clyde in 1966. She was 224-feet long with a tonnage of 1,500 tons. She had a very handsome superstructure with a graceful, gently curved front; she even had a small promenade deck. From the bows she could have been mistaken for a passenger liner.

I was given the spare cabin on board *Cassio*, which was grandly called the 'Owner's Cabin'. It was a good-sized and comfortable cabin with a porthole looking forward up the fo'c'sle so it was away from the noise of the trawl deck during fishing. It even had a small area of verandah deck outside the door for 'promenading'. I looked about the cabin for a parasol. But, there was not one there!

We sailed up the Norway coast in perfect weather with the crew working in shirt sleeves on the trawl deck getting the gear ready for fishing. I spent a lot of time with Jesse in the radio room learning about the operation of the radio skeds and the other work that the ROs got involved in. Their days were full; from the early morning calls to other freezers through to late night skeds and, in between, those the RO was calling up shore stations to collect messages from the company, sending and receiving crew messages to families for birthdays, anniversaries, etc. They also handled the other skeds between all company vessels on the grounds and, of course, the all important position skeds back to the company office once every twenty-four hours. When they weren't doing that they would probably be trying to fix faulty electronics.

In those days, all longer-range radio calls were sent and received in Morse code. It was fascinating to see the RO tapping away for hours on the Morse key and compiling the positions and catches of the ships. All the ROs were able to recognise each other by the way they used the Morse key. Every operator had a unique rhythm and firmness to their keying action so they always knew which ship was calling them before the ship identified herself. In between handling all of these calls, the RO was expected to keep all the radios and bridge electronics in top operational condition and to at least try and repair any piece of electronics that went wrong or broke down. If he could not fix it then he had to call me in the office with the details and I would contact the main service companies in UK. We would discuss the fault and get the necessary parts sent out to the ship so the RO could fix it or get a local electronics agent ashore to assist. This covered everything from the radios and radars to the warp tension meters on the trawl deck to the TVs and the film projector in the crew mess rooms.

During the run up the coast, I spent some time on deck with the mate, Des. He was a friendly, chatty Welshman from Tiger Bay in Cardiff. He had sailed with the skipper for ages and explained what was happening on deck. I liked Des a lot and we got on well. He was also the spitting image of the singer Kenny Lynch. Thankfully though, he did not sing.

Life on a freezer trawler was altogether much more comfortable than on the side trawlers. The ships were bigger, the accommodation was more comfortable, all the officers, the factory manager and the cook, all had their own cabins and the crew shared four-man cabins, all with port holes, rather than the six-, eight- or even twelve-man cabins on some of the older side trawlers. As the ships would be away for much longer, the freezers were fitted with better recreation facilities and they all had TVs and film projectors with a supply of films put on board for each trip. The atmosphere also seemed a bit more relaxed. I cannot recall any time on *Lord Lovat* when the crew sat together other that for a quick pot of tea while waiting to haul the gear.

Once on the fishing grounds off the North Cape, we received reports of good fishing further east, along the coast towards Russia. *Cassio* had several good days of calm weather and good catches and the mood on board was cheery and relaxed. Skipper Alfie always seemed to be in a happy mood and this spread through the crew. After a few days fishing, we moved back to the grounds off North Cape where a number of other BUT ships were fishing. By this time, Jesse and I had gone through all the issues of the daily sked routines on *Cassio* and it was time to change ships. The closest BUT ship to us was the *Pict*, fishing about 5 miles away. It was agreed that I would be transferred across by Zodiac boat later that day after both ships had completed their next hauls.

Pict was one of the top freezer trawlers at the time. She was a newer ship than *Cassio*, built in 1973 by Brooke Marine. The RO was Dave Poole, who I also knew fairly well as Dave was always happy to spend time in the office when he was ashore and discuss the different aspects of his job. The warm weather and clear days continued off the North Cape of Norway and the fishing, while not fantastic, was good enough to keep the skippers relatively happy. The *Pict* was a happy ship and had the same cheery atmosphere on board as I had found in *Cassio*. This seemed to flow down from the skipper, Jo Russel. The freezer trawler skippers were highly experienced and successful fishermen who had all spent many years as skippers in side trawlers before moving to the freezer fleet. They were well respected in the industry and had loyal crews who would sail with the same skipper for as long as they could. Obviously, the skipper wanted to keep the good workers in his crew and this developed tight knit and successful crews. This trust and professionalism engendered the happy relaxed atmospheres that I found on *Cassio* and *Pict*. The food was good and there was always something new to learn.

The *Pict* in BUT colours. (Photo with thanks to Walter Fussey of Hull, photographers)

The *Arab*, sister ship to the Gaul and both built originally for Ranger Fishing Co. of North Shields. (Photo with thanks to Walter Fussey of Hull, photographers)

The radio operators were not employed by the trawling companies but by the radio companies themselves. In those days, there were two main radio companies operating on the dock, Marconi and Redifon. The ROs were appointed by the radio company to the ships that had that company's radio stations fitted as they had obviously been trained to operate and maintain that make and type of equipment. *Cassio* had a Marconi radio fit so Jesse was a 'Marconi Man'. The *Pict*, however, had a Redifon fit and Dave was a 'Redifon Man'.

After a few days in *Pict* spent discussing the issues of skeds and daily reports with Dave and comparing notes with what I had learnt from Jesse, I needed to start to head for home as the office expected me only to be away at sea for just two weeks or so. The skipper started to ask around the other ships in the area to see if any ships were due to head home in the next few days. None were, but the *Arab* was due to go into a Norwegian port for bunkers in a few days. She was fishing nearby, so it was agreed that I would transfer over to her by rubber boat. I would then go ashore in Honningsvaag when she went in for fuel. The ship's agent would be asked to arrange my onward flights back to the UK.

As I went across in the boat, the *Arab* loomed up beyond the waves. She was a big, but squat looking ship with a BUT mid blue hull. There was no mistaking the workmanlike air about her, No nicely curved superstructures with promenade decks here. This instantly looked like a hard-working ship. She was also an identical sister ship to the ill-fated *Gaul*.

The *Gaul*

'Factory Trawler lost with all hands' screamed the headlines. We were now fishing in the area in which the *Gaul* had been lost. She disappeared without trace, with all hands, a crew of thirty-six, on 8 February 1974, while 'dodging' in severe weather on North Cape Bank off the North Cape of Norway. The wreck was subsequently discovered some years later in position 72 degrees 5 minutes north and 25 degrees 6 minutes east.

The *Gaul* was built for the Ranger Fishing Company in 1971 as the *Ranger Castor* by Brooke Marine in Lowestoft. She was a big trawler, over 200-feet-long and with a gross tonnage of 1,100 tons. When she was built, she was the latest word in deep-sea factory trawlers. She was bought by BUT two years later in 1973, along with a number of her sister ships, which were also renamed using the names of ancient tribes or peoples (*Kurd*, *Kelt*, *Arab*, etc.). The loss of such a new and modern ship, well-designed and crewed by experienced trawler men, was met with disbelief in the Hull fishing community.

As often happens when no wreck is immediately found, rumors and fanciful explanations start to emerge as to what has happened. The *Gaul*, sadly, was no exception and in Hull the relatives and friends of those missing were treated to

The *Gaul*, lost with all hands on 8 February 1974 off northern Norway. (Photo with thanks to Walter Fussey of Hull, photographers)

the full range of the media's fanciful imaginations in all their glory. One national TV channel even produced a TV documentary that included such nonsense as saying that the Gaul had been boarded and captured by the Russian Navy as she was a 'Spy Ship' and had been taken to a remote Russian Fjord. They even claimed that the crew was all OK and captive in Russia. The TV offered no explanation as to how the Russians might get aboard a high-sided stern trawler in a Force 9 Gale! They claimed that she could have been sunk by a submarine that had surfaced directly underneath her and holed her. None of this nonsense helped anyone and rather than get caught up debating such nonsense with the media the Company adopted a sensible 'say nothing' approach until a proper enquiry could take place.

Others, who knew what fishing in an Arctic winter really was like, and who were wiser, followed the more logical possibilities. All the TV talk of Russian submarines capturing the *Gaul* was totally disregarded by the men who sailed in her sister ships.

At the time of her loss she had been 'dodging' in very bad weather. Trawlers 'dodge' the weather when it is too bad to fish and the skipper wants to stay in the same area. When the weather gets too bad, all fishing is stopped and the factory deck is shut down. The crew, apart from those on watch, will use the time to turn in and catch up on sleep. The ship goes slowly into the wind and weather and then turns and runs down wind to the other end of the grounds and then turns and goes back into wind so that she remains in the same area. As winter gales in the Arctic can last for days, steaming in one direction all the time would result in the ship ending up miles away from the grounds, so they 'Dodge'. The weather on the day the *Gaul* was lost, as reported by other trawlers in the area, started off with rough seas that had been built up by easterly winds of Gale Force 8, and which increased through the morning to Force 9 or even 10. The seas also got bigger. They had built up across the long fetch of the Barents Sea and at the time of her disappearance, three exceptionally large waves were reported by a number of other trawlers in the area. These waves crashed across the front of the trawlers, which were steaming into the wind, and caused considerable damage to bridge windows and other parts.

The official report at the time concluded that the *Gaul* had capsized as a result of excess water flooding up onto her trawl deck from astern as she ran down wind and down sea. I asked the skipper of the *Arab*, Peter Abbey, about his thoughts on the loss of the *Gaul*. He was clear in his mind that she had been broached; i.e. hit by a big sea from the side as she was trying to turn back across the wind to head back up into the wind. He felt that perhaps the ship had been caught halfway round the turn by an exceptionally large wave and rolled over downwind. Once over, the power would probably have tripped off automatically and there would be nothing that anyone could do as they would all have been thrown off their feet in a moment. His view and the view of his colleagues was that this was the likeliest cause. He also felt that there must also have been some other factors involved, such as large amounts of water swilling about on the factory deck, which is directly below the open trawl deck. Such amounts of water swilling about a ship's deck is called 'free surface' and is extremely dangerous as it makes ships very unstable very quickly. This might have occurred if the pumps that drain the factory deck had been turned off or if the drains had become clogged after the factory had been shut down when they stopped fishing. Another contributory factor was the possibility that a door on the trawl deck near the stern ramp, which faced aft and which was not visible from the bridge, may have been left open and this would allow water to flood down into the ship if she was overwhelmed by a big sea. In that case, and, if the ship was in the middle of turning back into wind and was broadside on when one of the larger waves struck her, and if she had free surface water on the factory deck, then there would be nothing anyone could do.

Subsequent experiments carried out by the National Maritime Institute using a large detailed scale model of the *Gaul* concluded that water on the trawl deck alone could not have caused her to capsize and that this could only be a contributory factor. Their conclusion was that the factory deck below must have had excessive flooding as well. The wreck was found in 1997 and an underwater survey was carried out in 1998. What they found was that she had not been captured by Russians or holed by a submarine. The hull was intact and the door at the aft end of the trawl deck was indeed open as were some engine room ventilators in the ship. Some offal discharge chutes were also found to be in an open position but as these were free swinging flap doors then nothing conclusive could be proved. Certainly once the ship had been rolled over and was under water then these chute doors could possibly end up in an open position allowing more rapid flooding; but that in no way proves that they were a cause of the disaster as some have tried to make out. In all other respects, she appeared to be as one would be expect a trawler dodging in bad weather to be.

The *Arab*

As the *Arab* was a sister ship of the *Gaul*, I was excited at the prospect of seeing how this class of ship compared with stern trawlers such as *Pict* and *Cassio*. *Arab* was built in 1971 by Brooke Marine and was identical to the *Gaul*. Unlike the *Cassio* and *Pict*, however, she was a 'filleter'. This meant that she was able to fillet the fish she caught before it was frozen. All the skin and fish heads were reduced to fishmeal and bagged up on board. Because two frozen fillets from one fish take up roughly a third of the freezer space that a single, whole, frozen fish would, this means that it takes about three times as long to fill her hold as a block fish freezer, which merely gut the fish then freeze the whole body including the head and skin, etc. In turn, this meant that the filleter trawlers took two to three times as long to catch the same tonnage of finished product so tended to be at sea much longer. Whereas a block freezer would expect to be at sea for anything from forty to sixty days, a filleter would expect to be out for sixty to a hundred days.

Arab looked a solid and workmanlike ship and her design appeared to be well thought out with good accommodation and she seemed to be more spacious than the *Cassio*. She was also a fine sea ship. During the first twenty-four hours on board, the weather changed for the worse and I was able to experience a Force 8 gale in the *Arab*. It did not bother the ship at all. She ran down sea in this Force 8 and I watched from the bridge for ages but the seas never even threatened to run up the ramp onto the trawl deck. She did not stop fishing and there was nothing to indicate to me that this was anything other than a fine sea ship.

The one thing I noticed almost immediately however, was the mood of the ship. What a difference in ship's mood from *Pict* and *Cassio*. *Arab* was gloomy and the whole buzz that existed in *Pict* and *Cassio* was not there. Everyone seemed sullen and withdrawn. The skipper continued fishing the North Cape Bank catching only medium hauls of fish. The RO, a Redifon man, was uncommunicative and did not seem to be interested in helping me understand his job. He and the skipper hardly said a word to each other, again not the norm as these two people spent a lot of time together at sea and were often good friends. He chose to leave the industry soon afterwards. Meals were eaten in a gloomy silence and I tended to pass the time reading. At the time I was reading that super book *The World of Suzie Wong* by Richard Mason. Having spent time in Hong Kong and having visited Wanchai where the book was set, I was transported back to the sticky heat of a lively, bustling Hong Kong and the street markets and nightlife of Wanchai while I was sitting on a freezer trawler on a grey and gloomy Arctic Ocean.

By the Monday morning, the *Arab*'s skipper decided that it was now time to refuel and we went into Honningsvaag, a small town at the northern tip of Norway and the closest town to the North Cape itself. I went ashore with the ship's agent and I watched *Arab* as we drove round the bay to the town: her blue hull and white superstructure dominating the small port. The agent put me onto a bus to Lakselv, the nearest town with an airport, about two-hours' drive away. From there I flew back to Oslo, then home via London.

Scottish Boats

We were always looking at new electronics equipment that was coming onto the market and I had to try and evaluate whether or not it had any benefits for the fleet. This covered navigation as well as fish-finding equipment. The best way to do that was to go to sea in boats that had already had the new equipment fitted and talk to the skippers about whether it actually improved their catches or not. As they say in fishing 'If it does not catch you any more fish then it is a waste of money', as all the money needed by the company to run itself has to come 'Out of the Cod End'. I therefore spent time visiting Scottish boats and meeting their skippers and going to sea with a few of them. These included Skipper Buchan in *Lunar Bow*, a newly-built purse-seiner fishing for herring in the Atlantic to the west of the Orkneys Islands. She had a brand-new sonar that was creating a lot of interest in the industry.

Chris, a friendly salesman from Kelvin Hughes in Hull (who had sold the new sonar), and I arrived on the quayside at Fraserburgh on a wet and windy Sunday night. Some of the boats were starting up their engines and deck lights were coming on around the harbour. Crewmembers arrived in taxis, some were dropped off by their wives. Some were carrying boxes of groceries for the trip, others just a holdall. Other boats lay dark and silent, their crews safely tucked up in bed at home. Chris and I were warmly welcomed by the skipper as he arrived and we were taken on board. We were given a mattress each on the deck of the main crew cabin. We sailed just after midnight, as Scottish boats traditionally do not set sail on Sundays. Once we had cleared the harbour I settled down in my sleeping bag for the rest of the night.

We headed north and, as we cleared the Pentland Firth and sailed out into the Atlantic, a strong gale quickly developed from the west. It soon became too bad for any attempt at fishing so the skipper sought shelter in the lee of the Orkney Islands. Seasickness had set in again for both Chris and I so I was glad when we ran for the shelter of the islands. We got inside and anchored while the gale blew itself through. Eventually, after a few hours, the gale and the seasickness had passed by and we set off again.

The new sonar had a screen like a radar display and it gave a 360 degree view of the surrounding waters as the beam was transmitted out in all directions at once and we started looking for herring. There were other boats in the area now also looking for herring. The sun came out and it turned into a beautiful clear day with a big blue Atlantic swell rolling under us and a fresh breeze was blowing. In the clear light we could see, low on the southern horizon, the cliffs of Caithness in sharp detail.

The aim of purse-seining is to catch mid-water, or pelagic, fish by laying out the net around the shoal. The boat encircles the fish by going round the shoal to the end of the net that was first put in the water and hauling it in. The net hangs like a giant curtain down into the sea and around the fish caught inside it. When the other end of the net has been picked up, a rope that runs through the bottom of this curtain is hauled in until the bottom of the net forms a big bag, or purse. The top of the net is then drawn in as the boat lies alongside it and the fish are brought on board by big pumps or by brailing them in using small crane nets.

The skipper found a big herring shoal with the sonar and after carefully working out the wind direction, the direction the shoal was moving in and being aware of the other boats working in the area; he positioned his boat ready to slip the net. The crew were already on deck and with one yell of 'Let Go' out of the wheelhouse window, a big, red, rubber buoy was thrown over the stern. This was attached to the net and the net then ran freely out of its stowage area in the stern. The *Lunar Bow* steamed to starboard round the shoal and, with the aid of the sonar, the skipper was able to keep the shoal and boat in the right positions. Without another word from the skipper the boat came up to the buoy and the purse was hauled in. The ends were drawn up and the catch of herring was brailed up and into the fish tanks in the boat. The whole operation was done with just two words of command.

The fishing continued for three or four days until the skipper felt he had his quota of fish and we headed for home. However, it was realised that we had more herring than we were officially allowed to land under EEC rules. Therefore, to avoid paying a hefty fine for exceeding his quotas, the skipper had no choice but to dump a quantity of fish back into the sea. This fish dumping is something brought on by the EEC and the Common Fisheries Policy and is regarded by all as a total nonsense, if not a crime.

Picket Busting

On the fish dock you had to turn your hand to anything to get the job done. I discovered what this involved during a strike by shore workers on the fish dock.

I cannot even recall what the strike was about but I know that the pickets at the entrance to the docks prevented many of the electronic service company vans driving onto the dock. Therefore, to keep the trawlers running and ready for sea we had to find another way to repair faulty equipment. When we had a fault on equipment, such as a radar set or an echo sounder; I would take the report from the RO and go and talk to the service engineers in their workshops. They would show me on a similar set in the workshop what the problem might be and what the broken part looked like and how it fitted into the equipment. I would then go back on board the ship and try and identify the bit with the fault. As this was in the days before mobile phones so, if I had any queries I had to go all the way back up to the office and call from there. Once I had found the right printed board or module I had to dismantle the set, take it out and, without being seen by the pickets, get it round to the electronic company's workshop for repair. The next day, after it had been repaired, I did the same thing in reverse. As the pickets roamed the dock during the day we did some of this work at night, by torchlight if necessary. Of course, if I got the wrong bit then we had to do it all again!

Deep Sea Trawling and The Common Market

Britain had always had the best fishing grounds in Europe and had controlled her own stocks and managed her own quotas. After we joined the EEC or Common Market, Britain had to fall into line with the requirements and wishes of all the other fishing nations of Europe. This meant that we had to share our traditional UK grounds and that meant smaller quotas in our own waters while foreign boats from Spain, France and elsewhere could come and happily fish alongside our boats. Many traditional British near-water fishing grounds all around the UK were opened up to our European brothers who eagerly came in large numbers. A number of grounds ended up being fatally overfished. There were no other viable European fishing grounds that we could have access to that would balance this out.

The EEC Common Fisheries Policy has always been a very sore point in the whole fishing industry and I am not expert enough to try to explain it other than to say it was well known within the industry, before we joined the EEC in 1975, that the Common Fishery Policy was not going to help the UK fishermen in any way and that it would spell the end of the UK fishing industry. That came to pass.

The distant water industry, based mainly in Hull and Grimsby, was decimated by a combination of factors, of which the Common Market's Common Fishery Policy was one. Other factors included the fact that older freshers or side winders, built in the boom years of the 1950s and early 1960s, now required replacement, or at least expensive hull surveys and refits, to comply with modern insurance rules; the ever increasing cost of fuel oil; the extended fishery limits out to 200 miles in Iceland and Norway: the reduced fish quotas where they could fish as well as the new EEC CFP. Since the 1970s, we have witnessed the total disappearance of the deep-sea fleets from both the Humber ports, the over-fishing of traditional UK grounds by other countries, the continued reduction in catch quotas, the decline in the number of boats and the decline of the once flourishing boat-building industry, particularly in Scotland. On top of that, we have seen the introduction of the insane EU laws that force skippers to dump tons of good, but dead, fish back into the sea if they caught more than their quota allowance.

Time to Move On

As the Industry started to collapse in Hull, more and more trawlers were laid up and then sent to the breaker's yards. My work then became focused on de-equipping ships of their electronics and saying goodbye to ROs. The end was in sight and so I and many others bade farewell to fish dock, a sad end to a great industry and a fantastic community, that was brimming with fine people who understood what tragedy and hardship at work really meant but came out of it as kind, good people who always had time to help you. However, nothing lasts forever and we had to move on.

The prospects for work in Hull were poor. The decline of the trawling industry affected the economic climate of the town. To find work in the marine industry, I needed to move away from the area and I was lucky to find work in London working for one of the major Marine Electronics companies as a sales and marketing manager. This effectively ended my career in terms of working directly with ships and we moved south to start a new life in the suburbs, commuting into London and a nine to five world far removed from the sea and seven o'clock starts on the market. However, I was now working for a major international supplier of marine electronics to the shipping industry and so spent a lot of time talking to shipping companies and demonstrating new equipments on board ships and getting to know the world of the merchant marine.

From now on, major trips to sea would be as a passenger and so offered a new perspective. Whereas, before, any places I visited were because that was where the ship went, now I could choose the places I wanted to visit and select a ship to take me there.

CHAPTER 6

MV *Marco Polo* – The Antarctic

After the excitement of Hull Fish Dock, Doreen and I were working at building our new lives and careers in the 'Wicked South', well, London anyway. For me, the international marine electronics industry, and for Doreen, as an Air Stewardess for Sir Freddie Laker.

However, the tug of the Polar Regions does not go away and after a few years of dreaming and many months of gentle persuasion I convinced Doreen that we really should try and visit Antarctica. She was naturally nervous about some of the reports we had read of small basic ships and the Roaring Forties but eventually we found a trip that met both our needs. We both got such a thrill going to the Antarctic and being in the Southern Ocean, that we later did some trips to the Arctic on different ships and to different areas.

'South'

When I was about eight or nine my grandfather and I were chatting and I told him that I wanted to see icebergs. He went to his bookcase and handed me a brown-coloured book. 'Here you are, you might enjoy this.' The book was called *South* by someone called Ernest Shackleton. I had no idea what it was about and I thought it must be about the south of England. However, as he had said that he thought I would enjoy it, I read it. It was of course Shackleton's story of his 1914 Imperial Trans-Antarctic Expedition. Shackleton became my hero and I have since read it many times and all the other books covering the different aspects of that incredible expedition.

Shackleton and twenty-seven men sailed in his ship *Endurance* from Grytviken, in South Georgia on 5 December 1914 and headed south. The aim of Shackleton's expedition was to try and cross Antarctica, but the *Endurance* was trapped by the ice in the Weddell Sea before the party were even able to get ashore. After wintering in the ship, trapped by the ice, the ice finally crushed and sunk *Endurance* on 21 November 1915; nearly a year after leaving South

Georgia. They were then forced to live on the ice and drifted round the Weddell Sea in the ice pack for months until they finally arrived back at the ice edge near the tip of the Antarctic Peninsula. Here they launched the three boats that they had salvaged from the *Endurance* and kept with them on the ice. After struggling for days with gales and fog, sailing by day, sleeping on ice floes by night, if they could; they managed to reach a totally uninhabited and desolate rock called Elephant Island. They arrived here on 14 April 1916; dry land after fifteen months at sea and on the ice. There, they made a camp and Shackleton then set about going for help. He and five companions then sailed over 1,200 miles, in winter, in an open boat, the *James Caird*, from Elephant Island and made a desperate landing on the west coast of South Georgia on 8 May 1916. Shackleton, Capt. Frank Worsley and Tom Crean then became the first people to cross the unmapped, 3,000-metre high Allardyce Range as they had to get from where they had landed on the uninhabited west coast to the inhabited east coast to get to the whaling stations and help. Finally, almost eighteen months after the *Endurance* had sailed from South Georgia; Shackleton got back to the safety of the whaling stations and was able to take charge of the rescue of the remaining twenty-two men on Elephant Island. After three attempts to reach the Island, it was not until 30 August 1916 that Shackleton finally got through the pack in a Chilean tug, *Yelcho*. After five months on the Island, all twenty-two men were rescued safe and well. Ever since I read that book I have been in awe of Shackleton's achievement and have wanted to visit the Antarctic. However, in the 1950s and 1960s the only ships that went down to the Antarctic were the whale factory ships and the RN Ice Patrol ship, HMS *Endurance*. Expedition trips and soft adventure tourist ships had not even been thought of then. If I really wanted to go then I needed to become a whaler.

In the 1960s, Salvesen of Leith operated an annual whaling expedition to the Antarctic. It was mostly crewed by Norwegians but they collected a number of British sailors from the Orkney Islands and Scottish ports on their way. In those days, they took all sorts of people who would do the many basic, manual tasks on board the factory ship and the catchers. The key jobs on the whale catchers and most of the jobs in the factory ship were skilled or specialised and given to those with appropriate experience. In 1968, I wrote to Christian Salvesen in Leith asking if I could join their annual whaling expeditions to the Antarctic. I received a letter back from Salvesen saying that they were sorry but the previous year's expedition, the 1967 Norwegian expedition, had been the last one and they were no longer involved in Antarctic whaling. I was one year too late.

The Voyage

A few years after I left the Navy, I started to read stories in the press about expedition trips to Antarctica. The idea of expedition voyages had been started by Lars-Eric Lindblad, He was a Swedish explorer, who felt so strongly that people should have the chance to visit Antarctica that he set up his own company to run expeditions himself. He bought a ship and converted it for expedition work. He called the ship *Lindblad Explorer* and began trips from South America. I then read of a new company called Orient Lines, which had bought and refitted the old Russian passenger ship *Alexander Pushkin* and renamed her *Marco Polo*. In 1993, she was to make her first trip to Antarctica on a voyage billed as 'From Cape to Cape'. The ship was to sail from Cape Town in South Africa down to Antarctica and then land her passengers in Ushuaia in Chile, having sailed past both the Cape of Good Hope and Cape Horn. The expedition leader was to be Lars-Eric Lindblad.

The *Marco Polo* was built in East Germany for the Russians in 1966 and she and her sister ship, the *Mikhail Lermantov*, were managed by the Baltic Shipping Company running a regular transatlantic service between Leningrad (now St Petersburg) and Montreal. Both ships were of 24,000 tons and built for the North Atlantic. She began cruising in the Far East in 1975 and in 1992 was sold to Orient Lines and underwent a major refit in Italy. Her first cruise as the *Marco Polo* was down through the Suez Canal to South Africa which is where we joined her for her second trip. This was to be Lars-Eric Lindblad's largest and most ambitious expedition to Antarctica and on the biggest ship ever to go down there. Passenger capacity was reduced to half, to just 400, for safety reasons and to satisfy the demands for minimising the impact of tourism on the Antarctic continent.

The stab and dull ache of a dodgy tooth woke me in the night. We need to leave for the airport at lunchtime but I dash to the dentist in the morning before we set off. Nothing is found and I am given some tablets to take if it gets worse. We are due to fly from Heathrow to Paris and connect to an Air France night flight down to Cape Town. My tooth is still playing up and I spend our time in Charles de Gaulle Airport, a grey and most depressing place, looking for and failing to find, a shop that sells painkillers.

We arrive at the ship the following day and boarded her, by what must have been one of the longest and highest gangways in the world! It stretched out from near the top of the ship, like a giant feeler, touching the dockside some 30 yards from the ship. As we climbed up and up the gangway and into the ship, it seemed to go on and up forever. The ship towered above us while her new, blue painted hull and white super structure gleamed and shone in the warm South African sun. Thankfully, the tooth seems to have settled down. The ship is gleaming after its refit and we wander through the new public rooms, all clean new and

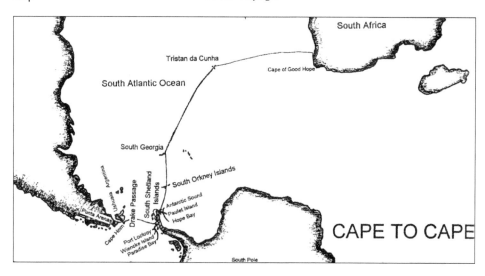

Sketch map showing the route of *Marco Polo* from Cape of Good Hope to Cape Horn via Antarctica.

Marco Polo, originally the *Alexander Pushkin*, at anchor off Grytviken, South Georgia.

decorated in soft, relaxing colours. Our inside cabin is comfortable, very roomy and with plenty of storage space. By the evening I am feeling fairly ropey again with my tooth and decide to go to bed early in the hope my tooth, helped by painkillers, will settle down. The ship is not due to sail until the following afternoon so that will give us the morning for some sightseeing in Cape Town.

I wake in the night feeling rough and feverish. I sleep fitfully until, at about five o'clock, I realise that my face has swollen to the size of a melon, or so it feels. I tell Doreen that I am feeling bad but she adopts her Florence Nightingale voice and says sympathetically 'Look, you are not having a heart attack so go back to sleep as there will be no one around at this hour anyway'. How I love her! She promptly goes back to sleep. I spend the rest of the night thinking 'Here I am about to go to the Antarctic for over three weeks with freezing temperatures and icy winds, and a bad tooth, a face the size of a melon and no dentist! Great!'

At 7.30 am I am first in the queue for the sickbay. The doctor looks at me. 'Oh! We don't have a dentist here.' Is that his remedy? However, we do find the ship's agent, who arranges for me to be taken to a local dentist in his van. Dr Van de Merve is a good man. He identifies the offending tooth, which has abscessed and drains it without any fuss. The relief as his drill cuts through the tooth to relieve the pressure of the poison is wonderful. He asks me where the ship is going and when I tell him he says 'Oh dear!' in a doom-laden tone. I panic as I think he is about to ban me from travelling but he decides that he needs to work harder to clear out the remaining poison and he sets too again squeezing my face and gums a lot harder with his fingers and thumbs of both hands. With that all done, he stuffs cotton wool into my bad tooth, gives me a big packet of penicillin tablets and sends me back to the ship. We sail an hour later. That night after dinner, Doreen and I stand together at the stern rail and watch the lights of Cape Town get smaller as we head off past Cape Point, the Cape of Good Hope on our 'Cape to Cape' voyage via Antarctica.

On our first day at sea the weather deteriorates and it is deemed too rough to hold lifeboat drill. I spend the day taking life easy, trying to read and eating penicillin tablets. During the day I realise that I have left my camera somewhere out on deck during the day. I report it to the Purser. I assume that I must have left it out on deck when I came back from the dentist and as I was not totally 'with it', and forgot to pick it up. It never turned up but we at least had Doreen's Olympus Trip as a back-up.

After a few days the weather improves and my face returns to its normal size. I begin to feel a bit more human and have a full American breakfast to celebrate. It is a nice sunny day and we see our first albatross, a yellow-nosed albatross, which spends most of the afternoon wheeling around the stern of the ship. Our first call is at Tristan da Cunha where we are to go ashore for the morning. Ships normally lie off in an open roadstead near the settlement of

Edinburgh and all stores and people are transferred by small, open boat as there is no sheltered anchorage and certainly no harbour. However, today, there is a big swell running into the settlement and the ship is rolling heavily as she stops off the coast. The local boats come out and try to come alongside but the heavy swell makes it difficult for them to approach the ship. The captain correctly deems it too dangerous to transfer passengers to small open boats with the 10 to 12 foot swell running. The trip ashore is therefore cancelled. Even so, there were passengers who thought they knew better and complained bitterly to ship's staff that the brochure had said they would go ashore at Tristan da Cunha!

Southern Ocean

South Georgia is 1,400 miles away from Tristan da Cunha and way down in the Southern Ocean, deep in the Roaring Forties; home to endless gales and huge seas. The Southern Ocean is a vast, mystical place, a place of mariner's tales and empty loneliness. It is an ocean where only albatrosses and the strongest and best-sailed ships can survive. The ocean begins to live up to its reputation. During the next day, the sea gradually gets up as the wind increases from the south-west. A large, low pressure area is moving towards us and we are told to expect heavy weather. As the morning goes on, the ship starts to pitch and broken seas wash across the fo'c'sle as the ship slides down into the troughs between the growing waves. Her bows throw masses of white water aside as she pushes her 24,000 tons down and forward into the next wave. In spite of the howling wind, it is a sunny day with blue skies and scudding white clouds. A few albatrosses still circle the ship as well as some Cape petrels and prions. The albatrosses, on their long thin wings, wheel round the waves with one wing tip millimetres from the water but never ever touching it. Then they swing up to catch more wind and without any apparent movement at all they wheel round in a wide circle and start again. They glide motionless for hours, skimming across the wild, roaring ocean and the breaking seas.

The clouds cast hard, dark shadows onto the waves as they fly across the sky in a headlong race with the waves towards the east. It is a rough night, with shudders, bangs and crashes echoing through the ship as doors slam and loose items finally let go of their hold and crash across the cabins. In the morning, we go up on deck to find that the wind is now up to about 40 knots, a full gale and howling out of a clear blue sky. It is spectacular. The seas have built up and some of the waves are about 40 to 50 feet high. The ship has slowed down and is still pitching as she tries to hold her course. If we have an engine failure now the seas and wind would knock the ship down and capsize her in seconds. From the open deck, the waves appear like moving mountains ranges of water as they come sweeping towards the ship with a threatening, hypnotic effect.

You cannot take your eyes away from them. The ship reaches the bottom of the trough and the wave mountains rear up high above us. As we climb our way up the slopes the rest of the range comes into view and the wind howls louder as we reach the exposed higher slopes. We can again see the vast expanse of range upon range of waves, with their tops blown off leaving white tails streaming from them. The decks tilt forward as the ship begins her slide down the far side and into the next deep valley, the wind drops and it gets quieter down in the shelter of the next mountain of water as it appears ahead and begins to towers above us. So it goes on, hour after hour.

We are now truly in the Roaring Forties and can absorb the atmosphere of the place, the biting wind that races round the planet and the great, white-crested waves that rear up menacingly and then ignore us as they remorselessly march towards to the east. I have never seen seas like this, the white crested waves and the deep, dark troughs between them stretch out in lines like dark, snow-flecked hills, out into the vast emptiness as far as the eye can see and then further, much further. The sense of emptiness and loneliness of this ocean is awe-inspiring. The albatrosses wheeling round astern of the ship only add to the extreme isolation of the place. If there is another ship or a yacht out there then we will never see it in the vastness of this chaotic spray-coated ocean.

It is now definitely getting colder too with a real bite in the air. During the afternoon we are told that we are at the half way point to South Georgia and I see the first 'sooty' albatross, or Grey Mantled sooty albatross to be correct.

By the evening the wind is at last dropping and the motion of the ship is a little easier. The waiters set the dining room for dinner. We hope that we are now past the centre of the low pressure system and things will improve. At its peak, it was a full Force 9, gusting to 10. The following day dawns sunny and much calmer; the sea is down to state 4 and wind down to about Force 4 or 5. We have a clear, crisp horizon and a sharper edge to the wind. Aerobic classes start again up in the gym and the restaurant is definitely busier too.

South Georgia

The cold, wet, clammy fog wraps itself around the ship. Ten days after leaving the UK, we excitedly go on deck to see the mountains of South Georgia as we make our approach to the island, but we are met by this all-enveloping fog. It swirls around the ship and most passengers stay inside, but we decide to go on deck and tuck ourselves in behind a metal screen, out of the wind. Then, there is a cry from forward. 'It's clearing!' We look out from behind our shelter and in a matter of seconds the fog starts to thin as the ship passes through the entrance to Cumberland Bay. We move out to the bow as we sail out of the solid fog bank and enter a calm, sun-filled, blue and white world. There before us is the most beautiful sight: the open expanse of Cumberland Bay, its blue peaceful waters extend away to left and right. Directly ahead, across the bay, the white, jagged mountain peaks of the Allardyce Range are bathed in sunshine and stretch away north and south with vast sweeps of drifted snow covering their sides. Glistening, silent glaciers come from the mountains down into the bay. Looking astern, we can see the fog bank lying like a solid grey wall on the sea and our wake emerging from it. The huge Nordenskjold Glacier emerges at the southern end of the bay. Cumberland Bay is more like an inland sea than a bay, as the land closes right round to the entrance. It is a calm and serene scene, with the sun warming the green shore line, white clouds gently drift along the tops of the mountains and then clear from Mount Sugartop, above Grytviken, to allow it to look down at the newcomers. A little further to the south, the highest mountain on the Island, Mt Paget, remains aloof and hidden in the clouds.

South Georgia was officially discovered by Captain cook, who landed here and claimed it for Britain in 1775. He named it 'Isle de Georgia' in honour of King George III. The *Marco Polo* anchors off King Edward's Point but not without a little difficulty, as the windlass seems to be playing up as they veer out the cable. The old, Norwegian whaling base of Grytviken lies at the head of a small bay just beyond the point. As we leave the ship by boat the storm damage is evident and the blue paint on the bows and hull has been sucked and stripped off by the seas, leaving a rust red finish that does not really enhance the ship's looks.

Once ashore at King Edward's Point we feel the gentle warmth of a summer's day as we pass the time with a group of young elephant seals who have decided that the main track is a good place to bed down for the afternoon. Some small penguins waddle by on their way to the beach. We had been told by Lars-Eric that under no circumstances must we get closer than 15 feet to any animal. The only problem was no one had told the penguins or seals that. We walk round the bay and arrive at Grytviken.

Whaling was first started here in 1904 by the Norwegian Carl Larsen. He identified the area as a good spot for shore whaling stations when he was Captain of the *Antarctica*, the ship carrying the Swedish Antarctic Expedition in 1902 under the Swedish explorer Nordenskjold. Larsen returned here and built Grytviken, which was the site of an earlier base for seal hunters. Their blackened blubber boiling pots were still lying along the shore when Larsen arrived. The name Grytviken means 'Pot Cove' in Norwegian. By 1912, there were seven whaling stations on the east coast of the Island run mostly by the Norwegians and the British but some were run by Argentineans and the South Africans. However, by 1964, all whaling had ceased as it was no longer economically viable and the stations were left to fall into ruin. Three of the old whale catchers that never left, the *Dias*, the *albatross* and the *Petrel*, are still here, aground and half submerged in the shallows beside the rotting flensing plan. The *Dias* and the *albatross* lie together derelict, silent, rusting and forlorn while further round the bay the *Petrel* sits in a similar state, untouched, since the last whalers left in 1964. At its peak, nearly 300 men lived and worked here including the crews of the whale catcher boats. There is a small museum in what was the station manager's house, run by a couple who live on their yacht, which is berthed at the jetty. They look after the base and are most helpful and show us the way round.

There is wreckage all around as a lot of the old station has been dismantled and the hazardous materials cleaned or removed; but a lot of the iron and steel and the remains of the heavy machinery is still lying around. In addition to the huge wooden flensing plan, where the dead whales were hauled up, the blubber cookers, and the storerooms are exactly as they were left. The most notably building is the beautiful, little, white-painted Norwegian chapel. It was built in Norway and sent out to Grytviken in kit form by Carl Larsen, where it was rebuilt, including two bells. It is as clean and lovely as it must have been in the days when the whalers used it on Sundays. The chapel sits just apart from, but incongruously close to, the main factory area where the massive slaughter of huge whales, the noises of winches and saws, the yells of men, the screams of cutting tools and the smell and steam of boiling whale blubber would fill the air all season long. In the store rooms by the jetty there are still large coils of the whale line that was attached to the harpoons.

The highlight of the trip ashore is the visit to Sir Ernest Shackleton's grave. He died here of a heart attack in 1922 after arriving on the *Quest* for another expedition. His grave is in the whaler's small graveyard on a hillside just along the beach from the whaling station. The graveyard has a smart, white-painted, palisade fence around it to keep the seals out. Shackleton's grave has a stone surround with gravel top and a plain, rough-hewn granite tombstone. It says simply:

To the dear memory of
Ernest Henry Shackleton
Explorer
Born 5th Feb 1874
Entered life eternal
Died 5th Jan 1922

A further memorial to Sir Ernest Shackleton lies round the bay at Hope Point on a small hill overlooking the whole of Cumberland Bay. It is a stone cairn with a white cross on it and was erected by the men of the *Quest*.

I wake up and lie still, listening for the throb of the engines. There is no noise. We should have sailed late last night to go to the Bay of Islands but there is no indication that we are at sea at all. I go on deck and find we are still at

Above left: Sir Ernest Shackleton. (Library of Congress)

Above right: The grave of Sir Ernest Shackleton in the Whaler's graveyard in Grytviken.

anchor in Cumberland Bay. It turns out that the windlass motor, which we had noticed had not been too happy when letting out the anchor, has decided that it certainly won't be hauling it in. For the present we are stuck. If we cannot get the anchor in then we cannot sail away! They could of course break the cable, put a buoy on it and leave it on the seabed and try to recover it later; but that would be a last resort. The engineers set to work to change the motor from the starboard windlass for the dead one on the port windlass. Once they have done this and heave in the anchor, we can sail but now with only one working windlass. The work will take all day and so gives us an extra day to explore the area. Some of us go with one of the ornithologists to look for the nest site of a sooty albatross. To our delight, not only do we find it, but there is a sooty sitting on the nest. They are big and beautiful birds but they are not as big as the wandering albatross. Their heads and body plumage is a soft charcoal grey that looks like velvet. Their delicate eye markings give

Shackleton's *Nimrod* leaves Cowes in 1908 for the Antarctic. (J&C McCutcheon Collection)

them an inquisitive, but nervous look. This one, however, remains firmly on its nest and allows us up to our 15-foot limit. Its nest is on a cliff face and, by carefully climbing down to a nearby grass ledge, we are able to spend ten minutes or so watching the albatross and enjoying the view of the bay from its prime nest site.

The next few days are spent visiting the fantastic wildlife of South Georgia. We visit the colonies of millions of king penguins, small colonies of sea lions and all of their attendant smells. There really is nothing quite like the awful smell that comes from a colony of sea lions. Penguins are bad, but sea lions are worse! At the King Penguin colony we see a curious sight. A leopard seal has come ashore and is lying by the water's edge. Normally, a leopard seal would swim along the beach by the penguin colony and attack any passing penguins. The king penguins in their manner of haughty, but interested gentlemen, waddle up to about 5 feet from the leopard seal and stand for a few minutes staring at it and examining it closely. The seal just lies there unconcerned. Yet once in the water they would have swum as far away from it as they could. We visit a wandering albatross colony; where the nests are actually 2- or 3-feet high mounds of earth and grasses and are scattered over an open tussock grass-covered hilltop where the wind blows continually. The birds must have this wind to help them get airborne. They are huge birds. Close up I would think they are at least twice as big as the sooty albatross. Their heads are about 18 inches long and somehow they manage to fold their huge wings up so they become part of their backs. Like the seals, they are content to let us walk up and take their photos and they just watch us in an 'interested but I don't care' sort of a way.

We leave the magic of South Georgia and head further south towards the South Orkney Islands. We see the first iceberg at 57 degrees south. It is quite an impressive one too; on a grey cloudy day the iceberg is a silver gray colour with sides looking like sliced ice cream, a sculptured mass drifting along on its own in an empty ocean. Now we really are in the Antarctic!

Antarctica

The next morning we reach the South Orkneys, a beautiful string of small islands lying to the north of the Weddell Sea. In spite of a hazy sun the sight is spectacular, all gleaming whites, greys and blacks. The black mountains, grey mists and shadows, white icebergs and floes, and black sea all around us. As the icy sun breaks through gaps in the haze, the scene changes and different parts of the scene are highlighted in the bright sun while others vanish into the haze or behind a drifting berg.

On Coronation Island there is a large colony of Adelie penguins. These are small penguins with cute faces and round, white-ringed eyes. They clamber up and struggle over the big lumps of drift ice at the water's edge. They slip, slide and fall but always bounce up again and clamber back up the ice before they stand at the water's edge and look carefully out to sea for any leopard seals and waiting for on e of their braver relatives to jump in first. If he swims away without being attacked by a leopard seal then the others will happily follow. How on earth do they decide who will go first? They are all totally unafraid of humans and walk right up to within a couple of feet of people on the shore peering intently at these new strangers on their beach.

We leave the South Orkneys, heading further south, down into the Weddell Sea and for Paulet Island. The sky clears and the sun comes fully out and we see a spectacle of huge tabular icebergs lying in a flat blue sea. Most of them seem to have grounded as the sea starts to shallow near the islands. These bergs are massive with flat tops and vertical cliff sides. Some are tilted and lie there like a slice of ice cream cake on its side. It is hard to estimate just how big they are but certainly twice as high as the ship and at least half a mile long. They continue below the sea for at least four or five times as far as they do above the sea. The icebergs stretch away as far as we can see. We leave this rare and beautiful scene and turn in as it is now about midnight.

Into the Pack Ice

During the night I become aware of occasional faint scraping noises running through the ship. I listen, ice! We must have reached the edge of the pack ice. By four o'clock in the morning the noise has increased to a juddering and scraping clearly coming from the hull. Then it falls quiet and the engine vibration drops quietly away. I get up and go on deck to find that the ship is stopped in the middle of the pack ice. It is overcast and snowing with the visibility down to about 2 miles. The pack ice extends as far as I can see on all sides. The ship tries to move ahead again, pushing the floes aside with her ice-strengthened bow. There are no visible leads or areas of open water and the floes have closed right up against each other. At six o'clock the ship finally comes to a stop. Silence falls over the ship and the peace and beauty of the pack embraces us. Off to port, a large iceberg with big floes round about it lies trapped in the pack. Some of the floes around the ship are over 10 feet high and the pack has ridges running through it, some extending quite close to the ship. The ship had been trying to follow leads through the ice but these kept closing up, leaving her stuck with nowhere to go. The ship tries to get under way again at about seven o'clock, but with the floes like solid concrete blocks floating at the side of the ship and extending down about 10 or 12 feet into the water, this is impossible.

Lars-Eric comes on the PA. 'As those of you that have looked out can see we are stuck in the pack ice. I have spoken with the captain and we cannot get to Paulet Island so we must go back and find a way out of here. When the pack ice is this dense it is termed 9/10th pack and is impenetrable for anything other than an icebreaker. Also, the wind is from the north and if we stay here we could be in real danger of becoming trapped in the pack and with a large berg to leeward, this is not a good place to be.' Not the most encouraging wake-up call, but true!

The captain tries to manoeuvre the ship round but there is a real danger that one of the ice chunks will damage or even break the propeller. If that happens we could be here for a while. Gradually, by going ahead and astern and trying to turn the ship he eases her round and we start to back track through the ice that we have already passed through. Slowly, we head back to the north. Then, as we get into more broken pack ice, the swell increases telling us that we are now near to the ice edge, so we start to turn to the west.

Iceberg Alley

Paulet Island is a tiny island to the south of Joinville Island and Dundee Island on the north-eastern tip of the Antarctic Peninsula. Our approach from the north-east had failed. So now we make for the northern end of Joinville Island with the hope of passing round its northern and western edges and then south

Just one of many tabular icebergs in the Antarctic Strait, or Iceberg Alley.

through the Antarctic Sound from the north and reaching Paulet Island and its large Adelie penguin colony that way.

When we arrive at the sound at five the next morning the weather is still poor. It is foggy, snowing and there are icebergs everywhere. The sound is known as 'Iceberg Alley' by those that know. We finally get through but only as far as Hope Bay on the mainland. Here, there is an Argentinean Research station, and as the fog clears, there before us is the mainland of Antarctica, a mass of ice, snow and mountains in the sunshine. We are looking at a continent the size of North America with less than a couple of hundred inhabitants, most of whom are only there for the summer anyway. This is the last continent. This is what we have come to see and to set foot on.

Any hope of landing at Hope Bay is now dashed by the wind. A 40-knot gale rises up and the sea is soon a mass of white horses. The wind pushes the loose pack ice against the only shore that it might have been possible to get to in a Zodiac. So, after our voyage to this wonderful continent, the chance of a landing here is taken from us. We must try another place, another time. The ship again slowly turns and we head back up the Antarctic Sound passing close to some of a large number of huge tabular bergs, all of which have broken off the Larsen Ice Shelf, as they always do every year.

The plan to reach Paulet Island is now dropped and we steam across the Brantsfield Strait to Half Moon Island in the South Shetlands group. Half Moon is a small, low, rocky, crescent-shaped island with a sheltered shingle beach. Behind it, the high snow-covered mountains of Livingstone Island

Sketch map showing the Antarctic Peninsula and the places visited.

A cheeky chinstrap penguin takes a close interest in a bright-red coated seal.

provide a magnificent backdrop. Half Moon is home to a small colony of chinstrap penguins, so named because they have a black chinstrap marking running from their black caps under their white chins and beaks. They are small birds and some were struggling up the ice at the back of the beach while others were tobogganing down to the beach.

To watch them from their low level and to be more comfortable I lie down on the beach behind the ice edge and wait. After a minute or so, one of them stops on his way to the sea. He has spotted me. He leaves his pals and sets off towards me in a very businesslike manner. He gets to about 10 feet and then stops; peers at me from top to toe then he moves closer. He gets to about 3 or 4 feet away and stops again. What is he going to do? He peers even harder at me and I am sure that he is going to give me a peck to see if I will do anything. He then obviously decides that I am just a boring, bright-red seal and not of much interest, so he turns on his heel and marches back to his pals with his report.

At Last, the Mainland

We sail for Paradise Bay in Graham Land on the Antarctic Peninsula and arrive there at eight o'clock the next morning in the middle of a blizzard. It is supposed to be one of the most beautiful spots on the coast but due to the weather we see nothing of it. We go ashore and at last set foot on the mainland of Antarctica. This is a real thrill. Even in the snow and cloud it is a special and spectacular place as the Antarctic ice cap reaches down to the sea. High, vertical, forbidding white cliffs of ice and snow hang silently above the bay; their tops invisible in

Left: A brochure from *Lindblad Explorer*, the first expedition cruise ship. (J&C McCutcheon Collection)

Below: Marco Polo at Port Lockroy being watched by a gentoo penguin.

Above: Sketch map of the Neumayer Channel and the route taken.

Right: Sketch map showing the Le Maire Channel and Booth Island.

the drifting cloud and making them seem even more threatening. Bergy bits and small growlers sit in the waters off the beach and the only movement is from a few Gentoo penguins scuttling about the shoreline. The scene has not changed in thousands and perhaps millions of years; yet like all of Antarctica it is only in the last 100 years that man has known about it and only in the last twenty years that people have been able visit and to marvel at its fantastic isolation and beauty. The ice ridges from the main ice cap come down to the water's edge, leaving only a few feet of tide-cleared shingle beach to walk on. We walk round the small bay as far as we can and paddle in our boots in the crystal clear sea by a large grounded bergy bit.

Our voyage continues down the Neumayer Channel, a narrow channel running between Anvers Island and Wiencke Island, where we spot three large humpback whales swimming south and further down the channel we see some smaller minke whales. Both are baleen whales that feed by draining krill through the baleen strips that hang from the top of their mouths. Both species

Marco Polo enters a misty and gloomy Le Maire Channel.

are endangered but the humpback is more endangered as there are fewer of them than the minke whales. After a scenic sail down the Neumayer Channel, with its ice-clad mountainsides, we arrive off Port Lockroy on Wiencke Island, the site of a former UK base. The scenery in the islands is stunning. White mountains, with the sun playing hide and seek through the swirling clouds, the constantly changing light highlighting a different area of mountain and ice then casting it into grey, blue shadow. It is so still now, there is not a breath of wind and the sea is like a piece of wet, grey slate. Once ashore, the sun breaks through to reveal even more spectacular mountains, many of which have not even been named let alone been climbed.

The following day, we pass through the spectacular Lemaire Channel between Booth Island and the mainland. It is shorter, but narrower, than the Neumayer and often choked with ice so we are lucky that it is clear for us. The black, snow-scattered, near-vertical mountain sides rise straight out of the sea on both sides of the ship and vanish into the mists above. The engine noise of the ship echoes back off the rock walls as we slide slowly through the still, black waters.

Drake's Passage and Cape Horn

We exit the strait and enter the Bellinghausen Sea. After reaching 65 degrees 12 minutes south, we turn north and head for the Drake Passage and Cape Horn 600 miles away. It is Christmas Eve and, as we turn towards the north, the fog descends and Antarctica rapidly vanishes into the mist. After a short while it might not have been there at all. It is easy to understand how early explorers failed to find it for so long. My lasting feelings were that I must go back again and I still plan to one day.

'This bacon is not crispy!' Clearly others on board had other things to worry about! When we went down for lunch we found ourselves sitting near to two middle-aged English ladies who we had seen about the ship. They never seemed to be too happy about life. Today, they were both arguing with the waiter about their club sandwiches. 'It is not properly toasted. The crispy bacon in it was not crisp and there was too little dressing on the salad. This really is not acceptable.' Here we are in Antarctica, at the southern end of the Drake Passage on Christmas Eve with a storm forecast, and their major interest was the bacon in their sandwich.

On Christmas Day, the westerly wind rises again and the sea starts to get up. The ship is due to be off Cape Horn at about four o'clock this afternoon. However, with the wind and weather deteriorating, there is a concern that we will not see the Horn. By early afternoon, a big beam sea is making the ship roll and waves are starting to come over the bow. The spray lashes across the upper decks and rattles on the windows. The upper decks are soon put out of bounds. At about a 3.45 p.m., disregarding the out-of-bounds warning, people start to go out on deck to try and see if we can see the Horn. Ahead of the ship all we can see is a grey murk. Suddenly, a woman in a yellow parka points excitedly out to starboard and we follow her arm. There, off the starboard bow, emerging from the cloud, is the instantly recognisable dark shape of Cape Horn. A hunched mass of rock, its sharp, pointed peak and sheer southern face point defiantly to the south. The wind continues to rise, up to 40 knots with the seas getting up to 20 or 25 feet high. It is a brilliant sight, to actually be here seeing something that you have only ever read of in clipper ship histories or lone yachtsmen's journals. Now we are there seeing it with our own eyes. The sun breaks through and, in spite of the spray and the howling wind, it shines on the Horn itself. This legendary lump of rock that has been written about by many but seen by few is the last piece of land at the tip of South America. So many sailing ships have been wrecked and sailors' lives lost at its feet and on the islands close by, while trying to sail round it. Most of them are unrecorded, ships that were just posted 'Missing'. Of those that did get round it, either after the long run from Australia, or going the other way, to windward, coming from Europe and going up to Chile and the west coast of America, most never even saw the Horn. Either they were too far south or the Horn was lost in clouds or darkness. Some of those ships that tried to sail round it to the west spent literally weeks tacking to and fro across the Drake Passage trying to edge past the Horn. Some gave up and turned round then sailed eastwards downwind all the way to the west coast of America via the

Cape Horn emerges through the murk, the graveyard of many ships and sailors.

Indian Ocean and past Australia, just to save the ships from the pounding that the seas off the Horn could give them.

The *Marco Polo* holds her course heading north-west as if she is carrying on in to the Pacific Ocean. When she is about 3 or 4 miles west of the Horn she turns to the east, down wind and sea and steams past Cape Horn. We sail 'Round the Horn' on Christmas Day. In the traditional maritime sense of the old wind jammers, we have not sailed 'Round the Horn'. The Horn lies at exactly 56 degrees south and in the days of sail to claim that the ship had sailed 'Round the Horn' she must sail from 50 degrees south in one ocean round to 50 degrees south in the other. However, we have sailed 'past' Cape Horn. Once we are clear and the fearsome Horn falls astern we go below, back into the warmth for some Christmas 'cheer' and a piece of Christmas stollen cake; something that the sailors on the wind jammers would not have been able to do.

Once past Horn Island the ship turns north and heads for Ushuaia at the eastern end of the Beagle Channel. The ship is soon in the lee of the islands that are the last remnants of the southern tips of the Andes as they disappear beneath the Drake Passage before they re-emerge as the Antarctic Peninsula. Once in their lee, the sea calms down considerably and the wind drops away. We even managed a short stroll on deck before the formal Christmas gala dinner. What a day!

Beagle Channel

The final leg of the voyage was up the Beagle Channel and out into the Pacific Ocean then back into the Cockburn Channel before turning into the Straits of Magellan. This whole area is spectacular, with pointed high mountains,

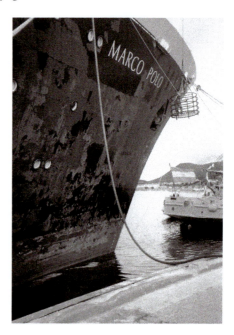

Marco Polo at Punta Arenas showing off her lost paint caused by the storm in the Southern Ocean.

glaciers and natural forests. We had a fantastic, calm, sunny day for our trip through the Beagle Channel, which, so we were told, is highly unusual. The guides kept saying 'This weather never happens. It is always cloudy, very windy and wet here.' The Beagle Channel, named by Charles Darwin after his ship, seemed to go on forever, with hundreds of islands and rocks along the way. Navigation must be difficult but thankfully the water is deep. So we found our way into the Cockburn Channel and then into the wide expanse of the Straits of Magellan. The mountains had gone and the landscape was flat and agricultural with just low hills in the distance. The Strait was wide and we could not see the other side.

Throughout the voyage, Lars-Eric Lindblad kept us fully up to the minute with his chats from the bridge, telling us what was, or was not, happening and why we were going to do whatever it was. He was a wonderful man and so enthusiastic about everything. His enthusiasm was contagious and his love for and concerns over Antarctica were very evident. He was determined that Antarctica must remain a pristine reserve and must not be damaged in anyway by tourists, industries or others and, equally, he knew that only by taking people to Antarctica will the general public develop strong feelings for the preservation of the continent. He was, I am sure, always trying to get Captain Eric, from Norway, to take the ship into places that the captain would rather not go but between them they made sure that we always did something memorable and exciting, and we did get to most of the places that Lars-Eric had hoped to take us. The lectures on board all carried this message throughout the voyage as

Sketch map of Tierra Del Fuego showing the route of *Marco Polo* to Ushuaia, through the Beagle and Cockburn Channels then into the Straits of Magellan and on to Punt Arenas.

well as providing masses of information about this fantastic continent, such as details of its geological history as well as its exploration and its wildlife. Every day we seemed to learn something new about penguins, seals, whales or albatrosses. Lars-Eric was a true champion for the Antarctic with his 'Leave only footprints and take only memories' motto. It is thanks to him that the controls governing visiting ships and how people behave ashore were put into place. Lars-Eric sadly died in 1994.

We finally docked at Punta Arenas and left the ship. They wanted us off the ship so they could clean it for the next trip later that day and so we were taken for the afternoon to The Cape Horn Hotel. The ship organised a buffet dinner for us that evening at an out of town eatery before we were taken out to the airport for the overnight charter flight back to Miami, via Santiago. Unfortunately, everyone who ate the chicken dishes at the buffet went down with chronic food poisoning on th e flight. The aircraft toilets were blocked off as they were full and it then took over two hours before we could get off the plane in Miami as the US Port Health had to get the sick off to hospital and interview everyone else. Doreen and I had looked at the chicken but decided it looked dodgy anyway so left it alone. Thank goodness we did! We spent twenty-four hours in Miami and finally arrived home exhausted but elated after a real 'trip of a lifetime'.

Of all the places we visited and in spite of the fantastic ice caps, glacier fronts and mountains of Antarctica itself, South Georgia was the place that made the strongest impressions on me with its own climate, its history, the spectacular scenery and incredible wildlife. Now, there is a place I would really love to visit again.

CHAPTER 7

Professor Molchanov – NE Greenland

Oh Greenland is a dreadful place,
It's a place that's never green
Where there's ice and snow
And the whale fishes blow
And the daylight's seldom seen.

So goes one of the verses of a sea shanty about the Greenland whale fishery sung by whalers in the eighteenth and early nineteenth centuries. It is not a bad summary of Greenland in winter. It is a huge and inaccessible place to visit and parts of it are still virtually unknown to the outside world, in particular the east and north-east coasts.

The Vikings discovered Greenland in about AD 1000 and settled along the green, southern tip and up the west coast, but the northern parts on both coasts remained virtually uninhabited. Apart from a thin coastal strip, Greenland is totally covered in a vast, deep, ice cap. This ice cap is thousands of feet thick and where it breaks through to the coast massive glaciers tumble down into the sea, often at the head of long, deep fjords.

After the Vikings in the tenth century, the first European to venture up the east coast of Greenland was the English mariner Henry Hudson, of Hudson Bay fame. In the 1570s, in his ship the *Hopewell*, he was searching for the north-west Passage. Hudson named the area he was in at 73 degrees north as 'Hold with Hope' and this is the first English recorded place name in the area, although doubtless the earlier Thule and Inuit inhabitants had their own names. Hudson did not find the north-west Passage and on a subsequent trip in 1611, during another search for the north-west Passage, he worked his way up the west coast to the Baffin Bay area. There his crew mutinied and having overcome Hudson and the officers, they cast Hudson, his young son and seven men adrift in a small boat without food or water. They were never seen again.

It was then not until the early 1800s, when Arctic whalers started to sail in the area, that any interest was taken. Among them was a Yorkshire whaler from Whitby, called William Scoresby. In the ships *Baffin* and *Fame* he sailed along the east coast in his search for whales, but in doing so he logged everything he saw. Explorers followed; Douglas Clavering and Edward Sabine separately explored the coast and the place names reflect their work. (Clavering Oy and Sabine Oy, for example). Oy is Inuit for island. The whalers continued to make discoveries and added new names as they went; Jameson Land and Liverpool Land, an area of high, jagged, mountain peaks and fjords that is totally unlike Liverpool and the Mersey estuary. After that, several expeditions under Swedish, French and Danish leaderships charted the north-east coast giving European names to the places as they went. From the west, the American, Robert Peary, spent twenty-three years exploring the north-west coast and, in 1892, got across the ice cap to Kap Bridgeman on the very northern tip of Greenland. It was Peary who proved that Greenland was an island with no connection to any land further north. In 1907, a Danish expedition team, led by Lt Johan Pater Koch, got to Kap Bridgeman from the east, so completing the exploration of the coast round Greenland.

The Greenland ice cap was first crossed by Fridtjof Nansen and five companions in 1888. Since then, a few expeditions have crossed it, notably in 1988, when a multinational expedition which included a Russian glaciologist, Dr Victor Boyarsky, who we were to meet later, crossed the Greenland ice cap with dogs from the southern end to the north-west coast, (the long route) as a training exercise! They did this before they crossed Antarctica with dog teams in the 1989/90.

One of the reasons that I was keen to visit the north-east coast was the fact that, apart from the early explorers and whalers, very few people had ever been there. I wanted to see the seas, mountains and fjords that were familiar to whalers like William Scoresby. Scoresby came from Whitby and was a whaler's son who stowed away on his father's ship when he was ten. He became not only a famous and successful whaling captain but a scientist of note, for his work carried out in the Arctic. On his voyages he recorded all the information he could on the weather, ice, whales and the land. In 1822, a year when the ice on east Greenland receded to leave clear water up to the coast, he explored over 400 miles of coast line charting and recording the features and giving them names including, of course Scoresbysund. It is actually named after his father. Scoresby put all his findings and narratives of whaling into a famous two-volume work called *An Account of the Arctic Regions*. I wanted to visit the seas described so graphically in the whalers log books where they recorded tales of their boats being capsized, whales lost, overwintering in the ice in leaky ships, men falling into the icy seas and all the daily perils of nineteenth-century Arctic whaling.

The Trip

I had read of a trip, the aim of which was to sail west from Spitzbergen across the remotest part of the Arctic Ocean and the Greenland Sea, along the southern edge of the ice pack and then down the north-east coast of Greenland visiting what fjord systems and sites it could dependent upon the ice and weather. The ship was then to cross the Denmark Sraight, head south and land in Iceland. This expedition is based on the Russian expedition ship *Professor Molchanov*, a converted Russian research vessel and able to carry about fifty persons.

To join the ship for this trip we first had to get to Spitzbergen. We arrive in Longyearbyen, the main town in Spitzbergen, late at night after the flight from London via Oslo and Tromso. We are met at the airport by a tall, fair-haired young man, called Peter, who is over-enthusiastic and announces that he is our expedition leader. 'Get your bags quickly! It is late we must hurry!' A few of us look at each other with some concern. After getting our bags from the baggage area, we congregate around the bus and wonder what we are in for. The party are dropped off singly and in pairs at various hotels and hostels around the town. We noted that out leader was not for waiting to see if the customer was able to get into their hotel or not. As soon as they were off the bus with their bags he ordered the driver to drive off. Doreen and I are dropped off at an expedition hostel outside the town. The place is deserted and mostly in darkness apart from a girl in the reception area, who has waited just for us. Once she has given us our key she climbs onto her scooter and leaves for home. Our room is in a different building about 200 yards down the road. We find our way there and discover that the room has just one single bed. After a night with both of us crammed into this small single bed, we are up early to look round Longyearbyen before joining the ship.

Professor Molchanov in the still waters at the head of Scorebysund, Greenland. Formerly a research vessel, this Russian ship makes an ideal expedition vessel.

Map of north-east Greenland showing the route taken by the *Professor Molchanov*.

On the way along the road to the jetty, we talk to a Dutch couple, John and Margarete. John is a retired marine engineer in the merchant marine and has similar interests to myself. Margarete is a friendly and down-to-earth lady who allows nothing to go by without good reason. We discussed our arrival at the airport and the expedition leader's behaviour. We agree it is not a good start. As we walk onto the jetty, having met up with some more of our fellow shipmates, all we can see of the ship is the top half of her white superstructure. The *Professor Molchanov* is not big. She was built in Finland in 1983 for the Russian Government as a polar and oceanic research vessel. She was 72 metres long and 1,753 tons.

As soon as we are all on board we set sail. Our cabin is comfortable, but basic. We have an upper and a lower bunk, a small bench seat by a porthole, a desk and a bathroom with a shower. As we will only be in it for sleeping, it proves ideal, apart from the fact that the bunk is a bit on the short side for a tall fellow like me. The dining room is more 'canteen messing' than 'haute cuisine' but the food is simple but good and well cooked by the Russian cook. A small working deck at the stern, with a hydraulic crane, provides a good stowage and working area for the Zodiac rubber boats. The ship operates an open-bridge policy for passengers, which means that we are able to go on the bridge at any time. The skipper and watch-keeping officers, who were all Russians, are friendly and helpful and in spite of imperfect English they always try hard to answer any questions. We are relieved to learn that 'I am the Expedition Leader' Peter from last night, is not the leader, just the deputy leader. We meet the actual leader at the first briefing. He is a dour Dutchman called Rene.

The trip across to east Greenland is uneventful. The ice edge that we hope to see is reportedly some 100 miles to the north at 81 degrees and it is deemed by Rene, to be too far out of our way to get to even though everyone on board is keen to see the edge of the pack ice. We start to get to know more of our fellow explorers. There are a number of Dutch people and they are good company and we strike up friendships with them. There is Derek and Anne from Salcombe. They are a charming, easy going and friendly couple. Even though Derek walks with a stick, he is an enthusiast for the old Brixham sailing trawlers and spends most summers on board one. We also have a Japanese film actress, who we are told is very famous in Japan, but of whom none of us have heard. She travels with two male companions and everywhere she goes, on board or ashore, she clutches a soft toy polar bear. It turns out to be the only polar bear we see on this trip.

We spend our time on the bridge watching the Greenland Sea go by as we sail across a calm, empty ocean with just the odd small iceberg drifting in the sun. Because the ice edge was well to the north we hope that this means that most of the fjords are free of ice so we can visit parts of the coast normally cut off by the ice even in summer. Greenland is Danish and a large part of north-east Greenland is a vast national park and entry by non-Danish groups is not permitted. We need both a Dane on the trip and the permission from the Danish Government to land there. So, on our team, we have a Danish naturalist who has been asked to join the expedition to enable permission to be granted.

One of the other passengers with whom we strike up a friendship is a Swede, travelling on his own, called Per Magnus. He is a warm and friendly guy who runs his own polar travel business in Sweden called Polar Quest. He is here as some of his clients are on the ship and he is also keen to see how this expedition, run by the Dutch, works out as he is planning to run his own expeditions to similar areas. Per Magnus is calm, sensible and very aware of peoples' different needs and capabilities, and speaks easily and with confidence about running an expedition such as this. He gives us all a feeling of confidence. He naturally takes a very keen interest in the skills of our leaders on this expedition.

Sirius Patrol

Our land fall is Daneborg and we arrive there mid-afternoon on a dull but calm day. This area, even in summer, is very often ice bound. We anchor in an ice-free Young Sound. Here, low hills by the water quickly rise to high mountains as the fjord winds its way deep into the mountains. There are large patches of snow still lying on some of the hills and the higher mountains still have their white caps on, but the lower slopes and shoreline are all clear of ice. Daneborg is a Danish Marine camp, set up in 1950 and home to the 'Sirius Patrol'. It is the only military dog sledge patrol anywhere in the world. The name Sirius is taken from the brightest star in the constellation of Canis Major and known as the 'Dog Star'. From the station, the Marines carry out military surveillance and policing patrols throughout the year, round the whole of the north and north-east coasts, using dog teams in winter and boats in summer. The patrols are also a key part of keeping a military surveillance eye on what anyone else may be doing in the area. Greenland is on the route from Russia to the USA

Daneborg, home to the Danish Marine's Sirius Patrol and their dogs. The ship lies at anchor just off shore.

and in the Cold War there were concerns about what ambitions the Russians might have had for Greenland.

We go ashore there and meet some of the marines and their dogs. They have over a hundred dogs: big, strong Husky dogs, many of them bred at the station. The twelve or so marines live here for about two years at a time in modern, well-equipped huts that make up the camp. Needless to say, the whole camp has an aura of being well organised, as it has to be to survive without any outside contact for most of the year as well as carrying out the patrols and caring for the dogs. Their patrols consist of two-man teams with ten or eleven dogs to each team pulling one large sledge. As the sledges have to carry everything that the whole team is ever likely to need for many weeks at a time, including all the dog food, they can weigh between 300 and 500 kilos each. The patrols can often last up to four months; so the dogs are bred for endurance pulling rather than speed. These are not racing sled dogs but true beasts of burden. They are all highly trained and well cared for and all of them wanted to be petted and told how fine they were. At feeding time they all sit patiently by their bowls in their allocated spaces, with their food already down in front of them. When all the dogs have their bowls put out, then the marine gives a one-word command and the dogs are instantaneously head and shoulders into the bowls, eating furiously.

On their patrols they also check that the emergency huts in the area are properly secure from weather and polar bear damage. If a bear can smell any trace of food it will try to break into the hut and a number have been found totally wrecked by bears. The huts we visit on the coast are all of a similar style and size. They can be used by hunters caught out in bad weather or anyone who needs an emergency shelter. They are small but big enough for two or three people to use in an emergency and equipped with just a stove for heat and cooking and some basic food. They have a stock of firewood and always a box of matches on the table with one projecting out of the box so anyone with frozen fingers can get hold of it easily to light the fire. There is normally a bottle of whisky there too and some blankets or fur pelts for warmth.

Walks

Our trip takes us down the coast with several ventures ashore seeing walrus, white Arctic hare and musk ox on the way. We go on a number of walks into the interior, walking in remote, empty valleys and on hills that few people have even seen let alone walked. At Clavering Oy, once we are ashore, the leader divides us into two small groups. One group is to head for a walk around a hill while the other group could wander along the shoreline or immediate hinterland at their own pace. The hill walk group are a mixed age group with a few who are definitely senior citizens and others who are not that naturally athletic. We all want to see what we comfortably can of the place. The young deputy leader, Peter, is to lead this walk. Some of the party ask him if he knows the route and if it is suitable for us as we are all wearing the wellington boots we needed for the wet shore landings from the Zodiacs and not proper walking boots. He assures us it will be fine. Our enthusiastic young friend then sets off up a 40-foot high scree slope of loose rocks and stones. We scatter for safety as loose rocks slither and fall down the slope, landing and crashing all about us as he races for the top. We yell at him to stop but he is oblivious to us. This is not a good start. This splits up the group as we all have to wait until the loose rocks have stopped sliding and coming down on us before some try to follow him up the scree slope and others look for a better way round the hill. Once we have all got to the top we find that our leader has already set off across open ground, thick with clumps of tussock grass and wet, marshy areas. We let him race on and follow at our own pace enjoying the scenery and views. After a while he stops and, when we have caught up, he leads us up into the higher uplands where we do have fantastic views of the interior. A beautiful, wild, and empty valley seeming to stretch away forever, rushing streams pouring off the hills and musk ox grazing in the far distance by a wide rocky river. Beyond that the mountains loom and behind them the white flecks of the ice cap itself shine in the sunshine.

He leads us on across the moor where progress is naturally slow as there are no animal tracks to follow so we each cautiously make our own way through the tussocks and round the bogs and become spread out right across the hill top. Then we drop down the side of a hill into the main river valley. Peter announces from way ahead that we have to cross the river even though doing so will mean that we will have to find a different beach, for the Zodiacs to collect us, from the sheltered beach we had used to get ashore. The river is rock-strewn and fast running but thankfully today relatively shallow, about 3 feet at the deepest points. It is perhaps 50 or 60 feet wide but the river bed is made up of round, wet and very slippery rocks. In a flash, our young leader splashes across it and then sits resting on the opposite bank, proud of his efforts. The rest of us, however, have to select our own routes across, and while guiding and holding one another, ensure that the more elderly and less agile are able to make their way over without falling in or twisting an ankle. Eventually, we all make it and we head back towards the coast. Here, as we feared, the shoreline is both steep and exposed and the waves are high and crash onto the beach.

As we predicted, we are also now cut off by the river mouth from the other group and the Zodiacs. After a delay and radio mix-ups the Zodiacs find us. However, the waves here are too high for them to come straight onto the beach, but the crewmen try. Twice the Zodiacs are flooded as they try to get onto the beach bows first then finally they come into the beach stern first, which puts the outboard motors at great risk. This also means that we have to wade out further into the waves and time our boarding leap to try and avoid the bigger waves and surf. Two people are knocked over by the waves and need to be manhandled into the boat and end up in wet, crumpled heaps of boots, parkas, cameras and bags on the flooded floor of the Zodiac. Finally, everyone manages to get on board and we go back to the ship, albeit wetter than we had planned. However, the trip has shown us some fantastic scenery and the experience of hill walking in rubber wellies.

In north-east Greenland we are very isolated from the rest of the world. It is easy when you are on a well-run ship, with good food and warm bunks, to feel that nothing can go wrong. After all this is a just 'Soft Adventure' and nothing can happen to you. However, in remote places, such as this, a simple slip or a fall on wet rocks or wet grass can easily lead to broken bones and, if it happens when you are well away from the beach and the ship, this can quickly turn into a major survival exercise. If, when you fall, you are out of sight and hearing of anyone else you may not be immediately missed. If the weather then changes, or a radio fails to work, or a rising wind and heavy surf prevent the Zodiacs getting back inshore, then these factors will conspire against you as they often do in emergencies. A constant awareness of your circumstances is needed all the time. Even if in the event of a serious accident people can get you back to the ship then a hospital and qualified medical help are not available until the ship takes you to one, which may be many hundreds of miles away. Any good leader will always have all these factors under constant review and be aware of the capabilities of the weakest members of the team. It seems that our young leader must have been away from expedition leader course on the day they covered that.

The Fjords and Icebergs

Our first sightings of icebergs is at the entrance to Kaiser Frans Joseph Fjord where the bergs sit, silent and gleaming, in the sun on a mirror calm, blue sea. We sail past them and up Sophia Sound into the narrow Antarctic Sound, where the setting sun is turning the whole landscape a glorious warm, reddish orange colour. The bare red mountains rear up from the fjord and as the sun sinks so a hard black shadow slowly moves across the hillside and replaces the sunlit orange, as we continue deep into the fantastic fjord systems of East Greenland.

The following morning the ship anchors at Ymer Oy, an island deep in the fjord system. There is no wind, we are totally sheltered on all sides by the mountains. After a short walk ashore we set off in the Zodiacs to explore some of the icebergs nearby. Per Magnus takes one of the Zodiacs and invites his clients and a few others, including Doreen and I, to join him for a tour round the icebergs. Unlike our Dutch deputy leader, who proceeds to roar off round the fjord with his passengers hanging on grimly, Per Magnus hardly uses the engine. Now, when we are right alongside the icebergs and looking up at them from sea level we stop, switch off the engine and let the Zodiac drift on the flat, deep, black water. Then we just watch and listen and appreciate their size and beauty even more. The ice itself takes so many different forms. Sometimes it is a solid impenetrable white mass; sometimes it is totally transparent. Sometimes it is like a delicate filigree sculpture and riddled with holes. In some of the icebergs ridges and scratch marks show where they have torn at the seabed or land on their journey into the sea. In others we see straight lines of transparent blue ice running right through an opaque white mass. Most of them have erosion lines made by the sea water and waves washing at their bases and most also show signs that they have toppled over and capsized at some time as the water erosion lines rise up at acute angles from the present waterline. In the sun, the icebergs gleam and glisten with a dazzling whiteness against the black, shadowed sides of the fjords, yet when they are in the shadow they become grey and flat; losing all their angular shapes and lustre. All the time, as the sun shines warmly on them, there is a gentle noise of water dripping off the iceberg into the sea or gurgling as it runs down hidden channels deep inside the ice. Their colours vary with the light, from pure white through greys and vivid blues to pale greens. As we look down into the water, we see that the white colours gently give way to soft greens, then to deeper greens and blues before they vanish into the black of the cold, deep water. The icebergs come in all shapes; some are flat-topped, some are sculptured like giant statues, some have tall pinnacles and some are rounded and smooth, while others are rough and jagged. The icebergs are continually changing, their shapes change with perspective and viewing angles; their colours change with the sun, which throws deep, dark, blue shadows across the shaded sides of the iceberg that contrasts strongly with the bright sunny side. Every iceberg is different; every one of them fascinating in its shapes, its ice forms and its colours. Later, as we watch from the ship, one of the bergs that we had motored round earlier slowly rolls over and settles into a new position. Waves wash out from it as it settles.

We sail on deeper into the Kaiser Frans Joseph Fjord system right to the head of the fjord. This fjord is thousands of feet deep and the sheer-sided mountains along its side are thousands of feet high. This is a real fjord; long, deep, dark, brooding and silent with the mountain cliffs climbing vertically from the black depths up to unseen peaks behind the high shoulders of the cliffs that form the walls of the fjord. Big icebergs sit silent and unmoving in the black shadows of the fjord. As we move slowly through these deep shadows we are sometimes illuminated, as if by a searchlight, as a shaft of sunlight cuts through a gap in the mountains. Occasionally, we see a pure white iceberg sitting in a totally black background as the sun catches it against the deep shadow of the cliffs. It sits like an imperfectly shaped pearl on a cushion of black velvet.

Icebergs, one clear and one white, lie at peace in the sunshine.

No one speaks as we all stand on deck and try and absorb the sheer splendour of this fjord.

We leave the fjord late in the afternoon and head south down the Kong Oscar Fjord, a beautiful, wide fjord between Traill Oy and the mainland. Gradually, the mountains recede and the land opens out on each side as we head towards the open sea. Later in the night we are given a small show by the Northern Lights. For ten or fifteen minutes, the soft green, silky trails dip and ripple across the sky like a silk curtain, before they fade and leave us alone in a black, empty sea.

Dawn brings us to a white mountainous coast on a clear sunny morning. The ship rolls gently along in a sparkling blue sea. Away to starboard, we can see the jagged, snow-capped mountains of Liverpool Land. The chart reveals the mixed history of this area and the nationalities of those who came here first; with Kap Godfried Hansen followed by Kap Smith; Canning Land followed by Carlsberg Fjord.

Scoresbysund

We enter the biggest fjord system in the world, Scoresbysund. It stretches over 300 miles inland and comprises many islands and smaller fjords. Its entrance, between Cape Brewster and Cape Tobin, is relatively narrow at about 15 to 20 miles wide. As we enter we can see the mountains of Cape Brewster shining away to the south. We sail into the massive fjord and head for the main settlement of Ittoqqortoormiit, or Scoresbysund. It was set up in 1925 by settlers from

Left: A towering berg floats out of Nordevest Fjord into Scvoresbysund.

Below: Slow ahead as we weave between the icebergs.

Ammassalik, some 500 miles to the south. The aim was to enable them to develop a community using the traditional hunting skills of their Inuit forefathers. From the sea, the village looks attractive with the coloured wooden houses of red, blue, pastel green, some white, all sitting in a haphazard way on the hillside and with roads leading down to a small, sheltered quay. However, initial appearances can be deceptive. When we get ashore we find that the only road is a wet, muddy track, littered with old and broken sledges, old packing cases and bikes, while loose barking dogs roam the streets. The crew warn us not to pet them as these are not trained sledge dogs, but scavenging strays that wander the town. A small Inuit girl of about four or five years old follows us around at a distance, staring silently at us all the time. She is wearing a fantastic blue-black sealskin coat that reaches her feet and is topped by a fur hood. Wooden racks of drying seal, ox and polar bear skins are scattered around. Alcohol is clearly a problem for some here too; although we were assured that a moratorium on spirits has helped the problem. Of the 500 or so people only about thirty are actually hunters, the remainder that are in work are in social services of some sort and very under-employed. The locals are friendly and happy to let us wander about and look at their town but once we had done the tour the only thing to do was to go back on board. Per Magnus knows someone here and goes off to find him. The man was a hunter who had just returned from a trip up the fjord and reported that there are narwhals in Scoresbysund at the moment.

We sail that evening and head into the fjord but only after circling a large iceberg in the bay which is constantly changing colour as the sun sets in the west while we look at it from all points of the compass. The following day, having steamed up the fjord overnight, we are greeted by a majestic sight of many huge icebergs floating in the still waters of the fjord. The fjord at this point is very wide, more like an inland sea than a fjord. These bergs are all many times larger than the ship and we thread our way through them towards Norosti Bukta and Nordvest Fjord. We go ashore and for a couple of hours we just sit on a rock and watch, entranced as iceberg after iceberg drifts out of Nordvest Fjord into the main fjord. Although they are moving slowly, when we watch them against the background of the mountains they appear to be racing out of the fjord. Nordvest Fjord leads up into a mountain range known as the Staunning Alps and from where we are we could see why it is so called. The sparkling white peaks peep out over the nearer mountains, resembling a Swiss scene. At its head, the fjord is fed by the Greenland ice cap. It is impossible for the ship to find a way up Nordvest Fjord due to the number of bergs and the speed at which they are all moving. This is a one-way street. These icebergs are tens of feet high, some must have been well over 100-feet-high, and our ship is often lost behind them as she manoeuvres in the open water of the main fjord to avoid them. Later that afternoon, as we sail off to the west, we look back. The sun has now moved round and the icebergs have become silhouetted.

An iceberg with heavy scouring on its side. A sign that this part had once been at the bottom of the berg.

The sea has become a silver glistening mirror on which sits a monochrome of dozens of black icebergs.

We sail right up to the far end of the fjord system, or at least as far as we can. We stop near the top and a few of us go ashore for a walk up a little beautiful glen by the Rypefjord. Ellie, a spirited and chatty Dutch lady, who must have been in her eighties, led the way. I call it a glen because that is what it reminded me of, a lovely, empty, peaceful, Scottish highland glen. The slightly marshy glen floor is covered in wild flowers and tiny shrubs and berries, all of which seem to be blooming together and the rich colours of rusty reds, corals and yellows form sweeps of carpet across the rocks and the hillside. We have arrived at the height of the short summer and the glen is in full bloom. A small burn runs down the glen and its gurgling is the only sound to be heard. The hills above step up through raised moorland to the red coloured sandstone mountains basking in the sun behind the glen. We sit on a couple of warm rocks and chat to Ellie about the trip and enjoy the warmth of the sun in this beautiful spot.

Later that night we are very lucky to see about forty narwhals in the distance, but due to the ice we cannot follow them. Some hunters, who are camping in the area, come out to the ship that evening and tell us that they had seen a school of about 100 narwhals earlier in the day in the same location.

Our passage round the back of Milne Land is stopped by a field of broken pack ice made up of glacier bergy bits and small icebergs. The ship tries to nudge and push her way through but it proves difficult. That night, as the sun sets, the shadows of the hills to the west fall across the lower hills of Milne Land to the east and turn them black; but as the sun still shines on the snow of the higher hill tops it looks as if they had been set on fire, so brilliant is the sunset. Above the black shadow on the lower slopes, the higher areas are bright flame red then orange as they reach the summits. Here, they soften to yellows and merge with the pure white of the snow on the tops. All these colours are reflected back in the mirror-still waters of the fjord between the floating patches of ice. All too quickly, it fades as the sun sets and the black shadow quickly climbs the hill and puts out the flames, leaving a still scene with the ship surrounded by broken ice and black hills. After a few hours gently feeling our way through, we finally clear the ice and are able to continue down to the south side of the island and then east along the south side of Milne Island.

The Denmark Strait. The *Bismarck* and HMS *Hood*

After three days exploring the inner reaches of Scoresbysund we head out and into the Denmark Strait on a grey, rough and miserable morning. There is now an air of urgency on board as the vibration of the engine throbs through the ship, after days of gentle cruising, as now we are bound for Iceland. Also, a depression is coming up the Denmark Straight from the south and the wind is whipping up the waves into a lumpy and confused sea that makes the ship take on an uncomfortable motion. The clouds close down to the sea and all around us is now grey after days of pure whites.

It was through these cold, desolate and grey waters that, in May 1941, the formidable new German battleship *Bismarck*, (50,000-tons) and her escort, the cruiser *Prinz Eugen* (15,000-tons) made their run for the open Atlantic from Germany. They tried to creep down through the Denmark Strait, keeping close to the edge of the pack ice along this coast in the hope that bad weather and the ice would hide them from the Royal Navy. Their aim was to get into the Atlantic and harry the Allied Atlantic convoys. *Bismarck* had to be stopped; and it fell to the Royal Navy's pride, the fast battleship, HMS *Hood* (48,000-tons) with others to try and stop her. *Hood* was classed as a battle cruiser due to her high speed, but as she was the same size and had the same armaments as similar battleships of the time, but was 3 knots faster; she was effectively a 'fast battleship'. HMS *Hood* had been built by John Brown's in Clydebank in 1918 at the end of the First World War and was 'state of the art' in modern warship

Professor Molchanov moves carefully between the huge icebergs in Scoresbysund.

design and construction at the time. She was, at 48,000 tons, the biggest, longest and fastest warship ever built. She was armed with 8 x 15-inch guns, which exactly matched those of the new *Bismarck* when they met in 1941. The one weakness she had in 1941 was one that did not exist in 1918 when she was built. Her deck armour was not strong enough to protect her against the new higher trajectory shells used in the Second World War.

The two ships met in battle in the Denmark Strait on 24 May, after the cruisers HMS *Norfolk* and HMS *Suffolk* had located and tracked the *Bismarck* down through the grey murk of the Strait. The engagement did not last long. While closing the *Bismarck*, *Hood* fired her opening salvoes. To the Germans, these looked like great, bright suns in the Arctic sky. The *Bismarck* responded. In an early salvo, a modern, high trajectory shell from the *Bismarck* came straight down onto the *Hood*'s deck, penetrated the relatively thin deck armour and exploded in one of the main magazines. The ship was literally blown to pieces in an instant. Out of 1,419 men, only three survived. There is still conjecture as to whether the German shell penetrated the decks and went directly into the magazine or whether it exploded on the deck near a ready-use ammunition store and it was this explosion that then blew the hole down to the magazine. In any event the result was the same.

What must that battle have been like for the men on both sides in the icy waters of the Denmark Strait? With the grey mist and rain, the bitter wind off the ice to the north and the noise and vibration of the big guns firing, it must have been dreadful. There would be carnage inside the ship as shells hit and

Black icebergs. Icebergs silhouetted against a silver sea in Scoresbysund.

exploded in the ship. Flash fires would ripple through the passageways and compartments burning everything and everyone in their path, before anyone can turn out of the way, as the flames exploded into mess decks and gun turrets alike. The screams of dying and trapped men, burning steel shrapnel and white-hot splinters flying around, severing water pipes, steam pipes and electrical cables as well as cutting off power and access for those down below.

The enemy ship would be seen first by the frozen look-outs as a slightly darker grey patch in the patchy grey wall of mist and murk. 'Was that a patch of thicker

Sunset on the hills of Milne Land.

Icebergs floating off Milne Land at the West end of Scoresbysund.

mist or is there something there?' 'No, just a heavy bank of fog.' The lookout wipes his binocular lenses and looks again. The dark patch is still there but it is getting bigger and darker. It even has a bow wave! Suddenly a ship takes shape and detaches itself from the murk. It is not just a ghostly patch of fog in the far distance, but a solid enemy ship just a couple of miles away! The low, squat, grey hull and the tall superstructures of a modern battleship operating at full speed, its low sharp bows throwing the spray and waves aside as it sliced through the seas with its menacing, deadly main guns pointing straight towards you. It must have been an awesome sight. How the three men from the Hood survived is a mystery itself as, after the shock of the explosion, the shock of hitting those icy waters would numb and paralyse anyone, never mind any injuries caused by the explosions themselves. Hyperthermia would normally render a man totally helpless in seconds and kill him in minutes. The three survivors were picked up by HMS Electra a couple of hours after the explosion.

Bismarck was caught and finally sunk a few days later by swordfish torpedo aircraft from HMS *Ark Royal* and torpedoes from HMS *Dorsetshire*. When she sank, the *Bismarck* suffered an even greater loss of life than the *Hood*. 1,995 died in *Bismarck*, 1,416 died in the *Hood*.

North Cape of Iceland

Our passage through the Denmark Strait is less eventful and later that day the weather improves and we come up to a small school of four or five humpback whales feeding in the rich Icelandic waters off the North Cape. These grounds

A tall berg floats near the entrance to Scoresbysund.

used to be some of the best cod fishing grounds in the Atlantic and always had a number of trawlers from the UK and Europe fishing them. Today, apart from a couple of Icelandic trawlers in the distance, they now seem to be deserted. It was near here, in the Isafjord, that the Hull trawlers Ross Cleveland and Kingston Peridot were lost in 1968. The whales are escorted by about forty white-beaked dolphins that leap from the waters and swim all around the ship. The big, slow whales just carry on, occasionally rolling slowly over in the water to cast an eye over this new white member of the school and waving a long fin as they glide by. They swim under the ship and they appear placid and relaxed. We stay with the whales for over an hour, transfixed by the serene beauty of these great whales before we reluctantly head for Keflavik, our final destination.

This had been a strange trip in some ways. A polar expedition when we had seen neither sea ice nor polar bears. Yet we had seen some rare and fascinating things and been to places that few have been to before. The Sirius Patrol, the spectacular fjords of north-eastern Greenland, which few people in the world have ever seen and which are just as dramatic as the famed Norwegian fjords:

the vastness of the Scoresbysund fjord system and the fantastic icebergs that come from the ice cap into those fjords. Seeing narwhals, even in the distance is a rare event. To me, seeing with my own eyes, things that I have only ever seen pictures of in books and also things that few people have ever seen before is thrilling and satisfying and that makes the experience worthwhile. I recall standing on a small rise on one of the trips into hills and looking down over a crest onto a beautiful river valley, with musk ox grazing way below, the valley framed by hills and backed by great mountains with the ice cap behind it all and thinking 'Has anyone ever looked at this before?'

CHAPTER 8

I/B *Kapitan Dranitsyn* – Franz Joseph Land

From St Petersburg in Russia, take the night train that travels due north and, twenty-eight hours later, you reach the end of the line, Murmansk. Murmansk is the port that was the destination for many of the Arctic convoys in the Second World War and was, until recently, a closed city. It is the naval base for the Soviet Northern Fleet. If you then take a ship and sail due north across the Barents Sea towards the North Pole for two and a half days you reach a group of islands on the edge of the Polar ice cap that are nearer to the North Pole than they are to Murmansk. You will have arrived at Franz Josef Land; a land that, even today, few people have heard of and even fewer have visited.

Franz Joseph Land (FJL) is an archipelago of 191 ice-cap-covered, uninhabitable islands on the northern edge of the Barents Sea. It is about 800 miles due north of Murmansk and 550 miles from the Geographic North Pole. The islands stretch over 100 miles from north to south and about 200 miles from east to west. Franz Josef Land was probably first sighted by Norwegian sealers in about 1765 when they reported sighting land when they were well to the east of Spitzbergen. Then, in 1873, an Austro-Hungarian expedition set sail from Germany in their ship, the Tegettoff, to find the north-east Passage. The expedition was led by two men, Julius von Payer and Karl Weyprecht. They never found the north-east Passage. As they sailed eastwards through the Barents Sea, they were suddenly caught by early ice and the ship was trapped. They had no choice but to drift with the ice and pray that one day they would be released. One year later and still frozen in, they looked out over the rail at the endless white fog and ice and then, through a clearing in the fog, they realised that they were looking at two jagged cliffs appearing to the north-west. They named the new land after their Emperor, Arch Duke Franz Josef. They named the cliffs Cape Tegettoff, after their ship. Franz Josef Land was then subsequently claimed by both Norway and Russia until, in 1926, Russia issued a decree stating that it was Russian and imposed a ban on anyone visiting it. It remained closed until 2002 when the Russians allowed one or two small expeditions to visit the islands. Even now it can only be visited during a few

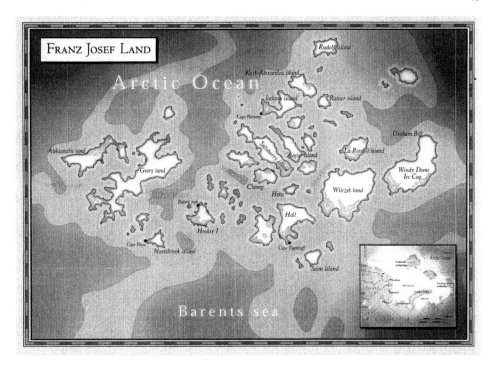

Map showing the islands of Frans Josef Land (inset).

brief weeks in high summer due to the ice and, even then, only by a Russian icebreaker.

But why would anyone want to go there? Firstly, because it is reportedly a beautiful area with all the islands having their own ice caps. Secondly, it is a haven for polar wild life – polar bears, walrus, whales as well as birds. Thirdly, it was where Fridtjof Nansen spent the winter of 1895/96 after his attempt to reach the North Pole from his Trans-Polar ship, the *Fram*. He, and his sole companion Johanssen, lived in a hole on a beach on Jackson Island for the whole winter. Having read of Nansen's exploits I want to go there and see the place. And finally, I want to go because it has the most northerly point of land in Europe or Asia, Cape Fligely, on Rudolf Island. Only the most northerly point of Ellesmere Island in Canada is nearer to the North Pole.

I wrote to Per Magnus at Polar Quest in Sweden. We had met him on the Greenland trip and I asked him whether he knew of any plans for expeditions to Franz Josef Land. He wrote back saying that he was in touch with a Russian Expedition Company that was thinking of mounting an icebreaker expedition to FJL the following year. 'If the icebreaker company, the Murmansk Shipping Corporation, committed to the trip, were we interested?' he emailed us. 'Yes, we are!' All went well, forms were filled in, deposits paid, visas sought and travel plans made. All was looking good but then, two months before the departure, the Murmansk Shipping Corporation cancelled the voyage saying there were not enough people wanting to go to make it worthwhile. Maybe they would plan it again the following year, if they got enough people. If not then the chances of anyone organising a trip to FJL were pretty remote and our chance to get there could have gone for good. We really thought that our chance had gone, but we had no choice, we had to just wait and see. Happily for us, the following year, the Russians did set up the trip again and this time enough people were interested, so we were on again.

Murmansk

The *Kapitan Dranitsyn* is a Russian icebreaker, operated by the Murmansk Shipping Corporation and based in Murmansk. She and her sister ships, including a fleet of nuclear-powered icebreakers, keep the northern sea route open throughout the year. To join the ship we have to go to Murmansk and that in itself is very special. Murmansk is the headquarters of the Russian Northern Fleet and a major submarine base. Having been in the Royal Navy during the Cold War and having sailed along the northern coast of Russia in RN warships and UK Trawlers, Murmansk is a place of mystery. You read about it in spy thrillers, or you heard of allied submarines watching the coast 'off Murmansk' but no one I knew had ever actually been there. What sort of place is it really? It is reputedly a desolate and miserable place where sunshine, food and happiness are scarce. You felt that military security ruled the town and all that goes on there and that greatcoat-clad, rifle-touting guards watched every street corner and anyone without the correct papers is a spy. The only people who lived there only did so because the Russian Government had sent them there either as part of the Navy or to support the Navy. Was it really going to be like that?

In Helsinki Airport, we meet up with the others going on the trip and then fly on by a special charter flight to Murmansk to join the ship. Per Magnus, who has arranged the trip for a total of about eight people, has sent one of his senior staff to accompany us. Her name is Carina, she is a slim, no-nonsense, Swedish lady in her early thirties, who tries hard to answer our questions and keep us together as a group. Most of the others on the trip are German with their own German guide.

We fly north, up over Finland and Lapland, before then turning east and descending across the Finnish/Russian border and the fells, birch forests and rivers of the Kola Peninsula to land at Murmansk. The airfield is deserted and there are no other planes in sight anywhere. Ours is the only plane in town. We go through Immigration where our Visas and passports are studied in minute detail. The arrivals hall is empty and we are shepherded straight onto a bus by a uniformed and serious-looking lady and told to wait in the bus. We wait and watch while the rest of the party are cleared and the luggage is taken by porters from the arrivals area and put into two lorries.

The terminal is a big and impressive three-storey, glass-fronted building. The airport car park outside the front of the terminal has about half a dozen cars parked there. No other cars arrive or leave while we wait. There are no signs to the short stay, or long-term car parks and no drop-off-only zones. No taxis, minibuses, no car-hire-courtesy buses, just the two buses for us pulled up in front of the terminal. Grass grows wherever there isn't concrete and the whole area has a sleepy, forgotten atmosphere that we have disturbed by our arrival. Eventually, everyone is on board and we set off towards the town. The scenery on the way is very attractive. The Kola Inlet is a long finger of water and runs deep into the countryside. We can see the wide estuary in the distance with green, wooded hills rolling down to the water's edge. Behind it, the low fells roll away to the west and the Norwegian and Finnish Border. Silver birches grow everywhere. As we get nearer to the town the Russian official tells us that we are not allowed to take any pictures of the town from the bus or even of the ship from the quayside. The buses take us directly to the ship and as the airport is on the south side of the town and the ship has been berthed at the southern end of the docks, we see nothing of the town itself except one roundabout and a few blocks of flats. Some are five or six storeys, made of concrete, while some are wooden, two-storey buildings that have been painted pale blue a very long time ago. The bus drives round the end of a warehouse onto the dockside and the *Kapitan Dranitsyn*'s black hull is suddenly there towering above us. She looks huge. We go on board to be greeted by a friendly, smiling Russian lady offering us cake and salt, a traditional Russian welcome. More staff show us to our cabins and we begin to settle in while we wait for the luggage.

The *Kapitan Dranitsyn* was built in Finland by the Wartsila Shipyard, which is world famous for building icebreakers. She was launched in 1975 but not completed for another five years. She is 12,000 tons, 25,000 hp and has a crew of sixty. She is one of a class of icebreakers designed for the Russian Northern Sea Route round the north coast of Siberia. This sea route is an important route for Russia and the icebreakers keep the seas along route open all the year round. This huge stretch of sea, from the Barents Sea, through the Kara Sea, the Laptev Sea and the East Siberian Sea give access to the main ports of Dikson, Tiksi and Pevek. The icebreakers need to be big and strong. In spite of all the claims about global warming and melting ice, the Northern Sea Route can still get blocked and ships can get stuck, even in summer. The ice is not as bad as in winter and it does retreat northwards in the summer, as it always has. But if the wind blows from the north, then the pack ice comes down to the coast along the north-east Passage.

The nuclear ships are even bigger at 25,000 tons and can generate 75,000 hp. They have a crew of almost 140. All the icebreakers have double hulls, with steel 48 mm thick at the bow. They also have a water-ballasting system between the hulls to enable the ship to be rolled by pumping water from side to side to free it if ice freezes to the hulls. An air bubbling systems forces high pressure air out through holes deep in the hull and prevents ice freezing to the ship. Special polymer coatings are used on the hull to reduce friction. Also, the ships can break ice going forwards or astern. Kapitan Dranitsyn is powered by a diesel-electric power system. She has three propellers, port, starboard and a centre line shaft. Her Captain, Sergei Papko, is an experienced icebreaker captain, having spent fifteen years on icebreakers in the northern seas. All her accommodation is within a main seven-deck-high superstructure unit that allows a high degree of noise insulation between it and the hull, so minimising the continual noise of ice breaking. She is well equipped for expedition work, having berths for over a hundred people and with a large dining room, lounges and a bar. She is very comfortable and a nicely decorated ship with comfy chairs and colour photos of Arctic wildlife on the walls. In addition, she has a well-equipped hospital, a gym, a heated indoor pool and a large, very hot sauna. The cabins are very comfortable, with two bunks, one of which folds up and becomes a settee during the day. There is a desk, plenty of storage space and a good bathroom as well as a large window that opens for fresh air.

We sail later in the afternoon. Murmansk is built totally down the east side of the Kola Inlet, between the hills to the east and the water, so it stretches a long way while, on the other bank, there is nothing but green woods and hills. The only bridge lies well south of the town and is the road to Kirkeness in Norway. I am amazed at how big the town is. Murmansk seems to stretch away for miles towards the sea. We pass the fishing vessel berths, where well over a dozen large, modern stern trawlers are tied up. Most look to be in good condition and some are obviously undergoing overhauls and refits, but some look derelict. We sail slowly down the Inlet past the industrial areas of the town, past warehouses, a power station and some large, forbidding, grey buildings that look from a distance like government offices. Along the hills behind the town is a series of tower blocks, which we assume are housing areas. We pass the commercial docks where the tops of freighters rise above the general collection of warehouses and cranes. We pass the ship repair yards where an icebreaker similar to the *Kapitan Dranitsyn* is in a floating dock. The Inlet widens and anchored off the port in the middle of the Inlet is a smart new freighter with a bright red hull and an icebreaker bow. The *Arctic Express* is one of a new class of cargo icebreakers operating along the northern coasts.

Gradually, we leave the last of the town and begin to see the start of the naval area. At the water's edge and out on the other side of the Inlet we can see a number of wrecks of submarines and warships that have sunk. They lie rotting and neglected, sticking out of the water. At one point, the last 30 feet of the stern of a naval patrol boat or corvette sticks vertically out of the water. There are no buoys around it to warn of its presence, so presumably all the local shipping will know it is there. Further down we pass the 'Atomflot', the base for the seven nuclear icebreakers. The nuclear icebreakers look very impressive, squat and workmanlike with their black hulls and rich orange-red superstructures. The first nuclear icebreaker, the *Lenin*, commissioned in 1959, is also berthed here. She is now decommissioned and has been turned into a museum ship. Nearby is the home base for *Kapitan Dranitsyn* and the other conventionally-powered icebreakers. As we pass the base, two sister ships of the *Dranitsyn* lie alongside. We wonder if the *Kapitan Dranitsyn* had been taken to the far end of the port for us to board her so that we would not see anything of the town or the port area from the bus?

High above on the hill stands the 'Alyosha', a giant, 35-metre high memorial, which was erected in 1974. It is a figure of a Russian soldier looking out over the port and it dominates the area. It commemorates all the soldiers who died defending Murmansk from the Nazis in the Second World War. Murmansk was put under heavy siege by the Germans, second only to Stalingrad, but Murmansk never fell and the Germans never captured it or the vital port and railway links.

Further down the Inlet on the eastern side we pass the closed naval city of Severomorsk. This is the headquarters and main naval base for the Russian Northern Fleet. As we pass we can see the base stretching out to the East round into a large bay. In the far distance, across the bay, ships and dockyards line the shore. The scene is dominated by the largest floating dock in Russia, moored near the main channel. The aircraft carrier, *Admiral Kuznetsov*, is in the dock undergoing maintenance, her ski jump ramp jutting out over the water. In addition to Severomorsk, there are six other small naval bases situated to the west of the Inlet hidden along the fjords and bays of the Kola Peninsula. It was from one of these bases, at Ara Bay, that the *Kursk* sailed on her fateful last voyage in 2000. During the Soviet era, there were over 200 submarines of all types based in this area. In addition, there is another large submarine naval base at Severodvinsk, near Arkhangelsk (Archangel) in the White Sea.

As we reach the entrance to the Inlet, the ship is ordered to stop by the Port Control and stay where we are, as a naval exercise is taking place with vessels leaving Severomorsk. We wait for about an hour or so before we are cleared to proceed. We finally come out of the Kola Inlet and reach the Barents Sea. As we head north, a westerly wind is blowing and the sea develops into a chop. The captain takes us well off to the west as we have been ordered to avoid the naval exercise areas just off Murmansk. It is not long before we are made aware of the one failing of icebreakers; they roll. As they cannot have any attachments on the outside of the hull as they do not have stabilisers or bilge keels and hence they roll a lot.

North

For two days we steam due north. During this time we are shown round the ship and meet our expedition leader, Dr Victor Boyarsky, a famous Russian polar expedition leader and the director of the Arctic & Antarctic Museum in St Petersburg. In 1995, he was part of an International Trans-Antarctica Expedition that crossed Antarctica using dog teams. They did so through the previously untravelled and coldest part of the continent, the 'Pole of Inaccessibility', as well as the Geographic South Pole. He has also taken part in many North Pole and Franz Josef Land Expeditions and runs the Russian ice station at 89 north, set up by Russia every year.

During these two days steaming we have time to explore this fascinating ship. At the stern there is a big, open, working-deck area and right at the stern itself is a 'V' shaped notch, about 10 feet wide by 4 feet deep, built into the stern and well covered with heavy, flexible fendering. At the forward end of this deck is the winch room where a powerful towing winch is housed. The ship is equipped as an ocean salvage and rescue vessel so it needs a powerful towing and salvage winch, and a number of special workshops on board. It also accounts for her having so much passenger accommodation. I notice a large, black, pressure cylinder, about 4 feet long and about 2 feet in diameter mounted on the deck, firmly fastened to the deck at its forward end and with a securing eye at the other. It lies on heavy wooden shock pads. Just as I am looking at this thing and trying to work out its purpose, one of the sailors, a thin, middle-aged man, appears from the winch room wiping his hands on a rag. He sees me looking at the cylinder and stops. I point to the black cylinder, 'Can you please tell me what that is for?' He smiles at me but does not speak. He seems to understand what I am asking and after a moment's thought, he kneels down on the deck, and takes out a small pencil from his dungaree pocket and begins drawing on the metal deck and explaining to me in Russian what happens. He is showing me that when they break ships out of the ice, the icebreaker backs the big V at the stern right up to the bow of the stranded ship. The ship is then secured hard and fast into the V at the stern of the icebreaker, hence the heavy wooden fenders. The securing cables are attached to the black cylinder. In the middle of his Russian I hear the English word 'Damper' and it all becomes clear. This cylinder is a form of giant spring designed to take up the sudden jerks and jolts that will undoubtedly occur during such an operation. I thank the sailor and we shake hands. He is delighted that I understood his explanation and I am delighted to have found the answer to my question with only one word of a common language.

Above the winch room is the flight deck where the small red and blue helicopter is lashed. I walk forward and climb the eight decks up to the bridge. It is one of the largest bridges I have been on. It is fully enclosed from wing to wing and with deck-to-deck head windows at the ends. The ship operates an 'open bridge' policy on these expeditions and the rule here is that passengers can use the starboard side, the crew use the port side. The starboard side has a couple of chairs and plenty of ledges to sit on and it even has a slave radar display. Down below, the dining room stretches across the width of the ship. It is bright, decorated in warm pinks and cream colours and always set for the next meal with pristine white table clothes. The bar, one deck below, is a light, warm and cosy area with plenty of easy chairs and a small, but well-stocked, bar in the corner.

The Islands

We arrive off the southern end of Franz Josef Land late in the afternoon. The sea is clear of any ice and as we come on deck to look at the islands, just off to starboard, two humpback whales spout a welcome for us. The islands stretch across our path. One of them, Bell Island, is easily identified by its distinctive steep sides and a bell-shaped silhouette. The islands are all low and flat-topped as all are covered in ice caps and cloud. The sun shines brightly on the ship and, as we get closer, we can make out the cliff faces and glaciers where the ice caps flow down into the sea.

We hope to make a landing at Cape Flora, on the south-west tip of Northbrook Island, but the heavy swell prevents this. It was here that Frederick Jackson set up a base in 1895 and where, in 1896, Nansen and Johanssen were rescued after overwintering nearly 100 miles further north. Maps of the islands did not exist then so they had no real idea exactly where they were. They were kayaking down through the islands hoping to meet a sealing ship or, if not, they planned to try and kayak to Spitzbergen, some 200 miles away across the open Arctic Ocean.

As they paddled along the coast of Northbrook Island they were attacked by walruses that drove their tusks into the kayaks and tore them badly. The two men just managed to get to shore and then spent four days repairing the kayaks with what little gear they had. As they finished the work and were about to set off again, Nansen thought he heard a dog barking in the distance. Johanssen did not hear it but Nansen set off on skis towards the sound. Perhaps he had been mistaken but he was sure he had heard something and so he skied on. Then, he heard it again and skied further and sure enough there, beyond a mound, was a dog and beyond the dog, a man. It was Frederick Jackson of the Jackson-Harmsworth Expedition, which had set up their wooden-hutted base camp at Cape Flora. The meeting was a miracle of chance. The Jackson Harmsworth expedition had left the UK long after Nansen and the *Fram* had been frozen into the polar seas so Nansen had no knowledge that there were any other expeditions there. It was the only one in the 191 islands at the time and had Nansen not been attacked by the walrus at that point or, had they sailed a few minutes before the dog barked they would almost certainly have perished trying to kayak to Spitzbergen. As it was, they went back to Tromso on a supply ship a few weeks later to be greeted as heroes.

I am disappointed that we can not visit the site of this famous rescue but perhaps before we finally leave we may get another chance to try and go ashore there. We sail on, up through the wide British Channel past George Island. The next morning finds us off Hooker Island.

Polar Bears

As we wake up we can tell from the noises that we are now in the ice. We look out and the ship is moving slowly through the pack. Then, right by the ship, we see fresh polar bear paw tracks in the snow-covered pack ice. They are leading away from the ship, off into the snow. The ship has just crossed their track. Later that day we see the bears. They are resting on fast ice in a large bay. They are probably about a mile away from us so the ship moves slowly into the bay, breaking the ice as she goes. When we are about half a mile away we stop in the ice and we wait. Sure enough, curiosity is getting the better of the bears and

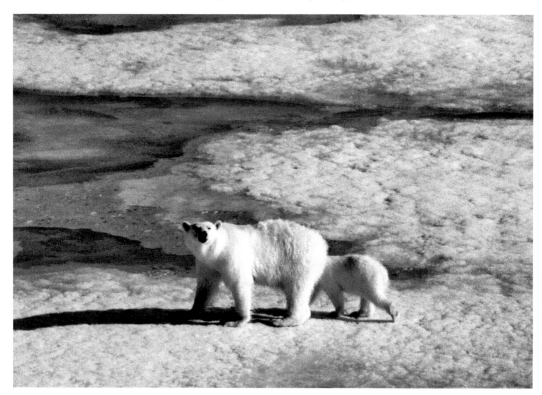

Polar bears. A mother and cub survey the ice for seals. (Photo by kind permission of Carina Svensson of Polar Quest)

they come out to see who we are. There are two of them, a mother and a cub. They walk right up to the ship looking hard at it: stopping then peering and stretching and sniffing to examine the new smells and sights that have arrived in their bay. Then they walk a few paces closer. The cub is timid, always carefully keeping its mother between itself and the ship as it peeps out from under her legs. We stand silently and excitedly on the fo'c'sle and watch them; the only sound the clicking of cameras and the sniffing and snorting of the bears. They walk right round the bows looking at both sides of the ship but not venturing further than the bow itself. After a while they become bored and wander off back to their resting spot. As we watch we can also see a number of seals lying on the ice all around the bay. The bears must have eaten recently or they would have been far more interested in the seals than in us.

The Ice Closes In

A shore visit to Tichaja Station, an old Soviet polar station on Hooker Island, showed the speed at which conditions can change. As we arrive off the disused station it is calm and the water is free of ice and we all land by the Zodiacs. On a gloriously sunny afternoon we are enjoying the wild flowers and the scenery and exploring the few wooden buildings that make up the station. I stop and look out to sea and notice that the ice is now moving in towards the shore on the tide. Looking along the coast I can see that a huge area of loose pack is now on the move and coming into the bay. We call to some of the others and head back to the shore. We warn the guys running the Zodiacs that the ice will soon be onto the shore but they seem happy to stay there. Half a dozen of us get a Zodiac back to the ship as it is clear that in a few minutes the shore will be cut off from the ship by the ice. Most of the others choose to stay or they have wandered further along the shore and have not noticed the ice. Already the ice is drifting past the landing point and there is a raft of ice between it and the ship. Driving the Zodiac back is not easy and the driver has a real job to pick a route through the moving ice floes, which by now are moving thick and fast along the shore. The floes are big, about 4 to 6 feet high, so it is difficult to see the route ahead and the Zodiac driver has to stand on the side to get any view of the way through to the ship. We get back, but we were the last Zodiac to make it. After a while it becomes clear that the ice is here to stay so the remaining people ashore have to wait there while the helicopter is made ready and they are then ferried back six at a time in the helicopter. Without the helicopter they would have had a long wait.

One of the sights of the Islands is Rubini Rock (Red Rock). This large, prominent rock, possibly a volcanic plug, rears straight up out of the water so it has deep water right up to its seaward sides. It is a haven for sea birds

Loose pack ice of FJL.

with thousands of kittiwakes, guillemots, little auks, and glaucous gulls nesting and screaming on the cliff sides. The captain takes the ship almost to within touching distance of the rock. His ship handling is impressive as the ship is in tidal waters but he keeps the bows close to the rock and just a few feet off, for over an hour. He keeps the centre screw running at slow astern and manoeuvres the ship forwards using just the two outer engines. This means that at any time he can put the outer engines to stop, and the ship will go straight back away

Kapitan Dranitsyn in the ice near Jackson Island. (Photo by kind permission of Carina Svensson of Polar Quest)

Doreen and myself out on the ice and dwarfed by the huge ship. (Photo by kind permission of Carina Svensson of Polar Quest)

from the rock on the centre engine alone. By doing this he is able to 'hover' the ship just a few feet off the rock for as long as he wants.

During the trip the ice conditions vary from clear water to heavy pack. None of it bothers the ship and we proceed as planned. The pack is made up of large flows, some with considerable ridging. The ridges are very jagged and in other places you can see where floes have ridden over one another to throw up peaks and cliffs on the ice. In many places, icebergs are trapped into the pack and drift along with it until they ground on the seabed and leave the pack to float on. All the while the land itself is ice locked. The ice caps meet the sea as sheer ice cliffs many tens of feet high and great smooth sweeps of ice take the eye across the icescape until they fall on another ice cliff edge or the broken area of crevasses where the ice twists round some deeply submerged rock many feet below. For all we can see we are looking at ice islands. In most cases there is no land or rocks to see. Everything is ice, complete islands many miles long and many hundreds of feet high made totally of ice. Watching the ice, either the pack or the land ice, becomes a totally absorbing occupation and we spend many hours just watching the ice crack, split and slide away from the bows as the ship moves relentlessly onwards.

On the western shore of Rudolf Island, high on the black basalt cliffs, sits the remains of the Teplitz Station. This was a Russian weather station that was only closed in 1995. It looks desolate and lonely, the two or three dark buildings black against the ice clad hill behind it. Here, they were quite literally the last people on Earth as beyond Rudolf there is nothing but ice until you reach Alaska.

Polar Ice Pack

There is rarely a week goes by now without some TV commentator telling us that because of global warming the Polar ice caps will have all melted by next Tuesday and actually it's all my fault for driving to the paper shop. This is usually on the basis of a photograph of a polar bear swimming in the sea and the commentator saying 'There I told you so, the ice must have all gone!' During this trip I asked our captain whether he had noticed the effect of global warming on the amount and extent of the ice. He said, without any hesitation, that in the fifteen years that he had worked in the Arctic Ocean, apart from the normal annual differences, he had not seen any definite changes. It is well known, and has been for centuries, that the amount of polar ice varies from year to year. In the summer of 2002 there was very little ice or snow in north-eastern Greenland. In Spitzbergen, in 2008, however, the polar ice was further south in June than anyone could remember. It is interesting too that, in September 2009, the papers and TV were carrying the story that two merchant ships had sailed through the north-east Passage and this was due to global warming melting the ice. What they did not report was that a Swede, Nils Nordenskjold, first did it in a sailing ship in 1878, or that two Royal Marines sailed and rowed through the north-west Passage the same month and reported there was twice as much ice as they had been told to expect by the weather bureaux. They had to drag their boat over the ice to get through. It is hard to know who to believe, the scientists who say that the global temperature changes are a reflection of the sunspot cycles of the sun, a well known and recorded phenomena, or the global warming disciples who believe that because we heat our houses we are guilty of melting the ice caps. As with all these things, there are merits in both sides and the truth probably lies somewhere in between.

Cape Fligely

On a grey, murky day we round Cape Säulen, the north-west point of Rudolf Island, which is dominated by two massive, ice-capped basalt pillars of rock rising high above the sea ice. The Russian explorer Capt Sedov vanished in this area in 1914 and a plaque on the shore commemorates him. We sail out into the Arctic Ocean and into the main pack ice. It lies across the ship's bows and

Cape Fligely on Rudolf Island. The most northerly point in Europe and Asia.

stretches as far as we can see. We are now out of the channels and, as we turn east, we are sailing along the north coast of the northernmost island. We are heading for Cape Fligely, the most northerly point of land in Europe and Asia.

Unfortunately, when we get there, the heavy ice means we cannot go ashore by boat and the low cloud, strong winds and constant snow showers mean we cannot go ashore by helicopter either. Doreen and I stand out on the cold, snow-swept deck and watch the Cape. It must be one of the most rarely seen and seldom visited spots on the planet. The number of people who have seen this point can probably be counted in the tens rather than hundreds. The ship moves round through the ice just off the point. We are now just 565 miles from the North Pole. From a mile offshore, the Cape itself is not the grand, high buttress of a headland you would think it should be as the last place on the planet. It is a fairly low point of land and ice that drops gently down towards the sea with only the black rock on the low cliff edges showing us that there is land there, as all as the rest is covered by thick ice. It is almost as if the land is submitting to the sea and ice and bending in submission before the Arctic wastes. The low cloud and snow flurries make the isolation even more total. To the North, the Arctic Ocean stretches away to the North Pole as a pack-ice-covered sea. The white ice merges with the grey cloud as the squalls of snow blow through. As the light plays on the pack ice it also plays tricks with your eyes. It creates effects that show ice-covered cliffs in the far distance. It is easy to see how the early explorers were fooled into reporting that a great continent existed to the north.

We wait for over two hours for the weather to improve but it doesn't. If anything it worsens, so we turn our backs on this memorable spot and head back towards the west. After the chill outside, we decide that a celebratory drink is needed to mark our furthermost north. On the way down to the bar we meet Victor Boyarsky. 'Come', he calls. 'Let us celebrate our furthest north with Vodkas! Large, neat and very chilled Vodkas of course! Nostrovia!'

Man Overboard

We head back through the Islands the way we have come as the sea to the north and east of Franz Josef Land is too dangerous as it has never been surveyed. Later that afternoon we clear the pack ice and reach open water off Jackson Island where, if the weather allows, we hope to make a landing. It is dull and windy but otherwise fine enough for a Zodiac landing. The crew start to get the Zodiacs ready for the shore landing and we are in the cabin getting ready to go ashore when the ship's alarm gives out six short blasts and we hear the running of feet past the door and urgent yells in Russian. From what we could understand later, the ship was stopping as we approached the landing beach. The deck crane lifted the first Zodiac from the deck and the driver was sitting safely on the 'T' bar that hangs from the main cable above the Zodiac itself. The Zodiac was craned over the side and was being lowered, but, as it got near the water the wind swung it round and up so one side dipped lower and was caught by the waves. Due to the speed of the ship, this flipped the Zodiac up in the air and the driver was knocked from his 'T' bar seat. He fell into the Arctic Ocean and was quickly left well astern of the ship.

Immediately, the other seamen on deck somehow clear the flipped Zodiac from the crane wire, and get another Zodiac in the water. We go out on deck, Carina is there and she tells us what has happened. The next Zodiac is already in the water and comes alongside the boarding ladder. Victor is there at the foot of the ladder and he leaps in with one of the seamen and they speed back to look for the man. The seawater temperature is -2 °C. The chances of survival are minimal unless the person is very lucky. The ship has now stopped and, from the ship's deck, we can just see the man in the water but he is drifting away astern in the waves as the rescue Zodiac races towards him. Those on deck are silent and helpless. Soon, the man is invisible to us and lost astern in the waves. However, with help from the bridge by radio, the rescue Zodiac finds him. By that time they reach him, the man is paralysed with cold and can do nothing to help himself. He has been in the water now for at least three or four minutes. Victor and his companion get to him and try to drag the deadweight bulk of a frozen, sodden seaman into the Zodiac as it rocks and tips in the swell. At last, they manage to haul him into the boat and set off back to the ship to get him back on board. We wait at the ladder to help but amazingly the man is able, with help from Victor, to get up the ladder himself. He is taken straight to the sickbay where he soaks in a bath for a while. He is a lucky man; just to have been found was lucky, to survive, very lucky. He was undoubtedly saved by the survival suit that all the Zodiac drivers wear. After a few hours in the sickbay, recovering his body warmth, he was fine. Needless to say, he was not short of offers of vodka in the bar for a couple of days. It was a truly sobering event, but, thankfully, one that turned out well.

Nansen and Johanssen

All this happened at the spot where Fridjtof Nansen and Hjalmar Johanssen spent the winter of 1895. In June 1893, Dr Fridjtof Nansen and a crew of twelve left Norway in the *FRAM*, a specially-designed ship, with the objective of testing Nansen's theory that the Arctic ice drifted from east to west across the Pole. They planned to deliberately let the ship be frozen into the ice towards the eastern end of Siberia and letting the ice's supposed westerly drift across the Polar Basin take the ship across the North Pole. This would prove that there was a polar ice drift across the top of the world. The *FRAM* was caught by the ice and frozen in mid-way along the Siberian coast in September 1893. This was probably further west than Nansen would have wanted but he had no choice. By February 1895, after seventeen months locked in the ice, the Fram had reached 84 degrees north and it was clear from the track that her drift, although clearly westward, would not take the ship across the Pole itself. Nansen then decided to make a dash for the Pole on foot. He and Hjalmar Johanssen, a superb international skier, set off for the Pole with two dog teams, sledges and kayaks, The sledges, tents, stoves, and kayaks had all been designed by Nansen. His designs have proven so successful that they are still used as the basis for similar equipments today.

At first they made great progress over good smooth ice, but then conditions worsened and the ice became broken with many ridges. Eventually, on 8 April 1895, Nansen had to admit that they could not get to the Pole and then safely back to Franz Josef Land with the provisions that they had. They had reached a new Farthest north of 86 degrees 13.6 minutes north, just about 240 miles from the Pole. They had always known that they would never be able to get back to the *FRAM* as she would have moved many miles in the ice by the time they would

Nansen and Johanssen, summer 1895. (J&C McCutcheon Collection)

The west coast of Jackson Island just as Nansen would have seen it, black rock peeping from the white ice cap.

arrive back; so they had set off with the plan to go to Franz Josef Land and take their chances of finding a sealer to get them home. If that failed, then they would make for Spitzbergen where they were certain to find human help. They headed back for the islands. During the trip, both their chronometers stopped so their navigation became a bit haphazard, but eventually, after many days, they sighted land. They could see mountains to the east but with open sea between them and the land. The problem was that they had no idea which land it was, as there were no proper maps. After a number of frustrating days waiting for the drifting and melting floes to carry them closer, they finally shot their last two dogs for food, launched their kayaks and set off by sea. They managed to get ashore on one of the islands in early August 1895, 146 days after leaving the Fram. But where were they and were there any sealers still in the area this late in the season? They soon realised that they were alone as the last sealers would have left the area by now as winter was about to arrive. They saw more islands to the south so paddled their kayaks down the sounds, with the sledges tied across the two of them to form a catamaran. On 17 August, a storm blew up. They struggled to get to shore through the heavy seas and drifting ice and managed to land on a lonely beach near a small cape. They landed on the one beach in the area where they could land their kayaks as elsewhere along the coast there had been nothing but sheer ice cliffs. As the weather worsened and the ice came in to the shore, they realised that winter had indeed arrived and they could go no further. They named the area Cape Norvegia (Cape Norway). They then settled down to spend the winter on the beach. The almost vertical cliffs behind the beach and ice blocking the sea meant that they had no choice but to stay there. Some walruses lying in the sea just off the beach were their first meal.

The small narrow strip of land above the beach offered little in the way of building materials so they dug out rocks from the ground to make a 3-foot deep

1. *Kingston Onyx* hauling her nets. She is shown in her Hellyer Bros colours. Originally she was owned by the Kingston Steam Trawling Co., before Hellyers took over Kingstons. *Photographic note:* Taken with a hand-held 400-mm telephoto lens from the deck of HMS *Keppel*.

2. *Chinstrap penguin.*

Above: 3. MT *Portia* in Isafjord in north-west Iceland. Isafjord was the scene of a double tragedy in the winter of 1967/68 when two Hull trawlers were lost in the same week due to heavy icing.

Left: 4. A lone Gentoo penguin on a stroll in the sun at Port Lockroy.

Right: **5.** Midshipman Gray taken by a shivering Graeme aboard HMS *Keppel* off Iceland in the winter of 1970.

Below: **6.** A Hull trawler fishing off Iceland. Decks and railings icing up as she rolls in the swell. Believed to be *St Gerontius*, owned by T. Hamlings. *Photographic note:* Taken with a hand-held 400-mm telephoto lens from the deck of HMS *Keppel*.

7. Icebreaker *Kapitan Dranitsyn* run by the Murmansk Shipping Company where she is based. Note the polar bear emblem on the funnel.

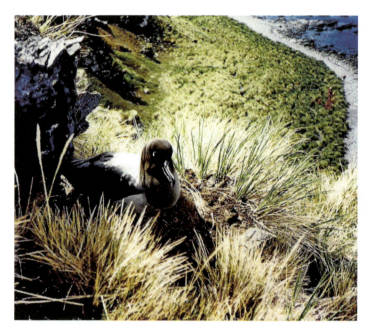

8. After a good walk and steep climb we found the nest of a light-mantled sooty albatross above Grytviken.

Top left: **9.** A zodiac motors past a grounded iceberg near Ymer Oy (island).

Top right: **10.** A small berg, 'like a white pearl sitting on black velvet'.

Bottom left: **11.** Doreen enjoying the air in the Greenland Sea on board *Professor Molchanov*.

Bottom right: **12.** Deep in Kaiser Frans Josef Fjord.

Above: 13. The bear retrieves his lunch from the ice edge and heads off.

Left: 14. Polar bear. (Photo by kind permission of Carina Svensson of Polar Quest)

Opposite, above: 15. Disturbed by the ships, the walruses stare at us in a totally disinterested way.

Opposite, below left: 16. An early-morning kill. Polar bears find their breakfast.

Opposite, below right: 17. Two puffins swim alongside the Zodiac.

18. Iceberg in the evening sun just off the village of Scoresbysund.

19. The 14th July Glacier in Krossfjord, Spitsbergen.

20. A walrus eyes us cautiously.

Fridtjof Nansen.

Cape Norwegia (Cape Norway). Nansen was able to get ashore here from his kayak on the only piece of beach in the area.

Above: The desolate narrow beach at Cape Norwegia showing the flat area at the top of the beach and the cliffs behind.

Below: The remains of the hut with the beach and sea beyond. Nansen's daily view for nine winter months.

The remains of Nansen's 'hole' or shelter. This shows the rocks they had to dig out to make walls and the tree trunk they used as a roof beam.

hole and built up a wall of rocks round the edge. They found a piece of driftwood to act as a roof beam across the top. As trees do not grow in Franz Josef Land this itself was a lucky find. That beam is still there. Then they covered the walls and formed a roof with walrus skins. These immediately froze solid. They called it 'the hole' for that is exactly what it was. They lived there in mind-numbingly-low temperatures of anything down to -40 or -50 °C, enduring the screaming storms during the long, dark, polar winter and living on polar bear and walrus meat. For most of their time though, they stayed inside the hole and slept.

Finally in May 1896, after nearly nine months in the hole, the sea ice started to break up and they continued down the coast in their kayaks until 100 miles to the south they had their chance encounter at Cape Flora with the Jackson-Harmsworth expedition and were rescued. After Cape Flora there was nothing but the empty Arctic Ocean. It was the last island on their route.

The *FRAM* itself completed her drift and came out of the ice west of Spitzbergen. She arrived back in Norway only a few weeks after Nansen. All the expedition team had survived and Nansen's theories about the Polar ice drift had been confirmed.

The Hole

As we are getting ready to board the Zodiac at Cape Norvegia, a polar bear is spotted walking along the beach. We watch and wait. If he stays there we may not be able to get ashore after all. It sniffs the air and wanders on then it walks

Salisbury Island from the north, a land totally covered in ice.

off over a rise so we carried on. From the sea, the Cape seems to be nothing more than a low rocky beach with steep, mountain slopes behind it. Ice and snow-bound crevices cover the cliff face and, above that, the ice cap comes down from the cloud to the very edge of the dark grey cliffs. The wind has got up a bit since we first stopped and the Zodiacs bounce from wave to wave and a few of us get a good dousing as we head into the beach. We land among large, hard and rough lumps of sea ice that clutter the shoreline and move around in the waves. Some walruses are idling in the breakers a few yards along the beach, just as they had when Nansen landed here just over 110 years earlier. They appear to be totally unaware of us. At the top of the narrow shingle beach is a raised and gently sloping area that stretches about 20 or 25 yards back up to the foot of some rough scree at the base of the cliffs. This raised area is made up of rocks and mosses with some grasses struggling to cling to the thin soil. In the middle of this grassy stretch we see an old log, bleached white and about 15 feet long. As we get nearer we can see that it is lying across a small hollow in the ground. The hollow is surrounded by loose rocks and stones. This is Nansen's hole. It was here that Nansen and Johanssen spent the winter of 1895/96. A plaque is mounted on a post some yards away. It commemorates, in Norwegian and Russian, 'Nansen and Johanssen's survival over the winter of 1895/6 at this point'.

I am now looking into the hole. It seems barely big enough for one man to lie in let alone for two men to live in it for a full polar winter. Dried bones of bear and walrus still lie by the hole. Although tiny, low wild flowers bloom in vibrant pinks and greens nearby, it is a desolate and depressing place. This is

August; what must it have been like through the dark of the winter night? The view from their front door is across the sound to the low ice covered hills of Salisbury Island in the far distance. It is a humbling experience to stand here where two men, through sheer determination, survived for so long. How tough, mentally and physically, were these men? And to do this after they had pushed themselves to the extreme trying to ski to the North Pole only to be defeated by lack of supplies: then racing back to find land and to try and find a sealer to take them home before finally realising that they had another nine months of winter to survive by living off the land.

Walruses

The three walruses are lying asleep on an ice flow in the middle of the sound. We left Cape Norvegia at about midnight on what is now a still windless night and encounter the walruses about four miles east of Cape Norway. From a distance they are reddy-brown, motionless lumps, like well-rounded sandstone boulders on the ice. The captain manoeuvres the ship so we drift to a stop alongside the ice flow. As we draw closer we can see that the boulders are made of leather and are very fat. The three great masses of very wrinkled,

Walruses on their flow drifting in the sea near Jackson Island.

Ice floes and ice caps, a typical Frans Josef Land scene.

The edge of the ice cap meets the sea in a cliff of ice well over 50 feet high.

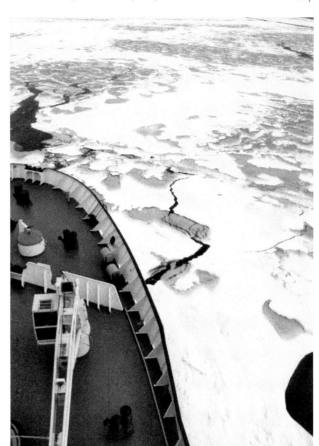

Right: *Kapitan Dranitsyn* breaks through the ice as she ploughs remorselessly northwards.

Below: Icebergs, glacier and mists. Near Hall Island FJL.

Sunshine and shadows as the mists swirl and roll across the islands.

A small bergy bit off the coast.

leathery, wobbly walrus slowly wake up and raise their heads to look up at the ship through small, round eyes that are both bleary and bloodshot. They each probably weigh well over a ton and are about 10 or 12 feet long. They all need a shave too with their prickly whiskers sticking out from their top lips. They belch and snort as the biggest one prods its neighbour with its tusk. These boys look as though they had a really good party last night and have only managed to get as far as this ice flow on their way home. One of them, bored by us already, starts to scratch itself with the ends of its flipper and then tries to go back to sleep. The other two start to scratch themselves now they are awake. They manage to avoid each other's tusks as they swing their heads about and start to move to make themselves more comfortable. Even a small movement of their head causes a ripple effect across their whole body as the fat under the thick, dry skin is set in motion. Ripples run out from the flow as they move about on it. Unlike seals, which look as though they are about to burst out of their skins, the walrus skins seem to be far too big for them, with masses of folds, creases and spare material. They look as though they are struggling to move about inside a great leather sleeping bag. After a while they decide that the ship is here to stay and as they cannot get back to sleep they will sit up and look at this strange, huge, black thing beside them. Even though we are no more than 20 feet from them and tower over them, they just lie on their flow and look quizzically at us without fear. They are totally unafraid and disinterested in us. When they are out of the water and dry like this, their skin is a reddish-brown colour and stands out in the Arctic white. This is unlike any of the other Arctic creatures which all tend to be white. However, when they slide into the water, they turn a glistening black and instantly merge into the black waters. It is such a very peaceful scene, the walrus, the ice floe drifting gently among others in the open waters and the panorama of the ice-covered islands stretching in all directions. We slowly move away leaving them to go back to sleep on their peaceful ice floe.

The next day we stop to go and look at a huge walrus colony. This colony is on the end of a spit of land and as we approach by Zodiac we can see the steam rising from this mass of over 100 walruses. Some of them are swimming about in groups just off the shore and as we approach they start to take an interest in us. About twenty of them swim across to the Zodiac and, when they are about 10 feet away, they stop and sit with their shiny, wet heads and tusks out of the water examining us. They get more agitated and concerned as we go closer to the colony and they start to move closer to the Zodiac. We decide that discretion is the better part of valour and move away. The walruses then chase us off, following the boat to ensure we did not go back. Knowing what we do about their skills at sticking their tusks through kayaks we make sure our rubber Zodiacs are out of their immediate range. We watch them for some time from a distance and it becomes clear that the walruses in the water are acting as guards for the females and young ones on the beach. Once we move away a little they were happy to watch us go. One of the other Zodiacs was not so lucky and a walrus did puncture one of the buoyancy chambers, although luckily not seriously and they were able to get back to the ship.

We leave them to it and motor quietly along a massive ice wall. At this point, the ice cap meets the sea and ends in a sheer wall of ice that is about 40 to 50 feet high and has the appearance of a freshly-cut block of vanilla ice cream. Here, we can see crevasses that run at right angles to the ice face, like knife cuts, running down through the edge of the ice almost to the sea level. Some have snow bridges across their top. Ice caves disappear into the ice and water drips from melt streams deep inside. Trying to imagine the vast quantity of ice that lies behind this half-mile-long ice front and the distance it goes back over the island makes us feel very small indeed.

Bentsen and Bjorvik

A day or so later, after sailing down to the south-east end of the archipelago, we come to Cape Heller on Wilczek Island. The day is very still but with a low cloud cover. The ice floes lie motionless all across the bay. The low cloud deadens any sounds so intensifying the silence of the place. It was here at Cape Heller that two Norwegians, Bentsen and Bjorvik, from the American Wellman Expedition of 1898/99 overwintered in a stone hut. They were an advance party for the spring expeditions and set up their camp in the late autumn. Unfortunately, poor management meant that they were left with insufficient provisions or proper equipment. They managed to build a good, solid, stone hut in which to overwinter but without sufficient materials to properly finish it they were forced to use walrus hides for the roof. The whole surrounding area is covered in loose stones ideal for building and their thick, dry-stone dyke walls still look fairly substantial even today. Tucked up against a small steep slope it was much more substantial in every way than Nansen's hole. Wellman and the main party were meanwhile living in proper wooden huts in the base camp at Cape Tegettoff. Like Nansen, Bentsen and Bjorvik had to live on polar bear and walrus but they did at least have a better-constructed hut than Nansen and Johanssen were able to build. Sadly, Bentsen died during the winter and as it was impossible to dig a grave in the frozen ground. Bjorvik kept his friend's now frozen body in its sleeping bag in the hut with him so it did not get eaten by bears, until he was rescued in the spring. Bentsen's grave lies a few yards away down near the shore. We try and imagine living in it through the long darkness of the winter, without food, proper stores or equipment and with just the dead body of your only colleague for company.

Cape Tegettoff

The south-eastern end of the archipelago is off to starboard, about half a mile away but wrapped in fog, just as it had been on the day that Payer and Weyprecht looked out from their ship only 133 years earlier. We wait for the fog to lift so we can go ashore at this historic point. As the morning goes on the fog does slowly lift and reveals the two tall, rock pillars that had never been seen by man before 1873. The Zodiacs are launched and we go ashore. Wellman set up his base camp here at the foot of the cliffs on a flat area on the spit of land that runs from the cliffs towards the twin pillars. All that remains are a few sections of the base of his wooden hut. It is ironic that there is more remaining of Bentsen and Bjorvik's hand-built stone shelter than the purpose-made, prefabricated base camp. Quickly, the fog descends again and we lose sight of the ship in the fog. We also lose sight of some of the party who have moved away from the shore and up towards the cliffs behind the beach area. Victor is keen to get people back to the ship as he does not think that the fog will lift. The dangers of one or more Zodiacs, each with twelve passengers, getting lost in the fog are very real. Zodiacs do not offer good radar targets so are very difficult to find in fog. Even in summer, the chances of survival here if a boat gets lost in fog are not good. Victor, who, as usual, is totally in charge, is down on the beach and orders the Zodiacs to only go back in pairs and to keep well in sight of one another. Doreen gets away in the Zodiac ahead of the one into which I climb. The Zodiacs find their way back with help from modern technology. Each Zodiac has a hand-held, sat. nav. receiver and can steer towards the sat. nav. position of the ship, this being passed to them by radio. Even so, malfunctions and errors can occur. The fog is now so thick that we lose sight of the Zodiac ahead and can only follow its wake. The trip back seems to go on forever. Surely, we must have passed the ship by now? Should we not turn round? Everyone in the boat is anxiously looking about to find any sign of the ship in the fog, then anxiously looking at the coxswain for reassurance that all is well. All we see is wet greyness. Shouts and calls come out of the fog but it is impossible to know from which direction. We motor on into seemingly endless fog, locked in our own cocoon of grey. The driver, while looking about all the time does not seem too concerned. Suddenly, a shaft of watery sun breaks through the fog just as a black cliff emerges above us. Where are we? But it is not a cliff, it is the ship and she is shining her powerful search light towards the shore so the Zodiacs can follow the beam back to the ship for the last few yards. We have made it. It is with a sense of relief that we all make it back to the safety of the ship.

Belugas

It is our last day in the Islands and on the last afternoon we are out in the Zodiacs again cruising along the ice edge when some distance away we see a movement of white on the black water. We watch for it again, and there it is, and then another. Round, white shapes are bobbing about. Excitement mounts as we all want it to be something that it may not be! We motor closer, slowly. There it is again, and another; now there is no doubt; we have finally found belugas, the rare white whales of the Arctic. We slowly motor over to them. They are feeding near the ice front and, as we watch, they surface for air, roll their backs and go down again. This is a magical, thrilling moment. They are not big by whale standards. They probably range between about 12 to 20 feet long but are pure white all over. This is the first time I have seen them in the wild. We get within a few feet of where they have been seen and turn off the engine. The sea here is black with mud and dirt washed out from the glacier a few yards away, so we can not see down in to the water. We sit in silence, watching and listening for any sound or sight to indicate that they were about to surface. They surface close to the boats to see what we are then carry on feeding down below. They are so silent that they always catch us unawares and they surface and breathe before we have time to turn round to see them properly. They always beat us. A stage whispered 'There!' from someone and as we turn, so the soft-looking, pure-white back rolls and disappears from view. When you see belugas in places like Sea World, where you can see them underwater through viewing windows, they always look as though their skins are too big for them, like a diver in a white, rubber, drysuit three sizes too big. The smiling, inquisitive look that they always seem to have and the sing-song noise of their call (they were called sea canaries by early whalers), make them enchanting animals. But, they are also very rare and sightings are few and far between. They carry on feeding undisturbed by our visit. Reluctantly, we leave them and return to the ship to gloat about our sightings to those who did not come.

Yamal

We had heard that the nuclear icebreaker *Yamal* was meant to be passing through Franz Josef Land and was possibly coming our way. She has just been to the North Pole and is on her way back to Murmansk. She is twice the size of *Kapitan Dranitsyn* and with three times the power. She should be in the same area as us as we move into one of the north/south channels between the islands. Patchy fog lies in banks around the islands and the view to the north is masked. Captain Sergei stops the ship in an area clear of fog and we wait. Then, as we watch, *Yamal* emerges through the fog bank. Her squat red superstructure,

The nuclear-powered icebreaker *Yamal* emerges from the mist near Hooker Island having been to the North Pole.

black hull and the distinctive shark's teeth painted round her bows are easily recognisable. Everyone comes on deck including the crew. One of the waitresses from the Dining Room asks to borrow my binoculars so she could find her friend who is working on *Yamal*. She does, and there are lots of girlie squeals and waving to and fro as the two ships lie stopped about a hundred feet apart. Other crew members find their friends or relations on *Yamal* and vice versa. As they do so, little groups of squeals and males calling across the water rings out. We are the only two ships in thousands of miles of ice-covered ocean. You tend to forget that in Murmansk the sole industry is the sea. It is natural that the crews all know each other and live close to one another. They will have brothers and uncles, daughters and cousins working on the merchant ships and icebreakers, trawlers and naval ships that operate out of Murmansk. We all take photos of the other ship as we lie still in the clearing in the fog. After a while, the *Yamal* slowly heads off on her way back to Murmansk, leaving us for our last night in these beautiful islands. Tonight is to be Russian night and the crew do not let us down with a decorated dining room, colourful table linen and a wonderful Russian meal, with borsht, beef, potatoes and of course, vodka! All served with pride and a flourish.

Murmansk Again

So, after many days in the most fantastic of places, we head back across the Barents Sea on the two-day steam back to Murmansk. Now it is time to pack our cases and get ready for the trip home. We arrive back in Murmansk during the night and wake up to find ourselves alongside the wharf from which we sailed. We sadly leave the ship and are taken back to the airport by bus. Even though we were the only flight of the day, the Russian authorities were unable to decide how we should be processed and which check-in desk to use. So, after a delay of nearly one and a half hours, we finally get checked in for the flight and checked out of Russia. They then call us forward to get on the bus to go out to the aircraft. I have both of our boarding passes in my hand. As we leave the building, Doreen is immediately behind me but is stopped by the security guard. He has decided that this bus is full and as I step outside the door is firmly shut behind me. I get on the bus then realise that I am holding Doreen's boarding Pass. This could be a problem! I get off the bus at the foot of the aircraft steps. A tall, serious and unhappy-looking security guard with a tall-fronted, peaked cap is standing barring the way up the stairs. He demands to see everyone's boarding pass. I show him both mine and Doreen's boarding passes. He looks blank. I point at the terminal and say 'Wife'. He does not appear to have even heard me but just grunts and gives me a look that said 'You stupid tourist', and then lets me get on the plane. 'Oh boy', I am thinking, 'what happens now when Doreen gets to the aircraft with no boarding pass? Will they let her on? Even if they do, she is going to kill me. Oh well, at least I have had my holiday and if she is not allowed on and is carted off to the local salt mines she won't be able to shout at me anyway so that's all OK.' The next bus arrives at the aircraft with the remaining passengers. I watch from the aircraft as she gets off. She gets to the steps and is stopped by the guard. Now the fun will start! She shows the guard that she has no pass, smiles at him and points at the plane and says something to him. The guard just grunts and she walks straight up the stairs! No passport check, no boarding pass, nothing, just a smile! When she sits down beside me, I am given a look that says it all; 'You stupid tourist!'

CHAPTER 9

The North Pole

Attempt to reach the North Pole with Victor Boyarsky

The idea that I could actually get to the North Pole had taken root the year before and it had started with the offer of vodka! Doreen and I were on board the Russian Icebreaker, *Kapitan Dranitsyn*, on an expedition to Frans Josef Land. The ship had reached the ice covered waters off Cape Fligely, the most northerly point of land in Europe and Asia. We were now just a few hundred miles from the North Pole, yet unable to get ashore on Cape Fligely as the sea ice prevented the use of Zodiacs and the low cloud prevented the use of the helicopter. Doreen and I stayed out on deck, wrapped up in our warm, down-filled parkas and fur hats, taking in the atmosphere of the place. We felt almost within touching distance of the Pole; it was there, somewhere beyond the white, windswept ice pack that now stretched, uninterrupted, all the way to the North Pole and beyond. Snow flurries blew round the decks and the wind moaned gently over the ice. The captain waited in hope that the weather might change and we could somehow get ashore, but at last, after hanging about for a few hours, he decided it was not going to improve, so it was time to move on. The ship turned back towards the west and we left Cape Fligely to its solitude.

The thought of going to the North Pole had always fascinated me. To stand on the very top of the world, in the middle of an ocean of ice, from where every direction was south and from where in every direction there was more, endless, floating ice. To be one of just a few thousand or so who have been there had always been a dream. However, it was also somewhere that I never really thought I would ever go. After all, I was no Ranulph Fiennes or Wally Herbert. I certainly did not have the Arctic skills and experience, nor the funding, to mount my own expedition; at nearly sixty, I was not going to be selected to join anyone else's. However, the fascination and the dream remained. Although I had been to the Arctic a few times before, I had never been onto the polar ice cap itself. Here at Cape Fligely, I imagined that this was as near as I would ever get.

We went back inside and away from the cold, windswept decks, and started down towards the warmth of the cabin to thaw out. On the way down we met Victor Boyarsky, our expedition leader.

'Are you coming to the bar for a vodka to celebrate the most northerly point of the expedition?' asked Victor, who was clearly heading in that direction.

'What a great idea! Of course we will.'

A few minutes later, as the pack ice drifted past the windows and Nostrovias (toasts) were called to celebrate the event, we settled down to enjoy the warmth of the bar, the vodka and Victor's company. The bar was deserted so the three of us chatted freely. After the second vodka Victor began chatting about his life.

Dr Victor Boyarsky is a polar legend in his homeland of Russia. He is a well built and bearded man, whose age was hard to guess but he looked every inch a polar explorer. He always has a ready smile and a friendly comment. He looks like a Russian bear with his big bushy beard and wild hair. We already knew from his presentations on board that he was a Doctor of Glaciology and had worked for a number of years at the Russian Vostok Base in Antarctica. He had led dog sledge expeditions across the Greenland Ice Cap from south to north, and skied across Antarctica with dog teams via the South Pole and the Pole of Inaccessibility. He had led trans-Arctic expeditions and crossed the Bering Strait in winter from Russia to Alaska as well. Victor is the Director of the Arctic and Antarctic Museum in St Petersburg and runs his own company, Vicaar, which specialises in polar travel and expeditions. He leads by example and as we had seen on this trip, keeps a firm control of his charges. Heaven help anyone who does not follow Victor's instructions! Victor inspires confidence and trust and everyone feels comfortable with him. During a man overboard emergency in Frans Josef Land, when a crewman fell from a Zodiac as it was being lowered into the sea, he proved that he leads from the front in a clear, strong and decisive manner.

As we savoured our vodka, he told us that each year he sets up and runs an ice station called Barneo on the polar ice cap at 89 degrees north, just 60 miles from the pole, on behalf of the Russian Government. I remembered the film Ice Station Zebra and recalled the icy desolation depicted in the film and the crazy, romantic notion of a tented camp floating on 2 feet of ice above the deep, cold, Arctic Ocean.

'I set it up for the Government and run it for the few weeks of spring that it operates. We have done this since 2002. Normally it is in April, depending on the weather. I also lead some skiing trips to the Pole from there and we can also use helicopters too.'

'But how do you build an ice station?' I asked. 'How do you start?'

Victor explained how the camp is run under the auspices of the Russian Geographical Society and his Company, Vicaar, do the work.

'First we fly two helicopters from the Taimyr Peninsula in northern Siberia to about 89-North and around 120-140 East. We have to refuel on the way and to do that we have a fuel dump on the ice at about 87-North, which is dropped by parachute from an Iliyshin 76 aircraft. We look for an area of large flat, solid, multiyear ice suitable for making a runway. When we find one, we land and set up a temporary camp. Then the Iliyshin makes a parachute drop with our two bulldozers and we start making a runway. Once we have bulldozed a flat area for the runway, and it has to be at least 1,200 metres long, we spray the whole runway area with seawater, pumped up through the ice, and leave it to freeze. Normally it needs temperatures of about -20 or -30 degrees Celsius to do the job properly. When it has frozen, an Antonov 74 flies in, bringing the rest of the staff, all the camp equipment and supplies. At the end of the season everything is packed up and flown back to Longyearbyen and then back to Moscow, where it is stored, until the following year.' He made it sound so simple.

Here was the man who had been to both poles and now who took other would be explorers to the pole. I heard myself asking a question.

'Could you take me to the pole?'

'Of course, of course! Why not?' Victor replied without hesitation.

'Seriously Victor, I am not a young man anymore and apart from the odd visit to the gym and a round of golf I am not anyone's idea of a honed, super athlete, nor a polar explorer. I have done some cross country skiing but only at the winter holiday level.'

'If you want, you can come with me', he said with a serious face, 'I will take you. I will give you proper training in Spitzbergen first and make sure it is all OK. Most years I take a small team of novices on a short two- or three-day ski trip, and cover the last few miles to the pole. I can add you to such a team, which I will lead. Of course it is important that we all have three or four days' proper training together in Spitsbergen before we set out. The others will all be of similar experience to you. Everything will be fine', he assured me.

'But how do we get to your ice station?'

'That is easy. We fly there from Longyearbyen, on Spitsbergen, in our excellent Russian Antonov 74.'

I was sold. I looked at Doreen and waited for that look. You know, the one that wives give their husbands that says 'And just what do you think you are doing?' Doreen sat still and was as entranced as I was as Victor spoke easily and warmly, as if going to the pole was no more than going to the supermarket on a cold day. I began to imagine that perhaps a dream could come true. All I needed to do was to make the commitment. Oh yes, and find the money! This trip would not be cheap. Doreen was totally for it and pushed me to say yes.

'The money is irrelevant', she told me back in the cabin 'We can find the money and once it's gone, it's forgotten! You will never get another chance like this and never forgive yourself if you do not go now!' As usual, she was right.

We met up with Victor again later that year at an event at the Scott Polar Research Institute in Cambridge and we discussed it all over again. I still had doubts that Victor would really want to take me with him. But he was still confident that there would be no problem.

'You are fit man, I will make sure all is OK and I will be there for the training and the trip'.

The plan was to fly from Longyearbyen to the ice station, then take a helicopter to about 25–30 miles from the pole. We would spend three days skiing the final few miles to the pole where the helicopter would pick us up. He emphasised that he would lead both the training in Spitsbergen and the expedition. If he had any doubts he would not let me go. As long as Victor was confident that I could do it, and as long as he would be leading the whole trip, then I decided I would do it.

'Talk to Per Magnus at Polar Quest, he will fix everything and he talks to my office a lot, so it is easy. You can pay him in UK money too, so no need for roubles', he smiled. Polar Quest is the Swedish travel firm run by Per Magnus through whom we had arranged the Frans Josef Land expedition. All I had to do now was get to Spitzbergen in April the following year.

Day 1, Sunday 15 April 2007

After months of impatient and apprehensive waiting, the day of departure finally arrived. Doreen drove me to Edinburgh Airport. It seemed a bit unreal, sitting in the car on my way to the North Pole. I felt nervous, excited and a bit scared; but of what, exactly? The cold? Failure? Falling through the ice? It was impossible to say.

'What are you nervous about?' Doreen asked. 'There will be no problem, Victor will be there and if there is anyone you trust, it is Victor!' She was right. Whatever it was I just wanted to get away and begin the trip.

I had with me with all the clothes and equipment that were on the endless list that Victor's people in St Petersburg had sent me. Stuffed in to my case were different weights of thermal underwear, fleeces, socks, tent socks, gloves, spare gloves, ski goggles. Oh, of course not forgetting the vital pee bottle for the tent. I would get even more specialist clothing in Spitsbergen from Victor's team there. I had been working on my fitness since last summer with regular gym visits and was feeling fit. But will that be enough? Time will tell.

Day 2, Monday 16 April 2007

After a restless night at an airport hotel in Oslo, I gave up trying to sleep and got up at about 5 a.m. I had some breakfast, returned to the airport and checked in for the SAS Longyearbyen flight. I was still feeling anxious but excited – the next time I came through here I should have been to the Pole, I told myself. I knew I would never get another chance to try to do this. I knew that once I got to Spitsbergen and met up with Victor and we started the arctic training all would be well. We arrived at Longyearbyen, having had glorious views of Spitsbergen's snow-clad mountains, gleaming in the sun as the plane circled round before landing. As the plane touched down, I was blissfully unaware of the events taking place far out on the ice at Camp Barneo, or of the difficulties that lay ahead.

I was due to be met at the airport by Alexei, who works for Victor as his Longyearbyen manager, but he was not there. Victor was also due to arrive that afternoon from the ice station. Then, amid the chaos of hikers, skiers, huge rucksacks, bags of all shapes and sizes, even pulk sledges fighting for space in the small airport arrivals area, I met Malena. Malena was the Polar Quest rep who was there to meet other clients. She saw my Polar Quest bag labels and came over. She was a happy and smiling blonde Norwegian girl, who chatted away while I waited for Alexei and she looked for her other clients. She worked at a hotel in Longyearbyen and does representational work for Polar Quest as well. Malena told me that everyone refers to the ice station as Barneo. Apparently it was a joke made by a radio operator about the weather up there when the station was first set up. He referred to the new station as the 'Borneo of the north', or Barneo as it is now called. She told me that there has been bad weather up there and things are disorganised. She gave me Alexei's mobile number and I called him. He was on his way.

After some time a breathless Alexei arrived.

'Sorry, it is chaos here.' He gasped, 'There have been no flights into or out of Barneo for over four days and the weather at the Pole has been bad for days and is still very bad. There is a big storm up there, Longyearbyen is full of scientists and skiers trying to get up to Barneo, there are no beds anywhere and I am trying to find beds for people who should have gone to Barneo but who are still here.'

Between Malena and Alexei, I pieced together the situation. Victor was stuck at Barneo and was now very unlikely to get back to Longyearbyen tonight, or even tomorrow. There were a number of skiing expeditions stuck up at Barneo waiting for the weather to clear so they could get back to Spitsbergen. There was also a number of skiing expeditions still out on the ice, up near the pole, and stuck in their tents in the storm. They had been there for three or four days, awaiting rescue by helicopter. In addition, a lot of the scientific work being done out on the ice had been delayed and they are trying to get more scientists out there with their equipment. To make matters worse, the ice runway at Barneo had broken. The floe on which it was built had cracked right across the runway in the storm, rendering it unusable. Victor's team at Barneo were having to clear snow and ice and make another runway in spite of the bad weather.

Likewise, there were a lot of expedition people in Longyearbyen waiting to get to Barneo. The welcome dinner that had been programmed for our team that night had been cancelled as Victor would not be back and some of the others on the team had not yet arrived. Alexei did not know where they were or when they would arrive. Alexei is young and enthusiastic, but was struggling with the total uncertainty of everything. He was trying to organise people and beds in town as well as getting the cargo and passengers to go up to Barneo. This of course was difficult as no one knew when the flights would restart. Things did not sound good and I saw my chance of getting to Barneo, never mind the pole, diminishing.

I had been booked into the Spitsbergen guesthouse, which was in a small settlement called Nybyen about a mile and a half out of Longyearbyen. Alexei said he would drive me there. He then decided, to save time, to get me kitted out straight away and so we went to Vicaar's warehouse in town, which was on the way. The building was fitted out with big wall racks that were crammed with every type of arctic travel item: tents, bed mats, small boat-shaped sledges called pulks, boots, kayaks, cooking items, food rations and everything in between. There, I met Eugenie, a young and friendly Russian guy who is a polar guide and expert skier and who was Victor's deputy on our ski trip. He was squatting in the middle of a mountain of items and stopped what he was doing to attend to me. Without any preamble he eyed me up and down, assessed my size, and started handing me things from different piles.

'Here, these are your bed mats, you need two. Here is your pulk, it is old but OK.'

He passed me an endless chain of various bags and clothes items. I left weighted down by them all and was told to go and try all the clothes on. The only problem was boots. They had none that were my size. We headed off for the guesthouse. Once I had checked in, it became clear that it was more of a hostel for local expeditions than a hotel. Each day snowmobile and skiing trips set off, or arrived back, at the guesthouse, and I saw other expeditions driving off up the snowmobile tracks on the other side of the valley as they headed off into the mountains of the interior.

Alexei drove off with the promise that he would get me some boots the next day, when the teams in Barneo got back, weather and flights permitting. I settled into a simple room which was warm, had a comfortable bed, and a wash basin, with the main bathroom and showers right across the passage. Faced with the prospect of being there for a few days, I resolved that I had better make it home. The guesthouse had no TV or radio in the rooms, and served no meals other than breakfast.

Day 3, Tuesday 17 April 2007

The next morning, after a good sleep and some breakfast, I set off to walk into town. The day was calm and sunny, the scenery spectacular. The steep sides of the valley reached up to snow-topped cliff faces, which peered down from both sides. The deep snow covered everything, including the road, so I slid more than walked down towards the town. On the way Alexei drove past in his van and stopped to pick me up.

'The news from Barneo is not good', he told me. 'The new runway has now been broken up by another storm last night. It will now be at least tomorrow night (18th) before any flights can get in or out. Some people still in Longyearbyen are now starting to cancel their ski trips to the pole and trying to get flights back to the mainland as they are running out of time, but the flights back to Oslo are all full. Others are waiting in Longyearbyen to see what happens. There are still teams stuck out on the ice in tents as well as those already in Barneo trying to get out'.

He dropped me off and I walked to the warehouse to tell Eugenie that the clothes seemed fine but do not forget the boots. He had heard that the weather forecast would be good from Friday (20th) for a few days. That was the planned day for our flight north, so we might be OK. Would Victor get back here before then? I wondered. In the meantime there was nothing to do but wait. I was getting concerned at the lack of any special polar training, as my confidence was dependent upon Victor's mentoring. As if reading my thoughts Eugenie said,

'Victor will not come back now at all, as he must stay at Barneo to sort things up there. Also the original teams have had to be changed as some of the novices have not arrived. The others in our team now should be a Canadian, who skis in the Canadian arctic, and another guy, but he has yet to arrive too.'

These did not sound like the beginners Victor promised!

'Maybe I can give you a little training later, if the others turn up', he added as a throwaway line.

The idea of going off on the ice with another guide, who did not know me at all, did not sound good. With no polar ice experience and no special training, it seemed folly to embark on a trip with Eugenie and his expert skiers, especially given the weather conditions up there at the moment. I headed back up the road to the guesthouse deep in thought.

I called Ralf at Polar Quest in Sweden to get their news and views. Their information, which came from Victor's St Petersburg office, tallied with what Alexei had been telling me. They were also in touch with one of their clients, who was actually stuck in a tent near the pole and had a satellite phone. They said that there would be no flights to Barneo before Thursday night and a number of skiing trips would have to be cancelled. Victor would definitely not be leaving Barneo while this crisis was going on and would not be leading our ski trip. If the trip happened at all, then it would be led by Eugenie but with different skiers as the other novices that Victor had in mind for his small team have failed to appear in Longyearbyen. This was all unwelcome, but it is the Arctic and this is how things are. Everything is governed by the weather. The advice from Ralf was to wait and see. If I got to Barneo, then let Victor decide what I should do then. There was nothing more I could do, so I walked back down to town and had a burger and a beer in the Spitsbergen hotel.

Day 4, Wednesday 18 April 2007

I met up with Alexei in the morning but he had no more definite news.
'The earliest flight will now be Friday, but chances are low. Victor is so heavily involved at Barneo trying to get the people stuck out on the ice safely back to Barneo by helicopter. There is no chance he will be able to leave Barneo'.

Alexei still had no word of the other two who are meant to be in our expedition team – it appeared that they had not arrived or may have cancelled before getting to Spitsbergen. 'Eugenie will lead a small team made up from you and two others. The Canadian man should arrive today and another guy.' Alexei also let slip a small gem.

'The other guy is a Russian skier who knows Eugenie well and has been on many such trips in Siberia.'

A Siberian skier!

My trip as originally planned with Victor would definitely not happen. Even the new trip under Eugenie might not happen. If it did, it would be without any training as his guys did not need any.

I decided that it was time to reassess the whole situation. Firstly, there would now be no training before the trip, as Victor would not be there. Secondly, Victor would not be leading the expedition out on the ice. Thirdly, the flights up to Barneo were far from certain and ski trips are a secondary priority to the scientists and their equipment. So there was no way of knowing when, or even if, the ski trip would go up to Barneo. Nor were there any plans for returning to Longyearbyen. I had to be back in Longyearbyen for my flight to Oslo on the Wednesday (25th).

Perhaps now I really had to decide whether to scrub the whole thing and start thinking about getting home, or wait and go with Eugenie and the Russian, whenever they could get to Barneo. Or, alternatively, see if I can find some other way to get to the pole, perhaps on my own. Eugenie still seems to think I am an experienced skier like the others. My inexperience could have serious consequences in the event of bad weather, a fall, or an accident on the ice. Even if my skills and fitness matched theirs, which I highly doubted, Eugenie was planning on having to ski over 50 kms, with pulks, over three days. My sole aim of this whole trip was to get to the North Pole, and the basis for the trip was to do it with Victor as a short ski trip. Now, that had all changed.

The weather and subsequent problems with flights to and from Barneo had now put any chance of even getting that far in severe doubt. Also my end date of 25th meant that unless I got to Barneo in the next couple of days, there would not be any point in going at all – if the weather changed for the worse again, then I would not be able to get back in time. If I missed the booked flight back to Oslo I would not be able to get another flight for days and would have to buy new tickets. Time was running out. What had started as a seemingly 'safe little jaunt' in the bar of the icebreaker, was rapidly coming apart.

There were stories emerging of a couple of ski teams out on the ice, who had been stuck in a tent in the storm for three or four days and had never got to the pole at all. They literally could not move from their sleeping bags and had run out of food and fuel by the time they were rescued. I decided to ring Victor's office in St Petersburg and discuss the situation with them. A lady there, called Victoria, told me that they were having huge difficulties sorting out which ski teams would be able to get to Barneo with all their pulks, tents etc and it might take some days yet before it was all sorted out. That was assuming that the weather up there improved and, more importantly, that the ice runway froze over.

'Victoria, if I decide to cancel the skiing part of the trip and just want to travel singly to Barneo, in the hope of getting to the North Pole by helicopter, will it be easier for you to get me on a flight to Barneo?'

'Yes' she immediately replied, "It will ensure you will get up to Barneo with the scientists ahead of any of the ski expeditions. If that is what you want to do then I will tell Victor at Barneo and get his agreement.'

She called me back later to say that Victor agreed with my plan and that it would be better for me to do it that way.

'Will that cause any problem for Eugenie?'

'No. He will still go with the other two skiers when we can get him on a flight.'

I set off for town to find Alexei. I found him talking to some clients in the Radisson hotel and I told him of my discussion with Victor's office and my decision to change my plan. By lunchtime and after more phone calls, Alexei confirmed that the first flight up to Barneo would be on Friday 20th, the day after tomorrow. Alexei got a call to say that Victor had arranged for another Antonov 74 aircraft to fly up from Moscow to try and help clear the backlog. They would then have two planes operating for twenty-four hours. Priority would be given to scientists and those going singly, but all the ski trips must wait. All this was assuming that the new runway froze properly and that the weather settled down for a few days to allow it all to happen.

I walked back to the guest house feeling happier that I had made the right decision and feeling comfortable with it. I might not even get as far as Barneo, or I could get there and still get stuck. Time would tell.

That evening I saw Alexei. He told me that Eugenie, the Russian and the Canadian would wait and leave for Barneo whenever they could. However, Alexei also told me that the weather was still bad at Barneo and the runway was still not finished. The temperature was only -9 degrees Celcius, so the ice was not freezing fast enough. It was still not looking good for anyone.

Day 5, Thursday 19 April 2007

I met up with Alexei in town and he wanted to know if I was still happy with my decision to cancel the ski trip and try to get to Barneo alone. I told him yes, that I had discussed it with Victoria and that Victor knew all this and had agreed.

'That is very good. Actually, I spoke to Victor last night and I know he agrees'. He continued, 'We now hope to start the flights tonight and four flights initially will be planned. I am planning for you to go on flight No. 4 which should be sometime on Friday afternoon. We do not know yet when the ski parties will go but it will certainly be after that. Victor will arrange for you to return to Spitsbergen probably on Sunday (22nd).'

This was great news. Things were starting to look up. Alexei had still not acquired my proper arctic boots but he promised to hire a pair for me the next day.

In the end there were no flights on Thursday night. More bad weather.

Day 6, Friday 20th April 2007

At about 2 a.m. I was woken by the sound of car doors slamming and people talking outside. Perhaps this was the first flight in from Barneo? In the morning, another bright and sunny day, I asked the receptionist but she said, 'No, it was a flight from the mainland that arrived late'. She did not know whether any Barneo flights had gotten away but thought not. I said I was due to check out and go to Barneo today, but did not know yet what was happening. She said I could use the room until I knew.

If there were no flights to Barneo last night, then the chances for my flight up today were slim. At 11.30 a.m. the hotel housekeeper was banging on my door telling me to check out. I was now getting into a tight corner. I knew that there were no hotel rooms anywhere in town and I could not get a flight out to Tromsø, even if I wanted to, as they were all full as well. My only hope now was to get to Barneo in the next twenty-four hours otherwise I was going to be sleeping on the floor somewhere. A strange thought occurred to me that the only possibility for a bed tonight was at the North Pole!

I checked out and spent the rest of the morning sitting hopefully in the reception building of the guesthouse reading a book. I was deep into a chapter when I became aware of someone rushing in through the door. I looked up. It was Alexei. 'The flights are starting today.' He called, 'We think the runway may be OK and the weather is better, so you will be on a flight this afternoon. Do not go anywhere and be ready to leave when I come for you.' He dashed out and drove off back down the road. Hooray! It might still happen.

Shortly after 2 p.m, Alexei returned and I climbed into his truck. Two other guys, who looked like scientists, were already sitting in the back. We finally headed for the airport but even now my plans were nearly scuppered by another passenger that Alexei had to pick up. It was a woman who caused mayhem by being late. She had gone off on a morning tourist trip, against Alexei's advice, and was late back. Alexei was furious. When she did arrive about ten minutes later, she told us that she had forgotten her reading glasses and had left them in the tour car. She insisted on keeping everyone waiting at her hotel until her glasses were found and returned! We waited and waited as time slipped by. Alexei had promised me that we would get to the plane on time, but had also said that the plane would not wait if we were late. When the glasses were finally returned she did not offer one word of apology or thanks to anyone. This selfish woman very nearly caused us all to miss the plane!

With departure time fast approaching, we arrived at the airport and found the departure shed full of people, with an especially noisy American group in front of us with their pulks and back packs – all very 'gung-ho' confident, loud and cocky. We were the last to check in, and no sooner have we checked in than they started to board the plane. Alexei rushed back into the departure area with a pair of boots. 'Your boots, I did not forget!' He handed them to me and rushed out again. I had completely forgotten about them. I tried one on and it was OK. The other one was not. It was too small. I then noticed that they were not only different sizes but not even a matching pair! By pulling out some of the insulating felt insole, which was there to keep my feet warm, I got it to fit!

We boarded the Antonov 74. This was a small Russian twin-engine plane with high wings and a cargo ramp at the back. The rear half of the fuselage was given over to cargo, and the front half given to seats and people. I managed to sit by a window but those in rows further back did not have windows. The Russians gave us each a small pack including a salami sandwich and a can of fizzy orange. There was no interest in the usual flight safety rituals. There were bags and parkas stuffed all around the exits and no concern as to whether we had seat belts on or not. There was nowhere to stow anything, yet as there were greater hazards ahead than the possibility of tripping over a parka, no one was really worried. There were more fantastic views of Spitsbergen as we flew north, then I could see the pack ice and the polar ice cap. There seemed to be a few thin leads but not much actual open water. After two-and-a-half noise-filled hours, the plane started to make a long slow and very gradual approach. It seemed to be flying low and level but was gradually losing height. Obviously this was one long-low approach to avoid slamming down hard onto the fragile ice and disappearing through into the ocean below. Would the new runway hold up? Would we crack it, or worse, just carry on down? We held our breath. Then we touched-down very, very gently onto the 1,200 yard-long ice runway. The touchdown was almost imperceptible, but the reverse thrust was not. The runway held, the engines screamed and snow and ice flew past the window as the plane braked hard, trying to stop before the end of the runway and the ice floe. We stopped at the very end by some oil drums which marked the limit of the runway. Just beyond them a deep crack showed the end of the floe.

As I climbed down the aircraft steps, the first person I saw standing at the foot of the steps was Victor. He greeted me with a big bear hug and huge smile!

'Welcome, Gordon!'

'It is good to be here Victor'. Victor took charge. We all gathered on the ice, got our bags and Victor pointed the way to the tents. He told us to use the wooden bridging boards across the cracks in the ice that mark the edges of the ice floes. We set off towards the blue tents in the distance. The woman who had lost her glasses set off ahead of the rest of us, on her own, and stepped across the crack. Suddenly, a voice boomed out across the frozen wastes. We froze on the spot. 'Do NOT walk over the cracks. I have just told you to walk on the board, so why you walk on the crack? It is very dangerous to step over the

Camp Barneo.

crack.' It was Victor some forty yards away, where he was still supervising the unloading of the plane. The woman trudged on, looking chastened.

From the landing strip the camp was just a collection of low, blue, rigid frame tents in the distance. Large letters shaped from blocks of ice spelt out Barneo with blue dye. As we drew nearer we could see that the tents were all surrounded by banks of snow, cleared for access round the camp and about 8 feet high. They also acted as wind breaks. Someone identified the mess tent and we headed there and waited. The tent was about 30 feet by 20 feet and had a thick padding material lining to it. The tables were set out canteen style and a serving table had both a coffee and a tea urn on it, as well as a basket of bread and some hunks of cheese. Victor arrived about ten minutes later and told us to eat, just as a short, thin woman wearing a white apron and a frown appeared through a door in the back of the tent, with a hot tray of stew. She put it on the serving table and vanished. This was dinner. No potatoes, no vegetables, just the stew. It was about 9 p.m. by now. I got some bread and cheese as the stew did not look too exciting.

Victor then organised the beds. 'Come with me to find a bed' he called. We set off in a group round the camp which is made up of about six or seven ten-man tents. At each tent Victor went in and then called out 'Room for three in here', or 'No room here try the next'. Gradually we all found a bed. I ended up in a ten-bed tent which had seven people already in it and in bed. The tent was dark inside. There were no lights as the twenty-four hour daylight provided a little light through the door. The beds were small camp beds with sleeping bags on top. I made out a number of bodies in the beds near the door. The only spare beds were right at the other end. A French man and his wife took the other two beds. Hot air was provided by oil heaters outside and these pumped hot air directly into the tents through eight- or ten-inch wide pipes that came into the tents about 3 feet from the ground. They only heated one end of the tent though, so those by the door froze while those by the inlets cooked. One inlet was right at my bed level. We learnt that the slumbering bodies were Italians, but we never discovered what they were there for as none of them spoke English and they always seemed to be in bed. Having found a bed for ourselves we gathered back in the mess tent. There were over a dozen people, some I recognised from the flight up, others I did not. Who they were, where they were from, was a mystery to me. But I didn't care as I was at ice station Barneo! We started to relax and chatting with each other when Victor called for 'Silence please. The weather is good now so we will go to the pole now. Please get coats on and come to the helicopter now.'

Victor led us out and over the ice to an old looking Russian helicopter. It was a faded orange colour with a thick blue band along the side. It was a Mil 8 Taimyr and could seat eighteen of us in the back. Its engine was already running as we scrambled in and sat on the metal-framed bench seats along the sides, like a van. The noise was deafening and conversation was impossible. There were no seat belts or safety briefings. We flew north for about half-an-hour or more over the endless ice and snow. The helicopter slowed down as the pilot looked for a flat area of floe on which to land. He finally found one and we landed, unexpectedly gently. We all got out onto the ice and looked around in a bemused, lost way. It was as if we all expected to see a brightly painted pole sticking up by the helicopter.

Victor took the lead and we set out, walking across the flat ice and struggling through increasingly ridged and rough ice as we followed Victor in his red parka and white fur-trimmed Russian hat, with his GPS in his hand. The ice ridges were about ten to 12 feet high. They were tall ice crags with deep drifts and holes full of soft snow behind them. It was not easy to clamber over the ridges as they stuck up at all angles, yet it would be easy to slip or trip and crack yourself on the head or twist an ankle. We all slowed down and started to move more cautiously. Luckily the thick parkas and trousers provided some padded protection from the concrete ice. The helicopter was soon lost from view behind the ice and we were now dependent upon keeping Victor in view to avoid getting lost forever out on the ice.

The ice and snow were deceptive and again I tripped over an ice outcrop that I could not see. Then, I stepped into a deep hole filled with soft snow but which looked like solid ice. I tried to look suave but gave up as we all seemed to be having trouble staying vertical. How on earth do you travel through this on skis and pulling a loaded pulk? The enormity of what I would have faced on the skiing trip dawned on me as I looked at the chaotic mass of jagged ice that stretched across the icescape. Here the ice floes had come together and thrown up these huge ridges and pinnacles as the forces of the ocean current beneath and the wind on the ice above drove the pack across the top of the world. After about twenty minutes we were strung out across the ice in a series of gasping, cursing bundles as we tried to keep up. Then we realised that, at last, Victor had stopped. He was staring at his GPS. As we joined him he said simply 'We are there'. 89-degrees, 59.999 minutes north. The GPS readings seemed stuck. We scrambled a few yards further. Then, in between a confusion of jagged ice ridges and surrounded by deep snow filled gulleys, was a spot where the GPS readings flickered for a brief moment to 90.00.000 north. I was on the very top of the world. This was the climax of years of dreaming, months of excitement and days of changing plans, but finally I had made it.

The GPS only showed 90.00 N momentarily, then flicked to 89 degrees 59.999 minutes north (it did not show seconds of latitude). As 0.001 mile is about two yards, and the ice is constantly moving, it only had to move two yards for the GPS to register it. It was 23.40 on the 20th April. We were all happy; we really had got to the North Pole. Victor called me over and pointed to someone standing nearby.

Gordon and Victor at 90 North.

'Come, give him your camera' he said to me, then he grabs me by the shoulders. 'Please, mister, take our picture' he ordered the man.

Victor and I had our picture taken together by a tall blue flag with 90 degrees N on it that Victor had brought along and planted in the ice. Then he took one of me alone with the flag.

A low midnight sun was shining through a hazy deep red sky with bands of thicker cloud high in the sky. Wherever we looked we could see ice. Every direction was south. It was hard to imagine exactly where I was standing, looking out at the endless icescape and trying to picture a globe with me standing on the very top.

A deep feeling of satisfaction started to creep over me, while I may not have skied the last 30 miles to get here, I was still here. It had not been without its frustrations, but now it was all worth it. Now I could say 'Yes, I have been to the North Pole'.

Who was first?

Who really was the first person to stand here? Polar explorers had tried to get to the North Pole since the 1800s when Parry led a British expedition north. Others followed. Americans, mostly up through the west side of Greenland and the Davis Strait, and the Europeans from the Atlantic and Spitsbergen, all tried, but no-one managed it and many died in the attempt. Nansen did get within about 240 miles in 1895.

Great mystery has existed since the American Robert Peary claimed to have reached the North Pole on 6 April 1909. His claim was countered by Dr Frederick Cook, another experienced American explorer, who claimed to have reached the Pole a year before Peary, on 21 April 1908. Both claims have been extensively researched and both found wanting. Cook's claim was found wanting in the lack of accurate navigational data to support it. Cook also claimed to have been the first to climb Mount McKinley in 1906, but that claim was later proved to be false, so his credibility was flawed.

Peary's claim was doubted as it seemed impossible for him to have travelled as far and as fast as he claimed, to get to the pole and back, in the time he claimed. Experts have since said that his navigational data got less detailed the nearer he got to the pole. He would have had to have travelled at three times the average speed of his whole march north, up to the point of sending back the last support party, to do it; the experts felt this was highly unlikely. In fact, on his return journey, he overtook some of his support team who had started back days before and from well south of the pole. Although he had a No. 2, Henson, and four Inuit with him, none were navigators and so were not able to confirm or challenge Peary's navigation. Peary claimed to have travelled in a straight line the whole way, but Henson states in his diaries that they had to make many detours to avoid ridges and open water leads. Tom Avery carried out a replica trip in 2004 and actually beat Peary's claimed time by five hours. Avery concluded that Peary could have done it. However, Avery's fastest run over five days was 90 miles. Peary claimed to have done 135 in five days. Peary had spent his life in the Arctic, mostly Greenland, where he mapped vast areas of the northwest and northern coast. He had tried to get to the pole twice before and failed on both attempts. This was to be his final chance as ill health and injuries were already dogging him, so he had every incentive to get there. However, the doubts remained and well-researched books have been written supporting or disputing both claims.

Nansen tried to sail across the pole in *FRAM*, but the ice took the ship well south of the pole and Nansen and Johanssen then tried to ski there from the *FRAM* but they had to turn back 240 miles short.

In the twentieth century many people have claimed to have flown over the pole, only to have their records proven inaccurate. Roald Amundsen is the first man to have proved that he had actually been over the pole when he flew over it with Ellsworth in the airship Norge on 12 May 1926. However, they did not stop and flew on to Alaska. A team of Russian scientists flew there by plane and landed in 1958.

What is known for certain is that the first properly documented expedition to the North Pole on foot was by an Englishman, Wally Herbert, in 1969. Wally Herbert's expedition crossed the Arctic from Canada to Spitsbergen via the pole. There have been nuclear submarines surfacing here, nuclear icebreakers visiting with tourists and of course, Victor's team and expeditions from Camp Barneo, since 2002.

G gets to 90 North

We stood and savoured the feeling of being on top of the world, a place where only a few hundred have stood before us. We explored the immediate area, trying to take in where we were and absorb the ice scenery. After a few minutes Victor called to everyone that it was time to go. As we set off back across the ice and ridges towards the helicopter, I caught sight of something in the distance moving behind an ice ridge. I watched for it to come into view again. A dog team with two skiers emerged from behind the ridges as they arrived at the North Pole. They were moving quickly, as if the dogs already knew a secret route through the ice. Victor went over and spoke to them but we never learnt who they were, only that they were Russian.

We got back to Barneo at about 2:30 a.m. As I got off the helicopter Victor took me aside and told me that the others on the helicopter were going back to Spitzbergen in a few hours, but he would like me to stay until Sunday so we can chat and I can see what goes on at Barneo. I thanked him as he has enough problems without me hanging around.

Sleeping was hard, even though it was 3 a.m. and my end of the tent was warm. I lay fully dressed on the top of the sleeping bag. In the night, however, it suddenly got much colder, and very quickly. Someone had propped the tent door open to cool the tent down! The Italians soon woke up and discovered this and closed it again as their end of the tent was now freezing. I lay there absorbing the fact that I was actually sleeping, or trying to, on the polar ice cap and that under me was just one- to two-metres of ice, then 1000 fathoms of the cold Arctic Ocean. The following night the generator that provided the hot air for the tents stopped. I awoke to find I was shivering and the world had gone silent. I lay there, trying to curl up inside the sleeping bag to keep warm, but failed. In no time I was freezing as the Arctic cold reclaimed the tents and draped a heavy blanket of very chilled air onto everyone. It took the engineer some time to get it going again but thankfully he did. The hot air was soon blowing again.

Day 7, Saturday 21 April 2007

After a sleepless night, I got up at 7 a.m. The sun was bright and I met Victor walking out on the ice. He and I were the only ones up. It was clear that everything that happened here was run and controlled by Victor. He himself was as friendly and approachable as ever. There was no evidence of a No. 2 or any hierarchy other than Victor and the rest! We had a coffee and chatted for a while. He said he was hoping to get Eugenie and his two skiers up to Barneo later that day. He said I was right to change my plans and he was glad I had.

The meals in Barneo were basic. A pan of porridge was put on the serving table at 9 a.m. and left there. Lunch at 2 p.m. was a pan of soup. Dinner at 9 p.m. was some form of meat. When I was there it was chicken pieces and rice, or Frankfurter and mash. I could only assume Victor had his own supplies as he was never seen eating in the mess tent. The 'glasses woman', who turned out to be a New Zealander, decided to leave lunch until later as the tent was looking 'a bit full'! Someone suggested to her that this might not be a good idea as once the cook cleared it there would be nothing to eat until tonight. She looked at him as if they were an idiot. 'Of course they will give me lunch later', she snorted loudly as she left. She came back at about 3 p.m. and found that there was no food left out, so she marched up to the door through to the kitchen and called out for the cook.

'Can I now have my lunch?' she asked.

'Niet. You too late.' replied the cook.

I managed to suppress a smile.

I walked out to the edges of the camp area, past the runway, where I could feel the true scale of the ice cap and its beauty. On one side of the camp there were high ridges and deep ice holes stretching out into the distance, I tried to climb through some of these to see what lay beyond but found that the ice, heavy gloves, concrete-hard edges and all the angles that the ice takes up made it a thankless and punishing exercise, so I returned to camp. Also, although polar bears were rare this far from the ice edge, they were not unknown and we had all been told not to stray too far from the camp.

Out past the ice runway, marked along its edges by black bin liners filled with snow, or by oil drums, the ice was flatter, but even out here it had big undulations and looked like snow-covered fields rolling gently into the distance. The light and the sun played tricks on the ice. In the sunlight the edges and

Icescape at 89 North.

depressions in the ice were clear, shadows showed you where things were and how far away. When the sun went in, everything merged into a cold, grey-tinged white mass and it was impossible to see any definition or depth to the ice forms. The ridges were softened by snow drifting up their faces but they showed their true selves by the hard translucent ice shining on the sides.

The ridges ran into the distance, like snow-covered hedgerows. The wind had made sastrugi form where it had blasted loose snow away from the ice and the hard ridges flowed in gentle curves across the surface. Out here, away from the ice station, I really felt that I was at the very end of the world. The only sound was the continual moaning of the wind and the gentle slosh of loose snow being blown across the ice. The sky was everything. The heavens formed a vast dome over the polar regions and the ice station could have been a million miles away. At the ice station end of the runway the floe ended in a clear, deep edge about a foot wide. Here, small leads existed where the edges of the floes didn't quite meet with their neighbours. They looked so innocuous. At one point you could step across without even thinking, but a few yards away where it might be 3 feet wide a simple jump could, with a slip of a boot on the ice, easily turn into disaster. Out here, with the wind blowing, no-one back in the tents would hear a yell from the icy water down between the floes. The ice at the edge is smooth and hard and rises eighteen inches above the water. To climb out unassisted in a heavy parka and boots would be impossible. A gentle walk could, in seconds, turn to death and no-one would ever know.

With two aircraft operating, the back log was cleared fairly quickly and Eugenie and his team arrived on the last flight of the day. They collected

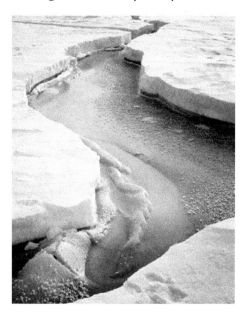

Open floe.

their gear then went straight to a helicopter that took off into the gloom and vanished across the wastes. They did not even stop for a coffee in the mess tent.

Day 8, Sunday 22nd April 2007

Up early again, I saw Victor in the mess tent having a coffee. I got one from the urn and joined him. We chatted about the bad weather and the ski trips. He was happier now that he had managed to get everyone who had been stuck on the ice back to Barneo and today the last would go back to Longyearbyen.

'It is always worrying, Gordon, with people out on the ice. It is very easy for things to get bad here and for a few days things were bad. It is easy to lose people in that sort of weather.' He said he was very sorry about not being able to get back to Longyearbyen and missing the training and the ski trip itself, but it had been impossible for him to leave and he was going to be unable to leave for some time yet while the rest of the backlog was sorted out. I told him that I understood, and anyway I was not too bothered about missing the skiing trip as Eugenie's new team seemed very professional. However, had it worked out according to the original idea we had on the *Kapitan Dranitsyn*, it would have been a fantastic experience. I was happy though, as I had got to the North Pole as he had promised me. He told me that later in the day, in addition to the Longyearbyen flights, there were some VIP flights due from Moscow and that we would not be able to use the mess tent while they were here. I gave Victor a bottle of vodka I had brought for him. He smiled. 'Thank you, thank you' he said, then tucked it safely into his parka pocket.

Later that morning a flight came into Barneo from Moscow. I walked out to the runway to watch it arrive. There were about a dozen VIPs who were all smartly dressed in military greatcoats or big civilian coats and fur hats. They stepped sheepishly onto the ice and each one was warmly welcomed by Victor. It was clear that he knew a good number of them very well. I assumed that they must be the power behind the ice station. Victor then led them all to the mess tent. Unfortunately this visit ran across lunch time so we missed out on lunch while the VIPs enjoyed their vodkas and snacks. At about 4 p.m. they walked happily out of the mess tent and back to their Antanov 74 and took off, back to Moscow. Victor said he could not tell us who they were, 'Just VIPs' was all he would say.

I dashed into the mess tent and grabbed a few left-over biscuits and a few chunks of cheese as it was still a long time until dinner. Just after the VIPs' flight disappeared, a second one came in. This was a military flight with security and Russian Special Forces people on it. The Special Forces flight made a very steep descent and landed with a thump on the ice and stopped at the end of the runway. A number of troops in thick heavy hooded military parkas got out and walked around. Then they too all vanished into the mess tent. They spent about an hour-and-a-half there then all took off again.

In addition to the main camp with the skiers and dog-team people passing through, there were different groups of scientists working in their own areas nearby. They were mostly Russian. They had their own small tents, or huts, close by to the main camp area. Some of the scientists slept in Barneo, some slept in their own camps. One French group had two divers and spent their days making holes in the ice floe so they could let the divers go down. It was a safer way than letting the diver go down in one of the open leads, because if the floes moved together then the diver had no way of getting back up through the ice. Another team from Moscow spent their time drilling small holes in the ice, which immediately froze up before they could get the next hole drilled. I never did discover what they were trying to do as the scientist spoke little English.

During a break in the day Victor called me over.

'I have arranged for you to go on the flight back to Longyearbyen later tonight. Is that OK?' 'That is great Victor, Many thanks.' If I had left it until the next day then there was an increased chance of getting stuck if the weather changed again.

'Good. Let's have a drink.' We went back into the mess tent and he produced the export vodka I had given him. With Nostrovias all round, we each had a couple of large ones and enjoyed the rare moment of peace in Barneo. I thanked him for getting me to the pole, especially after all the problems he had had. 'No problem, my friend, but the weather is forecast to get bad again soon, so it is better you go tonight.'

A ten-man sledging team arrived last night from further south on the ice. It was leaving for the pole. They spent the morning repacking their pulks before heading off towards the north and the high ridges that ran along that side of the camp. They struggled hard just to get the pulks moving, even over the flat ice surrounding the camp, and I watched as the pulks skidded around on the ice, banging into their skis and getting stuck on protruding ice ridges as though they had minds of their own. In the late afternoon a dog team of eight dogs and four people arrived. They stopped for a meal, quickly reorganised their sledge and headed off again towards the pole.

That night, after a long delay, the last incoming flight arrived and was turned round by the crew. I got my rucksack and walked out to the plane with Victor. The rest of the passengers consisted of a ten-man sledge team, who had been stuck out in the storm and had only got back to Barneo that afternoon, and one of Victor's people. I shook Victor's hand and climbed into the Antonov. The engines powered up and the plane thundered down the ice strip. Suddenly it lifted off and turned away to the south and Spitsbergen. The ski party were, naturally enough, in high spirits after their close encounter. Some of the guys had frostbite on their cheeks. These guys were all obviously serious skiers and were comparing their trip to ones they had done in the Canadian Arctic. This had been their final target, to ski to the pole.

We landed back at Longyearbyen at approximately 11 p.m., where Alexei met me and took me back to the guesthouse. I had no hotel booking for tonight, as the original plan meant that I would come back tomorrow, so I arrived knowing that I did not have a bed waiting. However, Alexei had said he thought I should be OK at the guesthouse if the reception building was still open. As I had left my suitcase with all my clothes at the guesthouse, it was the only place I could try. As we drew up outside we could not see any lights on in reception. The door was locked. I was too late. What to do now? At -15 degrees Celsius I was not about to sleep outside. I had an idea. Maybe there was someone still up at the Polarrigg hotel, as they seemed to have late night parties and I had met the owner, Mary Ann, so she might take pity on me. Maybe they had a spare bed or a mattress somewhere. Alexei drove me back to the Polarrigg hotel. Mary Ann was still up.

'Gordon I am so sorry, no. I have no spare beds at all. In fact I have one crowd sleeping on the floor over in the annexe'. I was about to turn away when she called me back.

'Maybe, if you don't mind, you could sleep with the Malaysians. They have taken over the meeting room over there'. Did I hear her right? Malaysians? She continued, 'You can sleep in their room if you can find some room on the floor.'

What are Malaysians doing in Longyearbyen? I wondered. 'That's fine Mary Ann, thanks. Where is their room?' She waved her arm at the front door, 'Just across the road in the annexe.' I picked up my bag and went back outside.

The snow was now falling heavily and it was difficult to make out what was hotel and what is not. I could just about make out three buildings through the snow. I looked around, but Alexei had gone. I climbed over the snow banks and headed for the nearest building. The door was locked. The next one looked like a garage or warehouse of some kind and its big double doors were also locked. So, I headed up the road for the third building. This was a wooden, single storey hut that looked more like a storage area than a hotel annexe. I tried the door. It opened. I went in. It was quiet. I found myself in a small corridor with doors opening off it. The first door I opened was the laundry and washing area with a toilet in the corner. I opened the second door and there were a number of bodies sleeping on the floor on mattresses. There were mattresses lying all around the floor, all with piles of clothes and rucksacks on them. Clearly there were lots more people from this room somewhere out there in the snow. Two big, noisy, blower heaters, in the middle of the room, were running at full power, and had turned the room into a hot house.

One of the bodies turned over and an oriental face smiled up at me from the floor and nodded as I indicated that I just wanted to sleep on their floor. I took off my parka and tried to decide where to lie. However, with the blowers on full blast, this was far too hot for me, so I decided to explore a bit more. I went out into the corridor again. It was pleasantly cool after the Malaysian room. I started opening the other doors. The first room was crammed with sleeping bodies. Like the Malaysian room, there were rucksacks, sleeping bags and boots lying everywhere. I quietly closed the door and moved on. The next door was small broom cupboard. Looks like I will have to sleep in the Malaysian sauna after all. I opened the last door. It looked like a small bedding and cleaning store room. It was freezing cold as it clearly did not have any heating, but it did have a single bed, with a mattress on it! The bed was covered with big boxes of linen and piles of clean towels. On a shelf on the wall there were even some duvets and pillows. The small window was quickly becoming snowed over as the storm outside increased and the snow started to drift against the hut. I had no intention of going out in that again so this must be home tonight. A shower and a change of clothes will have to wait until I got back up to the guesthouse in the morning, I shifted the boxes off the bed, kicked my boots off, pulled two duvets over my parka and fell sound asleep.

Day 9, Monday 23rd April 2007

In the morning, I woke to the sound of running water next door in the laundry area. I stretched out. I had slept well even if it was a bit cold. I got up and went back across to the main building. The first person I saw was Malena. 'Are you here too?' She asked. 'Yes, I slept in your bedding store!' She laughed, 'We had to turn away lots of people last night. There are absolutely no beds in town'.

'There's a good one in there' I said, waving at the store room. 'Can I get any breakfast here please? I am starving.' I realised that the last food I had was yesterday lunch and that was crackers and cheese in Barneo. Malena got me a table and then organised a good cooked breakfast. While she served my breakfast I asked her about the Malaysians. It turned out that they were part of a team of Malaysian skydivers who flew up to Barneo last night. They had commandeered the small meeting hall as there was nowhere else to go. The few bodies I saw were the support team guys. Their plan was to fly to Barneo, change into their sky diving gear and parachutes, then get straight into a helicopter and jump out from 6000 feet over the pole. Then when, and if, they all landed safely, they would be collected and flown straight back to Spitsbergen and so back to Malaysia.

I thanked Malena, bought some bread rolls in town and headed back up the road to the guesthouse, where I was hopefully booked in for the next two nights. I checked in, got my bag from the store and by 11 a.m. I was enjoying a hot shower and a shave.

Day 10, Tuesday 24th April 2007

A pure arctic day with blue sky and sunshine. I spent it walking around the town, shopping for odds and ends. I bought a present for Doreen from the supermarket-cum-gift-shop-cum-expedition-outfitters. I revisited the Arctic Museum and in the evening walked to the Spitsbergen hotel for a meal.

Day 11, Wednesday 25th April 2007

Malena rang me to say that Eugenie and his team had returned to Longyearbyen late last night; they just made it to the pole in three days and had been flown straight out from Barneo on the last flight. I met up with them for a coffee and chatted to the Canadian, Bill, and the Russian, Sasha, who went with Eugenie. Sasha was from St Petersburg, he knew Victor and Eugenie very well and did a lot of arctic skiing. He said that he was in Siberia in a tent earlier in the year in -54 degrees Celsius! Bill was from Toronto and spent his winters skiing in Quebec and northern Ontario. He had a cabin up by a lake that he used through the winter.

After they were dropped off on the ice by the helicopter from Barneo, the ice ridging was so bad it took them two-and-a-half hours to cover less than 2 kms. The ice drifted in the night and in the morning they found that they were 2 kms further south than the night before. On their second day they skied over 32 kms just to get round the ridges and hummocks, and actually only went north 3 kms. 'Well, the ice was drifting against us so it was a bit tiring' was Bill's laid back comment. On the last day they finally found some flattish ice and skied non-stop, for over fourteen hours, in order to get to the pole.

Eugenie told us that Victor had called to tell him that the steep landing by the Special Forces flight on Sunday had damaged the runway. It had cracked the ice and this had now split. The runway was out of commission again.

I left Longyearbyen and headed for home on the afternoon flight. I retraced my steps through Oslo and arrived back in Edinburgh on Thursday morning. Wow, what an adventure! I was lucky to leave Barneo when I did as I later learnt that the runway took 5 days to refreeze before it could be used again.

Was it all worth it? You bet it was.

CHAPTER 10

MV *Stockholm* – Spitzbergen – In Search of Polar Bears

Glaciers

There had been rumblings and cracking sounds coming from deep inside the 'July 14th Glacier' for ten minutes or more, echoing around the mountains at the head of the fjord. Derek and I were leaning on the rail of the ship, savouring the smells from the galley and letting the afternoon drift toward dinnertime. We had heard noises from the glacier when we had been ashore earlier, but after one small icefall it had all gone quiet again. Now it had restarted. We watched fascinated, but all was still, the water flat and the glacier face remained intact. These noises seemed to go on forever without any ice chunks or small ice bergs calving off. The noises subsided again. Then, silently and without any indication that it was about to happen, a number of large pieces of ice, each the size of a small house, together with hundreds of smaller lumps of solid ice, detached themselves from the glacier face and slid and fell towards the water. Some slid straight in and others tumbled and tripped on the lower edges of the glacier before falling into the fjord. The slapping sound of the ice hitting the water reached us and the scene changed. Birds took flight, and the ice wall became a blur of action as the ice fell and the water splashed up before it all fell calm again. Then we saw the wave. It was at least 10 or 12 feet high and rising. We watched and wondered what would happen when the wave, which was already radiating and racing out from the glacier, reached our small ship with its 8-foot freeboard?

The '*Stockholm* Plan'

It was over a coffee at The Scott Polar Research Institute (SPRI) in Cambridge that the plan had been formed. We were attending a Polar Quest reunion, kindly hosted by the SPRI, for the UK clients of Per Magnus's company. Some of the expeditions that Per Magnus runs in Spitzbergen are on a small expedition ship called *Stockholm*. Over coffee, a couple of the ladies, Jill and Angela, who I had

MV *Stockholm*. A former Swedish Government vessel now converted for expedition work.

met earlier in the year in Spitzbergen on another trip, said that they wanted to get a group of twelve together and sub-charter the *Stockholm* from Per Magnus for a private expedition around Spitzbergen and would Doreen and I like to join the party? The plan was to go early in the season and take the ship from Longyearbyen and see how far we could get round the top of the islands and look for wildlife and scenery on the way. The trip had to take place at the very beginning of the season as the ship was fully committed after that. In spite of the short notice we said yes.

Svalbard was first mentioned in old Icelandic texts and means 'Land of cold coasts'. It is the official name of the Island group. Spitzbergen was the name given by the Dutch explorer Barents when he discovered the island in 1596 and Spitzbergen means 'pointed mountains'. Technically 'Spitzbergen' is the name of the largest island in the group of 'Svalbard Islands'. Longyearbyen, on Spitzbergen Island, was set up as a coal-mining settlement by an American called, strangely enough, Mr Longyear. The relics of the old mines remain and one of the mines is still in operation. The Russians also operate a bigger mine further down Isafjord at Barentsburg, which is a totally Russian settlement. Today, during the summer months, Longyearbyen is a busy starting point for expeditions all over Spitzbergen and further afield. It retains a strong frontier-town feeling with most of the shops selling rations, boots, supplies, spades and big parkas.

Doreen and I arrive in Longyearbyen from Edinburgh after an overnight stop in Oslo. The others travelled up from London later that day and arrive well

The main saloon on *Stockholm* is a warm and welcoming area with polished wood and brass.

The main mess has a real feel of polar voyaging with old charts on the bulkheads and cabins opening off the mess and galley area.

after midnight. The hotel we have been booked into seems to be a theme hotel. It was, we thought, meant to resemble an old coal miner's hostel. The rough wooden top bunk bed I have is so designed that only a small and very flexible monkey can climb up to get into it, as I certainly can't. I am certain that the designer chappy has never tested the access himself and in the end I give up and drag the mattress off the bunk and put it on the floor.

The next morning we all meet up at breakfast. There are twelve of us. It is fair to say that none of us are in the first flush of youth. Doreen and I had been on previous trips with some of the group but others we have not met before. There are Derek and Anne, who we met on the Greenland trip. There are Jill and Angela who organised the charter with Per Magnus. They are two independent ladies who live their own lives most of the year but join up each year for trips together to far-off places. Then there are those who have never visited the Arctic before. Sarah and Anthony, who seem to have been to all the hot and sticky places like the Amazon. Sarah's mother Barbara, who is a lovely lady and who one afternoon towards the ends of the trip, when it was announced that we were trying for yet another Zodiac landing, decided that she had had enough and, said 'Fine, You all go. I am staying here in the Saloon on my own with a very large whisky.' No one argued and in fact some of us were quite envious. Then there are Amanda and Alex, who have also never been to the Arctic but heard all about it from Gill and Angela, and want to see it for themselves. In addition, Per Magnus himself is coming as the expedition leader and, with him, his wife Katarina; who as a director has a large role to play in the running of the Company. Both of them, as well as Per the skipper and Lisa, one of Per Magnus's full time Arctic guides who is based in Spitzbergen, have all led many expeditions in and around Spitzbergen so there will be no shortage of ideas as to where we should try to go.

The *Stockholm* is berthed across the end of the commercial jetty, dwarfed by a large merchantman lying along the main jetty. We are warmly welcomed on board by the captain, Per Engvall, as well as by Annika and Kjell, the stewardess and the chef, who between them run all the 'hotel aspects' of the ship, and the rest of the crew. After the safety briefings, we set sail down the Isafjord towards the open sea and into a strengthening south-westerly breeze, which gives us a few white horses and a gentle roll for our first night at sea.

The ship is a real beauty. She is small enough to get into the bays and small harbours but big enough to offer some degree of comfort for her twelve passengers and seven crew. Stockholm was built in Helsingbors Shipyard in Sweden in 1953 as a lighthouse tender for the Swedish National Maritime Administration. She is 40 metres long and has a gross tonnage of 361 tons. After her life in the Baltic she was saved from the scrap yard and bought from the Swedish Government by her current skipper/owner Per Engvall. He restored her and saw the potential in her for small expeditions to the Arctic.

Polar bears outnumber humans on Svalbard. (C. McCutcheon)

He converted and updated her for expedition work and to meet passenger-carrying standards and Lloyd's ice-strengthened standard A1. He restored the ship's interior to how she had been when she was new. This included the restoration of the beautiful wooden-panelled bridge front and interior and the wood panelling in the main saloon. To enable more passengers to be carried, he turned the original hold space into passenger cabins and a central messing area and linked this area through to both the bow and stern areas. This allowed her to carry at least twelve passengers. By 1998 she was ready to go.

Entering the mess it instantly reminds me of seeing Captain Scott's ship, the RRS *Discovery*. The early polar expedition ships had a very similar layout, with a central wardroom mess and cabins opening off it. A central skylight makes it a bright and cheery mess deck. The atmosphere in the *Stockholm*, with the old charts and pictures of the Arctic on the bulkheads, combined with the rich use of wood and brass, gives her a warm and adventurous feel. The cabins are basic but cosy. Ours has two wooden bunks, (that were exceptionally comfortable), drawers and a wardrobe for stowage and a small shower cum toilet as well as a small porthole. This we have to keep firmly closed, as it is only a few feet above the waterline. The whole cabin is painted white and is spotlessly clean.

A gale has sprung up out in the Arctic Ocean but we avoid the rougher weather by sailing up the Forlandsundet, a wide strait between Prins Karl Forland Island and the mainland. Dinner is timed so that we are in sheltered waters by the time

Map of Spitsbergen and the route taken. The route was, as always in the north, determined by the ice and not us.

it is ready. Dinner on the first night is a delight. Norwegian smoked salmon, beef tenderloin with port and truffle sauce and some good wines.

Our first night's sleep is interrupted by our first meeting with the wildlife. At four in the morning there is a tap on the cabin door and Lisa tells us that we are stopping to watch a group of about twelve walruses on a shingle spit on the island. I struggle up on deck to find I am the last, apart from Doreen who decides to stay in bed. The spit projects out into the sound from Prins Karl Forland Island and has an exceptionally steep shore. Because of this, and the fact that it is dead calm, Per edges the ship right up to the shore so that the bottom of the bow is just touching the bottom of the shingle bank and we, standing on the fo'c'sle, can almost lean over and touch the walruses on the shore. Not that we want to, the smell is enough and the continual belching and snorting is not conducive to getting any closer. Especially at four o'clock in the morning! A few bleary, red eyes peer up at us then close again. They are lying in a haphazard heap, overlapping each other with some asleep even though they have the tusks of others sticking in their side, or a flipper and folds of skins over their heads. Apart from an occasional glance they remain aloof and disinterested in our presence on their beach.

We continue sailing north up the strait, through the narrows and later that day we go into Ny Ålesund. This village sits on King's Fjord, a long, wide fjord running south-east inland from the sea. The village was set up by sealers who were looking for fuel during the First World War. They found coal and set up the Kings Bay Coal Company. Its offices still stand above the tiny harbour/jetty. Unfortunately, a number of mining accidents led to the deaths of many miners and in 1962 the mine was shut down.

Two Norwegian whale catcher boats are alongside when we arrive. They are easily recognised by their crow's nests and harpoon gun on the bow. They are reportedly hunting for minke whales, which Norway is allowed to do for 'Scientific Purposes'. These obviously include selling raw whale meat on Bergen fish market. They are fine-looking boats. Both look new and are made of varnished wood and are obviously clean and well cared for. There is, however, no sign of the whalers themselves as they are probably sleeping down below. Ny Ålesund is now a thriving polar research centre with scientists and students from around the world living there during the summer. It also boasts the world's most northerly post office, which sits among the other rust-red, painted wooden houses and buildings above the harbour.

It was from here that a number of attempts have been made on the Pole, particularly by air. A tall, metal lattice mast, which was the tethering point for an airship, stands on open ground about half a mile from the village. Amundsen and the Italian Nobile, together with the American, Ellsworth, set off from here in the airship *Norge N1* in 1926 and flew over the North Pole and carried on to land in Alaska. They were the first people to positively see the North Pole as well as the first to fly over it. A fine plaque and a bust of Amundsen have been set up at the base of the mast to commemorate the event.

Per and Per Magnus, are both keen to get up to the north so we reluctantly leave this delightful spot, leaving the two whalers resting gently against the quay. It has been a cold and breezy morning with snow showers blowing through. However, as we sail from the village, the sun comes out, illuminating a beautiful glacier on the eastern side of the fjord. As the sky clears, the sea instantly turns from grey to a sparkling blue. We sail out of King Fjord and up

Proceeding up the coast of Albert 1 Land on a brilliant sunny day.

the coast of Albert 1 Land, the sun shining down on our small ship, which is no more than a dot in the vastness of the dazzling sea. After half an hour, the after deck resembles a cruise ship lido deck, with bodies lying in the sun everywhere. The only difference is that these bodies are not in swimsuits, but have heavy boots, parkas, hats and gloves on as well as sun glasses. It is a fabulous afternoon. The sun shines down and everywhere we look there is another fantastic view. We have a flat, calm, glistening, blue sea and white, snow-clad mountains and glaciers edge down to the sea under a clear blue sky. The gentle murmur of the engine continues as *Stockholm* heads further and further north. Spitzbergen might only be a speck on the map but when you see it on days like this, when you can literally see for miles and miles, you realise what a vast wilderness it is; a wilderness of endless mountains and ice, empty of any form of human life. As the afternoon slips by, some people snooze on deck as the ship rolls along and the soft vibration of the engine helps relax us all. Some creep quietly below for a snooze in comfort and others sit in the bridge and chat with Skipper Per until drowsiness takes over and they also sneak off below. Per continues to sit contentedly in his chair in charge of his own ship, going where he wants to, in to the far reaches of the Arctic. I chat with Alec and Amanda up on the fo'c'sle, sitting under the bulwark and sheltered from the wind but still in the warm sunshine. They cannot believe either the weather or the beauty of the Arctic on their first trip. Like many in the Arctic for the first time, they expected snowstorms all the time. So, the afternoon drifts gently by, at every turn another spectacular view of Albert 1 Land, another glacier creeping to the sea, another ridge of snow-covered mountains climbing away deep into the interior. Another fjord, this time Magdalene Fjord, opens out to starboard, still, silent and empty in the sunshine.

The peaceful afternoon drifts by as we sail up the coast taking in the beauty of the islands. By early evening we reach the north-west tip of Spitzbergen and enter the narrow, twisting Sorgattet which separates Dane's Island and Amsterdam Island from the mainland. The towering black cliffs climb above us as puffins and little auks flap furiously along the cliffs to their burrows and nests. This whole region was used by the Dutch, Scandinavian and British whalers in the seventeenth century and many of the place names reflect the history. This particular area is called Smeerenburg. Smeer is the Dutch word for blubber. So, this was Blubber Town. It is a low, flat area backed by low hills. It was set up in 1614 as a tented camp. They would catch the Greenland whales from small rowboats as the migrating whales passed through the islands and drag them ashore on the shingle beach and reduce them to oil in huge pots or coppers up to 2 or 3 metres wide. The Danes were also trying to establish a base here and there were disputes between the two nationalities. After the first years when they lived in tents, in 1619, the Dutch brought wooden huts, bricks and building materials and the camp became more permanent. Smeerenburg grew to sixteen or seventeen wooden buildings with cobbled lanes, brick-based boiling ovens and even a small fort in the centre of the settlement. It is reported that at the peak of the industry in the 1630s there would be up to 200-300 men living here in the summer, working for seven separate whale blubber bases, each financed by a different 'chamber' or company, from Holland.

The Bears are Here!

We round the beacon on the end of the spit that has, for years, guided ships through the strait. Then, as we are passing Slaadfjord, a small ice-filled fjord on the mainland side, Per alters course into the fjord looking for a mooring for the night and we break into the fast ice that leads up to the Sallstrom Glacier at the end. His plan is to spend the night anchored in the fast ice below the glacier. The glacier is large and dramatic and in the early evening the sun shines through the mountaintops onto the glacier, turning it a gleaming ice white and leaving the glacier front and the fast ice in deep blue shadows. We are watching the scenery when someone notices a slight movement on the ice against the dark shadows at the base of glacier. Then, as we slowly move into the thicker fast ice, through the binoculars, the slight movement resolves itself into two polar bears

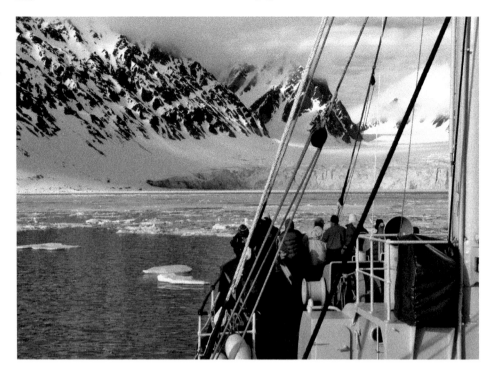

Stockholm edges gently into the fast ice in front of a glacier near Danskoya, north-western Spitsbergen.

The glacier front near Danskoya. The vast emptiness and remoteness of Spitsbergen is humbling.

A polar bear eyes up a potential dinner.

hunting along the glacier front. Eventually, when we are well into the thick fast ice, Per stops the ship. All falls silent, the sun slowly sinks lower and the bears continue their search along the deep-blue shadow of the glacier front as we relax on deck. The day is completed by another superb dinner and fine wine.

'The Bears are here!', Annika cries from the galley. We rush up on deck as quietly as we can, grabbing cameras and coats on the way. There, just a few yards in front of the port bow, are the two bears. One is a mother and the other is her cub, but probably about a year-and-a half old. They are staring and sniffing, moving and stopping. Then, when they see us emerge, they snort quietly and wander away for a few paces, then turn and nervously wander in again. The main deck of *Stockholm* is low, with only about 8 feet of freeboard at the lowest point, so we are almost down at eye level with the bears. They come right up to the side. The mother's fur is a glistening white and champagne yellow while the cub's fur is pure white. It looks so soft as the sun shines through the individual hairs and fibres of their fur. Four jet black eyes pierce and X-ray us, and everything they see, as their black noses are constantly working to take in every scent. Four small, round and rather cute ears listen to everything that is said (listening perhaps for an invitation on board for dinner). The loudest noises on the ice are their giant, pigeon-toed paws, as they gently crunch on the ice, and the sound of their breathing and short snorts as they savour the smells from the galley. On board, twelve passengers and all the crew are transfixed and silent. No one dares move or breathe in case we scare them off. Slowly, they become bolder and stand with their noses right at the deck level, peering through the rails. What will they do? Will they try to get on board? If they decided to there was no way to stop them. One jump and they will be on deck in a furry heap of hungry, prime carnivore. Will one of the peppermints in my pocket be acceptable? The smells from the galley of the shrimp, marinated in chilli and ginger, starter and the Asian fish dinner, with white wine sauce, as the main course will undoubtedly be more attractive to them, so my peppermints are probably safe. They do not appear to be threatening in any way, just curious and interested, and they hold eye contact with us until a movement along the deck distracts them. As we are watching the bears, an Arctic fox, half in and half out of its white winter coat, trots round the ship. It is half the size of a normal fox. It is obviously following the bears to collect any scraps from whatever meal they find.

Finally, the bears grow bored and wander off across the ice astern of the ship, still sniffing the air and looking for a better supper than anything a few tourists can offer. We settle down to our coffee in the mess deck and let our heartbeats return to normal.

Into the Ice

We sail again in the morning; having remained moored safely in the fast ice all night. No sooner have we left the fjord ice than we stop again to watch two male walruses on an ice flow near the fjord entrance. The early morning scene is magical. The two walruses are lying on an ice floe in the black waters of the fjord and behind them is the backdrop of the steep, snow-covered mountains and a glacier, all bathed in soft sunshine. As we move north through the strait, dead ahead of us, something is happening on a big ice floe. It is the two bears from last night and they have found their breakfast. They are devouring a seal that they have caught out on the ice. Blood covers the floe and it is easy to see that they have dragged the unfortunate seal onto a firmer part of the ice. The bears' faces are now bright blood red as they bury their heads in the seal's body and come out tearing and ripping pieces of flesh, blubber and entrails. Glaucous gulls scream and flap round the edge of the floe. Occasionally, one of the bears makes a move towards a gull to scare it away then returns to the seal's belly. Per edges the ship ever closer until, at about 100 yards, he feels we are close enough to see without being too close to scare them off so that they will lose the meal.

After a while, we move off and leave them to it – after all we have our own breakfast to get still. As we head out into the Arctic Ocean from the islands and turn east we can already see a wall of ice stretching right across the horizon. We are the first ship up this way this season so we have no detailed information from others who may have gone round before us. We steam towards the ice and enter it, with Per taking the ship in a careful but determined manner deeper and

Walruses lie on an ice floe off Spitsbergen.

Small sailing vessels at Longyearbyen, destined for the north of Spitsbergen. (C. McCutcheon)

Stockholm fast in the ice in a sheltered fjord allowed some leg stretching on the ice.

deeper into the pack ice, looking for a way through. Half a mile from the ship another polar bear is busy eating the last remains of a seal, with gulls circling him. He is a large male and he totally ignores us. He stays and chews at the last remains of the seal for some time before wandering off across the ice without a glance at us.

We try to see if we can find a route through the pack to the east all afternoon but there is no clear water. This is the fast winter ice that is still frozen to the land and has not yet retreated. Looking out across the ice through binoculars, the shimmer and reflections create hazy mirages that look like towering icebergs, or lines of icy cliffs of white skyscrapers in the far distance. As we had seen in Franz Josef Land, it is easy to start convincing yourself that there must be land and mountains out there. It is easy to see how the early explorers in the Arctic believed that there was a great undiscovered land to the north.

As it is still only early afternoon, we sail into Raudfjord, but heavy cloud prevents us enjoying the reported beauty of the place. Here, there is more fast ice, which is flat and clear of cracks and we are able to stop and go down onto the ice. The usual round of photography then ensues with people pushing the ship from the ice and stopping her with one hand, etc.

We sailed after dinner and as Per sees little chance of getting any further east he steams straight into the pack, heading due north. He is determined to

Two walruses escape the prying cameras.

As the vast emptiness of the frozen sea stretches across the ocean, a lone polar bear finishes his kill.

The mountains of Spitsbergen and the ice floes of the Arctic Ocean seen from the north.

get as far into the pack as he can and we have a sleepless night listening to the ice grinding past the hull, and feeling the juddering of the ship, as she smashes her way forward and as the ice falls off along the ship's sides. We imagine that there will be no paint at all left on the ship's sides by the morning. However, by morning and we are deep into the pack and up to above 81 degrees north. Soon after eight o'clock, Per stops the ship. The engines are shut down, silence falls and we go on deck to sit and watch as the Arctic world of the ice pack comes to us. It is a wonderful world into which we now find ourselves locked. Large floes of ridged and hummock ice lie all around. It is far too uneven and hummocky to venture out onto the ice as there are deep gaps between the floes that will be fatal if you slip and fall into the water as the floes are in slow, but constant, movement and they will close gently together over your head once you have gone through. Apart from that, the ridges are big enough to enable a bear to move very close to the ship without being seen and that will be a surprise that we might not want out on the ice. There is still no sign of any clear water or leads. The ship sits silent and still all day in the polar seascape while we let the atmosphere and the sensation of being where we are, in the ice pack north of Spitzbergen, sink in. I try to imagine Nansen and his men when they reached the point when their ship, *FRAM*, was frozen into the ice off Siberia and they knew that she would not be released for another two or three years, by which time the *Fram* would have crossed the Arctic Ocean. This would be their world, a world of white, white and more white, apart from the total darkness of the too-long nights of the Arctic winters. They were no radios, no contact with the outside world, and no way for anyone to even know where they were let alone to help them. They were absolutely alone.

Nearby, two walruses emerge from between the floes and lie on a larger floe. They, as usual, are totally disinterested in us and more concerned about settling down for a sleep than any threat that we might pose to them. Eventually, they grow annoyed at our presence, even though we were here first, and both slide gracefully off the floe and back into the water without a splash. They surface, look back at us, and then vanish into the deep. A few of us spend the morning in the bows of the ship just watching and listening to the pack ice as it moves in the slight swell and listen to the grinding and groaning of the ice pack and absorbing the atmosphere.

In the late afternoon, Per restarts the engine and we force our way back out of the heavy pack and move back to the edge. Here, we stop and take the Zodiacs out for an evening ride round the larger floes, looking for seals. A large bearded seal lies on one with its head sticking out over the edge ready for a fast escape if a polar bear comes by. He is a bit surprised to see us appear in the Zodiac but other than that he never moves a muscle. We are within inches of him but he is just not bothered.

We stop and haul the Zodiac up onto a larger floe so we can get a better view of the area. We have already lost sight of the ship. She is out there somewhere but she has already vanished behind the floes. The sun breaks through the clouds and shines on the distant peaks of Spitzbergen that lie low on the southern horizon and are bathed in soft sun light, while the views of some of the mountains are blocked out by the higher ice floes around us. As the sun drops behind the clouds so it brings cold air to the scene and the sea turns from clear and blue to onyx black and opaque and takes on a forbidding look. The sculptured ice statues of some of the floes now look fragile and vulnerable, while in the sun they had been dominant and strong, as the ever-changing Arctic light continually transforms the scene. We feel the chill and launch the Zodiac back off the ice floe. We find our way back through the ice floes to the *Stockholm* and gratefully climb back on board.

South!

It is clear that the ice pack extends right round the northern tip of Spitzbergen and that for all the captain's best efforts the *Stockholm* will not get through to the eastern end of the islands. It had been a deeply cold and late winter in the Arctic so we had expected the ice to still be quite far south. We are just too early in a season. After some discussion, Per and Per Magnus decide to head south and see some of the sights that lie off the beaten track south of Longyearbyen. It seems strange to hear someone say 'We are going south to 80 degrees north'.

The July 14th Glacier

We work our way slowly back down the coast and a day or so later we stop in Krossfjord, where the July 14th Glacier reaches the sea. We are soon in the Zodiacs again and are kept company by two puffins that land by the boats and spend ten minutes paddling along beside us about 10 feet away. They seem to have decided to escort us round their fjord. After watching another group of puffins perched outside their cliff-side burrows, we land on the beach about a mile from the magnificent glacier. Its ice front is about 90 to 100 feet high and is jagged and fractured. It stretches round the bay in an arc about a mile long. The ice at the top has broken into crags, towers and spires of ice, leaning out towards the sea as if waiting to dive in. Crevasses at the top edge open up as they reach the front of the glacier. There are other sections where raw wounds of bright blue ice have been left by ice that has broken away earlier. The light and sun gets behind these scars and throw a brilliant blue hue through the glacier. As the sun shines across the top of the glacier, some parts are a brilliant white while other parts that are shaded are deep blue. Cracks run down the face and at the bottom there are a number of small black caves. This fantastic mass of ice draws us to it like a magnet, regardless of our leader's warnings to take care and not go any nearer. After a short while, a few of us find ourselves at the extreme edge of the glacier face as it curves round at the edges of the fjord to form an ice bay. We sit on a low, shingle beach about 20 feet from the water and with the sheer rock of the fjord side at our back. We can hear the great murmurings inside the beast. Muffled cracks and roars echo round the fjord, but it was all going on inside; on the outside, nothing moves, the frozen exterior is keeping the inner turmoils locked in. This goes on for some time and we watch and listen as the glacier groans and grinds a few yards away. Then, another series of louder cracks and roars ring out and then stop. It falls quiet again, but a piece of ice the size of a house, with hundreds of smaller chunks, silently just lets go of the glacier face. It slides silently and gracefully down the glacier face then trips and falls into the sea. We stare transfixed as it hits the water. 'Run! Run!' someone yells. At the same moment, a 6-foot high wave generated by this relatively small chunk is charging along the beach towards us, pushing other floating chunks of ice along in front of itself. Never have people in boots and parkas moved so fast. We run back along the beach and try to get up to the highest point and round the end of the cliff where we can clamber onto higher ground. We all make it, just, and escape, unscathed. Over our shoulders we see the wave rushing by at amazing

The July 14th Glacier front and the narrow beach.

speed and force. By the time it reaches us it has diminished to about 3 or 4 feet. The wave subsides, peace falls on the fjord and it is as if nothing has happened.

As we return to the ship, anchored safely a mile or so away, and get back on board we can hear the glacier still groaning and roaring away like distant thunder. We stand on deck and watch in awe as a huge section of ice, about ten times bigger than the one we had seen from the beach, collapses into the sea. The spray dies away and we can see the wave the calving has generated. It is a serious one, at least 12 feet high we think. Had we still been on the beach it would have gone well over the top of our boots. We watch as the wave races out from the glacier, rushing up the cliff sides and inundating the beach where we had been walking just a few minutes before. The wave clears birds and flotsam as it goes. What will happen when it reaches the ship? We are anchored in a wide part of the fjord and by the time the wave reaches us it has dissipated most of its energy and it is barely noticeable. We breathe a collective sigh of relief and recognise how, by not heeding the warnings given to us, we could have found ourselves in serious trouble. The message is 'do not to mess with glaciers'.

On the way south we land on Prins Karl Forland Island to study a small group of walruses that have hauled themselves up on the beach and are mostly sleeping. While most are dozing in a walrus heap, one of the young males is in the sea just off the beach and has clearly seen us land and beach the Zodiac.

The world's most northerly train at Ny Ålesund. (C. McCutcheon)

He decides to take a closer look at our Zodiac and swims slowly down towards it. Per Magnus spots the danger and runs back. The walrus reaches the Zodiac and sniffs at it. Then he raises his tusked head over the low stern of the Zodiac by the outboard engine and examines the boat. He then starts to try and get on board the Zodiac from the stern by putting his head into the boat. Per Magnus arrives at the Zodiac and climbs in at the bow, picks up a wooden paddle from the floor of the boat and with a couple of sharp slaps on its nose persuades the young walrus to go elsewhere for his fun. While Zodiacs are very tough and buoyant, they are not designed to act as flotation rings for a ton of walrus. If it had succeeded it would have probably destroyed the boat and certainly knocked the outboard motor into the sea.

By the next afternoon we are much further south in Kaulenfjord. We are relaxing in the saloon having a peaceful cup of tea and enjoying the warmth of sun shining through the windows, and I am thinking that perhaps no one would notice if I slipped away for a nap, when two polar bears are spotted on the fast ice by the shore. We rapidly take to the Zodiacs to have a closer look. As we gently approach, one of them moves off. The other one, however, is obviously in two minds and it decides to stay and see what we are. It then comes quickly out onto the fast ice and continues towards us and the ice edge with a swinging, loping gait and a look of purposeful intent. Is it going to dive into the sea to investigate us more closely? Should we get out of here fast? We watch in awe as it gets to the edge of the ice, then it stops and picks up the red remains of

A walrus approaches the Zodiac looking determined. Will this one be friendly?

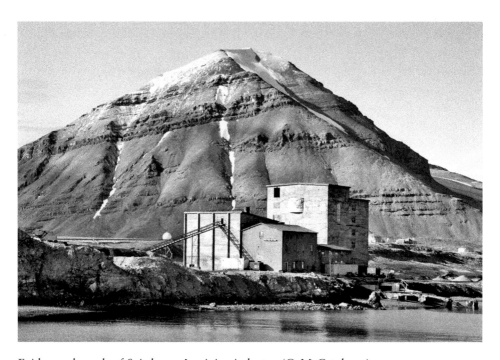

Evidence abounds of Spitsbergen's mining industry. (C. McCutcheon)

a seal carcass, which we had not noticed, and which the bears must have left there when they first saw us approaching. The bear has clearly remembered that it had left the remains of a seal on the ice and has returned to make sure we do not get it. We are able to sit in the Zodiac a few yards off the ice and watch this great beast as it comes out to the edge and collects the remains. It gives us a look that says 'This is mine, so clear off', then it trots off, with the remains of the carcass hanging from its mouth, to catch up with the other one, probably its mother, and together they wander off along the shore.

The day is spectacularly clear, the sun bright and warm, the visibility is endless and the scenery stunning. A few reindeer roam the lower slopes and Arctic birds are everywhere. The mountains all around the fjord glisten in the distance and the calm sea twinkle in the sunshine. Later that day we anchor in a bay by a huge shingle beach. Here, in the middle of nowhere, but not far from some old huts that had been used by whale hunters in the 1800s, we set up a BBQ at the top of the beach using some of the many thousands of tons of driftwood that for some strange reason have come ashore in this particular area. There is driftwood as far as you could see along the tops of the beaches. It is well dried and makes a grand fire. While the food and company are excellent, it is the aura that the place held that makes it magical. The perfect stillness and silence of the Arctic summer's night, the flat sea, the ship lying motionless at anchor off the shore and the mountains in the distance in the midnight sun. Everyone has come ashore and we leave the ship to herself for a few hours.

On our last day we meet up with some walruses, who decide to swim out and see us off. We spend a good hour drifting about them in the Zodiacs before we reluctantly move off.

So we ended this fantastic Arctic trip. It was made in many ways by the ship itself. The ship's warm and cosy interior, her history and the love that Per, her skipper owner, clearly had for her, all built the atmosphere on board and created an environment where we all felt privileged and lucky to be where we were. The intimate nature of a small ship, with just a few good people living closely together, engenders a strong feeling of responsibility as we had to depend on each other if trouble arises. This feeling is impossible to get on large cruise ships as the more people there are on the ship the less responsible one feels as there will always be others there first to deal with a problem. On *Stockholm*, we all felt that we were a part of the crew and not just 'passengers'.

CHAPTER 11

MV *Lofoten*

Arrival on board

The aircraft engine noise dropped away as we slowed for our landing at Kirkenes. The plane banked round and then the engines roared again. As it turned, my weight went against the window and I peered out and down into the gloom. All I could see below us was thick cloud. Then a few breaks appeared and through one of them I caught sight of a grey sea, with white streaks of windblown spray and breaking wave tops. There to the right in the distance was a tiny jetty and a small black hulled ship approaching it. The plane levelled out, the clouds closed in again, and the view was gone.

'You had better book early as *Lofoten* is a popular old ship with the enthusiasts and fills up quickly', the Hurtigturten sales person advised me on the phone. I had selected the *Lofoten* because she was the last typical Norwegian coastal voyage mail boat. All the other ships on the route today, there are fourteen of them, were much newer, larger and more luxurious in every way. *Lofoten*, however, exudes an air of mature dignity, small but beautifully formed. Her black hull and smart, sweeping bridge structure gave her the look of a small, aging aristocratic lady among her bigger, brasher, more upfront and modern pop star celebrity sisters.

I had wanted to go on the Norwegian coastal voyage ever since I had first heard about it as a child. I remember, when I was about ten, going into the Norwegian railways office in Cockspur Street, by Trafalgar Square, and asking for information on the voyage. The excitement of it was that the ships ran from Bergen in the south of Norway all the way to the most northerly ports in Europe, many well inside the Arctic Circle. The ships stopped at all the small towns and villages on the way, dropping off and collecting passengers, mails, and cargo. Originally operated by a number of separate companies, working from different ports with different sizes of ship, these had come together over the years and the Hurtigruten route established. *Hurtigruten* translates as 'fast Route' in Norwegian and is the name given to the service that operates from Bergen to Kirkenes and back.

Now, finally, fifty years after my first enquiry, here I was about to sail on *Lofoten* from Kirkenes to Bergen. After flights from Edinburgh, via Copenhagen and Oslo, I stepped onto a wet, cold and windy tarmac at Kirkenes. It was early October and the temperature was 2 degrees Celsius. The first snows of winter were already on the hills and the low-scudding clouds, which had prevented any view of the town itself from the air, were full of snow and sleet.

At the deserted and windy pier, the *Lofoten* was tugging at her mooring lines and grinding against the timbers of the jetty, eager to be off, as the northerly wind blew her hard against it. I descended the short gangway onto the deck and looked around. There was no one in sight. I went inside and down to the purser's office. A warm atmosphere wrapped around me, and a scent of marine diesel oil reassured me that this was a real ship. I got my cabin key from the purser, who warned me that it would be very rough outside and to be prepared for bad weather tonight.

I found my cabin one deck down on the port side. It was small with two bunks, the upper one folded up during the day and the lower one could be folded back to reveal a settee for daytime use. There was a small porthole right in the corner, over a tiny desk, and a little bathroom area. I was glad that my wife had decided against coming on the trip – the desk would not hold her lipsticks, never mind all the other makeups and hair sprays that modern women cannot live without. As for clothes storage, well, clearly we were meant to travel light. However, it would be ideal for me and I quickly unpacked my travel bag. A few minutes later I heard and felt the ship's engine start up, and the ship was soon straining against the fore spring as she tried to swing her stern out against the wind and depart stern first into the gale.

Lofoten was built in Oslo in 1964 and is a single-screw ship of about 2000 tons. She had none of the modern mechanical ship's aids, such as twin screws, or azipods, bow thrusters or even stabilisers! All her manoeuvring was done by the single propeller; she demanded the highest standards of seamanship and ship handling from her officers. *Lofoten* had cabins for 147 passengers but was about half full on this trip.

Settling In

Once clear of the jetty, *Lofoten* swung round into the wind and was soon steaming out of the Kirkenes fjord and heading for Vardo, some hours away. I set off to explore the ship. The small ship was warm and comfortable, without being in any way luxurious. There were two forward facing lounges with big easy chairs and polished wood panelling. A similar lounge at the stern afforded open views aft and gave access to the after decks. The dining room was a light, comfortable and pleasant room with wood panelling and blue upholstery; the smart white clothed tables already set for dinner. A polar bear skin graced one of the bulkheads in the main stairwell. As we headed north, out of the shelter of the fjord, the sea rose and the wind noise turned to a scream. I decided that a Stugeron seasick tablet was in order to ensure I enjoyed my first meal and had an undisturbed night.

I need not have worried about booking early as the ship was only half full for this October sailing. After looking around the ship, I sat down in the almost deserted lounge at the stern and watched the seas roll by. Out of nowhere an English voice assaulted me. 'Are you the one from England who's just got on?' I twisted round to see from where the voice was coming. It came from an elderly woman, sitting on the other side of the deserted lounge. She was half hidden by a pillar.

'Yes, I did join the ship today, but I have just come from Scotland.' She continued, 'Well you know what I meant, I am Chris. What's your name and where are you from exactly then?'

'My name is Gordon, and I live near Edinburgh', I replied.

'Oh I hear that's a nice place. Oh, by the way they have put us together at dinner.'

Clearly I was going to have company on this trip after all. Chris came and sat by me and we chatted for a few minutes. She was about sixty, of medium build and well wrapped up in a couple of cardigans. She told me she came from Farnham in Surrey, was a pensioner, a widow and was out enjoying herself. She then told me all I needed to know about the ship. She had got on in Bergen six days ago and was doing the round trip. Chris was clearly a real fan of Hurtigruten, the *Lofoten* and her crew.

The ship rolled along, pitching slightly, as we headed northward the dark day turned to an even darker night. As we neared Vardo Island the clouds cleared and a weak moon shone down onto a stormy, white capped sea.

'It will be rough tonight', Chris told me.

'Yes I can see that.'

'No, you don't understand', she said as though I was six-years old, 'This is nothing. Last night I was lucky to stay in my bunk it was so bad. You will see tonight!' She happily warned me. She did have a point, as after we left Vardo we would sail round the most northerly tip of Norway where there was no shelter from the northerly gale now blowing. The ship had come round this way last night in the middle of the gale.

At dinner that night Chris and I are joined by Sheila. She had also joined at Kirkenes, but just after me. We made a tidy British trio for the waitresses. The other passengers seemed to be mainly German with a few Norwegians. A young couple from Glasgow had a table to themselves on the other side of the dining room and kept themselves to themselves throughout the trip. Apparently, they came on the trip, on this ship, every year.

Vardo.

Lofoten was a quiet ship. The only sounds were the creaking of the ship, the deep throb of the engine, the howl of the wind and the quiet murmur of a passed comment between passengers, or the slap of a wave smashing against the bows and spray that rattled the windows. There was none of the 'ching, ching, ching' of slot machines, or a bingo caller shouting numbers into a microphone. No bands or groups noisily rehearsing, or any unnecessary announcements that you got on larger cruise ships. This was what I wanted, a real working mail boat doing its job.

The Northern Ports

We sailed into Vardo where without any noise, raised voices or announcements, *Lofoten* docked. A couple of new passengers boarded, five pallet-loads of cargo were craned on board and we sailed within minutes out into the wild and black Arctic night. We went out past the breakwater at the harbour entrance and began to feel the wrath of the gale, as Chris had warned. I prepared for a night of wild gyrations and being flung about the cabin. During the night we stopped at the ports of Batsfjord, Berlevag, Mehamm and Kjollfjord, but I never heard,

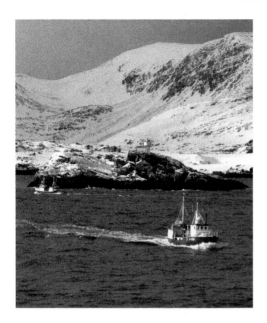

Fishing boats near Havoysund.

or felt, a thing and slept like a baby in my cosy little cabin. By morning the gale had died down.

At 5:45 a.m. the next morning we arrived at Honningsvaag, where it was still dark but the dawn was lightening the eastern sky. I had been here before. It used to serve as the main northerly point for servicing the British deep sea trawlers fishing in the Barents Sea off Norway, back in the 1950s, '60s and '70s, before the deep sea trawling industry died. In those days it was not often that a day went by in Honningsvaag without a British trawler or factory ship being alongside for fuel, or to pick up spare parts, or put a sick, or injured seaman ashore. I came ashore here to start my journey back to the UK from the factory trawler *Arab* in 1975 after I had spent a couple of weeks at sea. The town nestled on the south side of the island of Mageroya, which has as its northern point the North Cape of Norway – a popular tourist spot in the summer months, but not so much now that winter had arrived. We stayed for about half-an-hour then sailed and headed on south as a fine clear dawn broke over the eastern hills and the snow gleamed pink on the hills to the west. The storm had moved on leaving us in cold, clear sunshine and black clouds retreating in the distance. We called at the tiny village of Havoysund, before sailing round the corner to Hammerfest, classified as the world's most northerly town.

As we approached Hammerfest, the ship swept round a headland with a vast engineering complex being built on it. This, we were told, was to be the biggest natural gas processing plant in Europe and would supply gas to Norway and the UK. Hammerfest had been built on the fishing industry, with its own fish processing factories, but today there were few fishing boats about. I went ashore, (just to say I had been ashore) and walked along the skiddy, icy,

Lofoten at Hammerfest.

snow-covered streets for half-an-hour or so, window shopping, before getting back on board and seeking refuge in the ship's lounge with a warming coffee.

We then called at Oksfjord and Skjervoy, both tiny settlements tucked up small fjords. It was difficult to work out how people get to these places other than on the Hurtigruten. A glance at the map showed them to be miles from anywhere, at the end of very long and very winding roads. Oksfjord seemed to be held to the side of a mountain by glue. It had one street and behind that, the mountain face. In fact Norway seems to be one vast jagged rock on the edge of the Arctic, with thousands of rocky shards and splinters of islands scattered around the edge. There must be tens of thousands of islands and islets all along the coast. They offer fantastic harbours and sheltered areas for houses to be built. Houses and towns cling defiantly to these rocks, through all weathers and seasons, and the hardy folk earn their livings from fish and tourists. Up here in the North, the islands are grey barren rocks, some black and forbidding, but nevertheless beautiful with the snow and sunshine. After we sailed the wind increased and the sea developed into a white topped maelstrom, but the islands sheltered us enough so that although we rolled gently it was far from unpleasant and I enjoyed the dinner of smoked reindeer and roast pork.

Lofoten passed down through the fjords and passages between the islands that run all the islands. There was always something to see: another village, a small house all on its own by the water's edge, another mountain, snow fields

Church on the shore.

in the sunshine, passing fishing boats, or the daily excitement of seeing the northbound Hurtigruten ship rushing past us in the opposite direction. It was a daily event accompanied by one of the few announcements and tooting of sirens. Both ships always tried to sail fairly close to each other, if conditions permitted, to give the passengers some added excitement. Today it was the Vesteralen that passed us, her wet hull glistening black and red, and her superstructure dazzling white in the sunshine after being doused by a wild snow flurry.

Life Onboard

One Hurtigruten ship leaves Bergen every day of the year and stops at the thirty-two ports on the way to Kirkenes before turning around and heading back. Therefore, every day we passed one of the other ships somewhere along the way. The ships we passed were the new, bigger ships of 12,000–15,000 tons and fitted out like small cruise liners with multiple restaurants, bars, shops and spas. They sometimes offer night time entertainment with discos and cabarets as well. On *Lofoten* we made our own entertainment, even if it was just sitting with a coffee, watching the fabulous scenery slipping silently past the window, reading, or having a quick nap.

During the day I spent most of my time out on deck, even if it was bitingly cold. A small perspex shelter on the upper deck at the stern allowed us to keep out of the worst of the wind and still see everything. The ever changing scenery and weather made it impossible to want to go back inside. Snow storms swept down from the mountains, blanking out whole sections of the view, then they approached the ship. Their approaches were announced by white horses on the sea, then a swirling wind and finally a battering as the snow blew and billowed around the viewing shelter, while the ship drove forward through the storm. The world turned grey and damp, the cold nibbled at my neck, nose and fingers. The few of us that remained on deck stood in parkas, hats and gloves, watching as the snow eased and the sun emerged from the other side of the storm. The world was instantly blue and clear again. So we passed the time, until one by one we succumbed to the cold and went below for a warming coffee or something stronger. Or, just as we were about to move down below, another small port would appear round the corner and we would stay to watch the berthing, loading and sailing again. The Glaswegian couple, her with her pointed orange hat and he with his orange hair, beard and sandals, spent their time walking round and around the small deck.

The Hurtigruten ships are well organised and proficiently run. There are always two officers on watch at any time meaning that the captain also stands watches, which is unusual in deep sea ships. The captain, or chief mate, whoever was on watch, would bring the ship straight in alongside with the minimum of

The northbound Hurtigruten ship.

fuss so the ship stopped at exactly the right spot on the jetty. The one man on the jetty would handle the ropes; fore-spring first, so the ship could use this as a lever to bring the stern in, the bow rope was next before finally securing the stern ropes. Then he would jump onto his fork lift truck and in seconds have the gangway manoeuvred into position. He shot off on his truck into the warehouse. Then he shot back out from the warehouse with the first of the pallets of cargo that had to be picked up. He jumped down and man-handled the ship's lifting cradle, which hung on the end of the crane hook, under the pallet. As that was being craned aboard and stowed, he had been back to the shed and got the next pallet ready to load. Any joining passengers came on board while this went on. When he had moved any unloaded cargo off the dock into the warehouse he lifted out the gangway, let go the ropes and away we went again. During the whole activity not a word was said, no orders were yelled out and no panic ensued. This routine happened at port after port. I wondered what a British Trade Union representative would have made of it all! One-man operated docks?

The meals were good on *Lofoten*. The buffet breakfast had all you could want from warm rolls and eggs to cereals, herring and smoked salmon. At lunch there was always a choice of three or four hot buffet items as well as a cold buffet. Dinner was waitress served with a set menu. It was always fish one night, meat the next. *Lofoten* always offered good Norwegian cooking and plenty of it. At dinner Chris, Sheila and I enjoyed our evening chats catching up on the day. In spite of *Lofoten* being a small ship we often went many hours without seeing each other around the ship as we all found our own favourite spots to sit, read, knit, paint or just watch the world go by. So the evening dinner was a chance to catch up on the scenes of the day.

It was raining as we arrived in Tromsø, the 'Gateway to the Arctic', at midnight, sailing under the beautiful road bridge over the harbour in the dark but with the lights from the Arctic cathedral, sitting majestically up the hillside above the harbour, shining out through the rain. At the dockside a group of six joining passengers sheltered under the eaves of the dockside warehouse to keep out of the rain. A dockside streetlight illuminated the drifting curtains of rain. Once the gangway was in place, they ran across the quay and through the puddles to get on board keeping their heads down, their bags swinging behind them. The shafts of rain blotted out the lovely wooden fronted shops and houses of the town centre just beyond the quay, and only the masts of the fishing vessels moored in the nearby harbour were visible. Then we were off again.

So the voyage passed; day after day of ever changing scenery and weather, new villages and small towns appearing every couple of hours, twenty-four hours a day. The snow-covered mountains sweeping down to the shore or diving vertically down into the deep, cold Atlantic water of the fjords.

Tromsø, The Arctic Cathedral.

The Lofoten Islands

The ports rolled by, Finnsnes and then Harstad, capital of the Lofoten Islands. It is situated on Norway's largest island, Hinnoya and has about 25,000 inhabitants. The Lofoten Islands were the highlight of the trip for me. This beautiful chain of islands with their dramatic, jagged mountain peaks and narrow deep, sword-slash cuttings are only passed in daylight on the southbound trip. One of the nice qualities of the Hurtigruten is that what you see in daylight northbound is passed in the night when southbound, and vice versa.

We passed through narrow gaps that seemed far too narrow for the ship, but the officers steered us through without any problem. After a stop at Risoyhamn, the sun bathed the hills in brilliant autumn sunshine and we could see for miles up the valleys opening off the main channel. As we approached Sortland, a blizzard descended upon us. Snow flew everywhere and visibility dropped to nothing. The road bridge we were soon to pass under vanished, only to emerge at the last minute as we sailed under its sweeping arch. We docked and in minutes the quayside was inches deep in snow. However, the routine did not miss a beat. A fork-lift truck, manropes and pallets were loaded on and off. In Stormarknes, Hurtigruten have a museum showing the history of the company and even have one of the early ships, the old Finnmaken in dry dock had been preserved as a fixed exhibit. The main museum has a collection of ship models and paintings of the ships that have sailed the route over the years. Unfortunately there was not enough time to study them all and this would have to wait for another visit.

After Stomarknes we sailed through the Lofoten Wall. The ship appeared to be heading for a solid mountain range with no visible way through whatsoever, but as we finally reached the wall the ship gave a little jink to port, slipped past one island, then another jink to starboard and navigated round the back of another – suddenly there in front of us we saw a long passage opening up. This was the Raftsundet. It is 26 kms of dramatic mountain scenery. The low cloud and frequent snow flurries often blocked out the snow covered summits but when they cleared briefly they appeared even more dramatically right above our heads and revealed sides that fell straight down into the deep waters of the Sound. Everyone was on deck now, clad in coats, parkas, hats and gloves but video cameras whirred and cameras clicked as we made our way down this fantastic seaway.

The Lofoten Islands.

Trollfjord

More was to come. In spite of the bad weather the captain announced that he would take the ship into the Trollfjord. Trollfjord is a small fjord, just about 2 kms long and was the scene of a battle in 1980 between fishermen using modern steam-powered boats and those still using open boats with oars and sail. This detour was a real bonus as it is normally only done in summer and even then, only in good weather.

At the southern end of the Raftsundet, *Lofoten* swung round a small pine tree-covered rocky island and headed into a small fjord with no obvious exit. We seemed to have reached the top of the fjord and wondered if this was the Trollfjord. Someone said, 'I think we are going in there!', and pointed out to port. As she spoke, the ship swung to port and we looked at each other: 'Where are we going?' There were only rocks in that direction. 'Maybe we have a steering breakdown', I suggested to Sheila, who had appeared at my elbow on the upper deck. The ship rounded a rocky outcrop and we saw that there was a very narrow strip of water leading off between two sheer rock faces. Sheila looked concerned. 'Surely we cannot get up there and if we can how on earth can we get out?' I shared her concern! This seemed impossible even for our Viking captain! But we did. The ship glided into the eye of the rock needle and straightened up.

She was now aligned with the middle of the channel and we were heading right into the tiniest fjord in the world. The mountains came down to the water on both sides and we could almost touch the flat slabs of rock. Amazingly, as we entered the fjord we spotted a bright yellow kayak coming out. In it was a bearded man, in a bright-yellow oilskin and sou'wester. There was barely room for us to pass each other! 'What is he doing here? Where is he from? We have not seen a village for hours', Sheila wondered. The man skilfully tucked himself and his kayak against the rocks and allowed us to pass into the Trollfjord. He must have been annoyed as he would have thought that he had the place to himself and would not be sharing it with the 'Hurtigruten hordes'. Snow clung to the rough rock ledges and the sides towered upwards into the cloud as we moved slowly up the half mile or so of the tiny fjord. At the top, the fjord seemed to widen just a touch and the ship started to turn around. We all waited for the crunch – it seemed far too narrow to turn round in, especially with just a single screw ship. Slowly, without any fuss, the ship backed up a bit, eased forward again then backed up a bit more, and in doing so the bows slowly swung round and in spite of the lack of yells, graunching noises or expensive sounding crunches we realised that the ship was now facing back out of the fjord.

Later that night I took a walk round the snow-covered, slushy, wet streets of Svolvaer as the ship stopped there for a couple of hours. The town was

Trollfjord.

deserted on this cold and snowy October night, but it looked as though it was a really lovely spot. Tucked up against the mountains of the Lofoten Islands, it had its small harbour, pleasant town square, an interesting looking wooden church and cafes near the water. Another reason to come back, I thought, and do the northbound trip so I can see it in daylight! During the night we stopped at Stamsund and Bodo before we arrived at Ornes in a beautiful clear dawn.

Blue Nose Certificates

The sun was rising far beyond the white mountain tops, turning them black, and the eastern sky beyond was a brilliant blue. At about 11 a.m. we crossed the Arctic Circle, indicated by a large metal globe structure on one of the islands. Now we were back in the south. Later as we were having a coffee, the waitress came over.

'The Captain requests that you and Miss Sheila go to the bridge'. We looked at each other.

'What have you been up to?' I asked Sheila. 'I was wondering the same about you!' she said.

We need not have worried. In the tiny bridge with its big radar displays and the captain's chair taking up most of the space, was the captain in his uniform, the officer of the watch and one of the waiters with a tray of wine.

'Because you got on in Kirkenes,' began the Captain, 'you missed the ceremony for crossing the Arctic Circle, so we do it for you now.' With that Sheila and I were presented our Blue Nose certificates. We shook hands with the captain and the OOW, and were offered a glass of wine to celebrate the event. How very civilised and thoughtful! We were both very pleased that the captain took so much trouble for just two passengers. We stayed and chatted about the trip and the weather, and enjoyed our wine before thanking the captain and leaving them to their bridge.

As we sailed south with further stops at Nesna and Sandessjoen, the winter turned to autumn. The hills were now coloured with reds and browns, and the snows had retreated to the higher slopes. The sun seemed warmer too. At Bronnoysund we had about an hour to go ashore. It was a beautiful, peaceful Sunday afternoon, and I walked along the quay and up through the town and to a small marina. I caught up with Sheila on the way back. She had been window shopping. Sheila spends her time on board sketching and painting the passing scenery, but refuses to show anyone her handiwork. Chris likes just sitting in the lounges chatting and knitting. She did not bother coming ashore but always wanted to know what we had seen or done when we got back.

The polar bear watches from above.

A glimpse of the new ships

That evening was the captain's dinner. It was a fine affair with complimentary wine. A party spirit descended and we all enjoyed the evening. As Chris does not drink she gave me her wine. A starter of scallops was followed by roast beef and then a raspberry soup! (That's what the menu said!). We were finishing dinner when we realised that we were docking in Rorvik. As we secured, today's northbound Hurtigruten, the *Richard With*, appeared around the corner. I went ashore to watch. She was 11,000 tons and seemed huge. She berthed without fuss directly ahead of *Lofoten*. Her black and red hull and bows dominated the dock and *Lofoten* was dwarfed by her. In spite of her size, the *Richard With*, named after the founder of Hurtigruten, is far from the biggest ship in the fleet. The latest trio of Midnatsol, Finnmarken and Trollfjord were the biggest ships in the fleet at 15,000 tons.

As both *Lofoten* and *Richard With* were staying there for an hour, we were allowed to go on board the *Richard With* and have a look around. What a contrast with *Lofoten*! On the *Richard With* the large, wide gangway was deployed hydraulically, as was the huge ramp for cars that opened alongside it. No need for cranes here. The fork-lift truck just drove inside the ship. On board, she was a gleaming floating palace of modern polished decor, chandeliers, glass display cases, expensive gifts, shops, bar areas and even a night club. A big and comfortable looking dining room was situated at the stern and took up most of the rear of the ship. This was a cruise ship, *Lofoten* was a mail boat. It was that simple. If I ever take my wife on this trip, then this was the ship for her.

The Southern Ports

Our next call was Trondheim and a three-hour stop, the longest of the trip, allowed time for a pleasant walk around the town, which is dominated by its lovely cathedral. Trondheim was the home of Eric the Red, who founded the Viking communities on Greenland. The town is situated at the head of a lovely wide fjord and many miles from the open sea, but has been a major trading town on the Norwegian coast for centuries. Many old merchant's buildings, homes and warehouses built alongside the river have been preserved as well as many local streets and houses – they all add to the history of the town. All are wooden and painted in the lovely pastel colours of pink, blue and green that Scandinavia does so well.

A long and pleasant morning sail down the Trondheim Fjord finally brought us back out to the open sea where we found a fresh breeze and a few white horses; *Lofoten* relished the change and rolled gently along as we headed for Kristiansund. This seemed a charming town. It appeared to be built on an island, with the town centred round the attractive port area on the landward side. A number of graceful, high concrete arch bridges seemed to link it to other islands and the mainland. Many different types of ships clustered round the busy docksides, from fishing vessels to oil supply ships, to ferries and small yachts. We only stayed a few minutes but by the time we left and headed out again, the earlier breeze had grown to a half gale and waves smashed against the ship's side. A dinner of a fish soup, halibut steaks and prune mousse took our minds off the weather. Before we had finished dinner we had arrived at Molde on what was now another wet and dirty night.

During the night we stopped at Alesund and Torvik, but I was up early for the last morning at sea and our arrival at the tiny village of Maloy. After the final call at Flora and some delightful autumnal scenery as we wove between the islands, we found ourselves heading up the Bergen Fjord for our final destination.

Arrival in Bergen

Houses, lodges and chalets by the water appeared round every corner. There were small ones, large ones, some with boathouses and some with their own jetties. All looked neat and trim against the greens, russets and browns of

Typical coastal hamlet.

the hills. Most of the passengers were on deck on what was now a lovely late-summer's day. The sun shone, the sky was blue and *Lofoten* steered a straight track towards Bergen. We had sailed from winter into summer and it was almost warm again too. Chris and Sheila went below to pack and I leant on the rail and enjoyed the last few miles of this fantastic trip. We came under a suspension bridge and turned into the huge outer harbour of Bergen. Ahead was the old town with the mountain behind, the offshore supply ships docked along the quays, the ship repair yards and all the hubbub of the city. It seemed a different world from the one we were now used to of small villages and towns, one man on the quay and endless mountains. As the ship manoeuvred into her berth, the traffic noise from the city centre invaded the quiet decks. Our voyage on *Lofoten* was over. How much longer will she go on before she is retired? She will have been in service for fifty years in 2015. Not for a little while yet I hope, as I would love the chance to sail on her again. As an experience of life on the Norwegian coast as it used to be, it was superb, as a restful voyage and a chance to relax, it was brilliant.

We docked on time and as usual, without fuss, at the modern Hurtigruten terminal in Bergen. Designed for the new, large ships, the terminal towered over *Lofoten*, which looked a little lost as she sat quietly at the quay. The telescopic

View from cabin porthole.

passenger walkway gantries that connect the terminal to the large ships sat uselessly high above. *Lofoten's* stubby gangway, as always, was put straight from the deck onto the dockside. As we disembarked, I said cheerio to Chris and Sheila, who were staying in hotels near the airport tonight and had an early morning flight to London. I had a more leisurely start for my flight back to Edinburgh, so I was booked into a hotel in the town centre. I found a taxi and climbed in.

This had been a fantastic trip and one that I do intend to do again, but the other way. Whether I do it on *Lofoten* again, which is a super ship, or one of the new ships with Doreen, time will tell.

CHAPTER 12

Fram and Antarctica

Our first visit to the 'great white south' was in 1993; we promised ourselves that one day, if we could, we would return to the Antarctic, in particular to South Georgia. Exactly twenty years later we managed to keep that promise. When returning to some places, they look and feel the same as the last visit, but in the Antarctic that is not the case. The ever-changing weather, the constantly changing light and vast amount of stunning scenery made us decide that we would have to try and go back. We knew that even if we retraced our exact steps from 1993, we would see the place in a totally different way with totally different impressions and memories to take home.

This time we would sail to the Antarctic in the Norwegian ship, *Fram*, owned by the Hurtigruten Company. *Fram* was named after Nansen's ship *FRAM*, in which he made his historic, Trans-Arctic ocean passage in 1893. Nansen believed in the theory that the arctic ice pack moved in a great circle across the Arctic Ocean; the theory was formulated after the remains from a ship, which had been wrecked in the ice of eastern Siberia, was discovered on the coast of Greenland. Nansen sailed along the Russian coast and allowed the ship to get frozen into the ice and be carried by the movement of the ice pack right across the top of the Arctic. It took three years, but the *Fram* finally emerged from the pack ice of Spitsbergen. In Norwegian *Fram* translates as 'forward'.

We sailed from Buenos Aires due south to the Falkland Islands, then across the Southern Ocean to South Georgia. From there the ship would sail down into the Antarctic, visiting the South Shetland Islands and the Antarctic Peninsula, before re-crossing Drake's Passage to Ushuaia in Argentina, where we would disembark.

We had a few doubts about sailing to the Falklands from Argentina, given the political shouting and gesturing that had recently taken place between the UK and Argentina. However, although UK flagged ships did have a few problems during the year and some were denied entry to Buenos Aires, *Fram* was a Norwegian ship and no such problems existed. In fact we had an Argentinian on board with us. One of the German groups on the trip had brought their own guide with them from Buenos Aires, a young guy, who was pleasant and charming to all and who had not been born at the time of the Falklands War. However, he fervently believed that the Falklands should belong to Argentina.

MV *Fram*

Fram was built in 2007, in Italy, for the Hurtigruten Company of Norway. She was designed as a coastal ferry for the Norwegian coastal voyage, along with her sister ships in the Hurtigruten line. She is 11,647 gross tons, and 114 m long. She is ice class 1A and has a service speed of 13 knots. She can carry 318 passengers, but this is limited on Antarctic voyages to meet shore landing requirements. She had been modified for polar expedition work with her 'polarcirkel' boats, as her specially designed small 'zodiac' boats are called. An especially fitted-out dock for boarding the boats extended from the ships side at sea level. Storage areas for the polarcirkel boats, maintenance areas, as well as a passenger changing area with numbered storage pegs for everyone's boots and heavy polar suits, were all close to the boarding dock. This facility prevented wet mud and dirt being tramped from the shore back throughout the ship.

The *Fram* is beautifully fitted out with bright, warm décor and beautiful artwork throughout. There are many paintings and models reflecting her polar pedigree and connections. Our cabin was spacious and functional with two single bunks, and although not luxurious by cruise ship standards, it was clean, had a big window and cosy bathroom – in short, everything we needed.

Sailing

We sailed from Buenos Aires at noon. Once clear of the harbour, the ship steamed out into the enormous River Plate. It was a beautiful, sunny day as we sailed down the buoyed channel of the Plate Estuary, passing the occasional merchant ship on its way up stream. The river here was so wide we could not see the other side, but the narrow channel kept us aware that sandbanks could not be far away.

That evening, as we were finishing dinner, we felt the ship slowing and looked out to find that we could see the distant lights of Montevideo out to port. We were now at the mouth of the mighty River Plate. The pilot was heading ashore, leaving us to head out into the South Atlantic. At 13 knots it had taken ten hours to sail down the river from Buenos Aires.

We sailed past the site where the German pocket battleship *Graf Spee* scuttled herself after being cornered by the Royal Navy during the Second

World War. Somewhere out there was a buoy that marked the wreck site, but darkness prevented us from seeing it. Over the next few days as we sailed south in beautiful sunshine, with gentle, following breezes and a rolling sea, we got to find our way about the ship. We attended lectures on birds, whales, the story of the original *FRAM*, the Falkland Islands, as well as going on a visit to the bridge. The good weather put everyone into a relaxed and happy mood and as we cruised further south towards the colder weather and as the lectures continued, so our knowledge of the Southern Ocean and Antarctica grew. We attended fittings for foul weather gear and rubber boots and learnt the right way to board a polarcirkel boat.

The Falklands

The Falklands Islands are now well known as the scene of the 1982 Falklands War. Before then there were a number of people who could not tell you where they were let alone anything about them. They lie about 300 miles to the east of the southern tip of South America. The first recorded landing was by the English captain, John Strong, in 1690. The islands were then uninhabited and remained that way for many years but with England, France and Spain all making visits. However, the British eventually occupied the islands and in 1833 set up a garrison there to reassert Britain possession; the islands were declared a Crown Colony in 1840. Since then they have been inhabited by British people who made their living from ship repairs and sheep farming. Argentinian sentiment that the islands should belong to them festered until they invaded the islands in 1982. Long before the conflict between Great Britain and Argentina they were well known for their wildlife, particularly birds, fishing resources and sheep.

    I woke up and looked out of the porthole and I thought we were in the Hebrides. I saw hilly, heathery, misty islands with gorse bushes in bloom. Surely this was the Scottish islands, not the South Atlantic? In fact after a few days at sea, we had arrived at the western end of West Falkland, off Carcass Island. Carcass Island is named after HMS *Carcass*, which visited there in the late 1700s. We had arrived on a cold, breezy day, *Fram* anchored off a long, sweeping beach and we were taken ashore. The polarcirkel boats look like the usual rubber 'zodiacs' that most ships have for ferrying passengers, but they have rigid, tubular metal-side sponsons and a metal floor. They can only seat eight passengers, whereas the more common and larger rubber zodiac boats have rubber sponsons and can cram in as many as twelve or fourteen people sitting along the sides. The benefit of the polarcirkel boats was that they had a fixed structure at the bow which incorporated a set of steps down into the boat. To board it from the ship, the boat was nosed into the end of extended dock-platform and passengers simply walked down three steps into the boat.

This was much easier and safer than the normal over-the-side zodiac loading routine. However, the rigid sponsons meant that these craft banged hard against the waves without any give, and made for a teeth-rattling ride in choppy seas. Zodiacs, with their soft rubber sponsons, bent, flexed and gave to the waves and made for a much more comfortable ride.

Once ashore we really could have been in Scotland. The gorse was in full bloom, filling the hillsides with great clumps of bright yellow blooms. We followed our guides up to a house, set back from the shore, on a raised grassy area. Here, the lady of the house, Lorraine McGill and her husband Rob, had prepared a gigantic afternoon tea for their visitors. We all had tea, biscuits and cakes in their house. She had cakes for all! There were scones, cakes, biscuits and cupcakes. We were told that that when a visiting ship was due, it is customary in the Falkland Islands for the local residents to make tea and offer it to the visitors in one of their houses. In fact, as Rob and Lorraine were the only inhabitants of Carcass Island, they seemed to have drawn the short straw! It was most welcome and very well received, but I do believe they were left with a lot of cake to eat!

The Albatross Colony

The following day, we were up early as we were going ashore at West Point Island. The island is home to the Napiers, whose family have lived here since 1879. The island is not far from Cutlass Island, at the western end of the Falkland Islands. The ship anchored in a small, well-sheltered bay called Hope Bay. We disembarked by polarcirkel boats at a small stone jetty and set off to walk past the house and up the hill at the back of the bay. At the top of the rise the landscape opened out and we could see rolling down-lands stretching away to the horizon. We followed the wide sheep trails along the hillside and across more open hills before, after about three quarters of an hour, we came up to a low pass called Devil's Nose. Here, the hills came in and the tracks converged to meet at the end of a dry stone wall. We joined a muddy track that took us down beside an expanse of tall tussock grass. Once at the top of the pass, the valley started to drop away downhill and we could see the other side of the island with the sea in the distance.

After about one hundred yards one of the guides, stationed at the end of the stone wall, stopped us, made a 'shush' sign, and pointed down into the grass. There, behind a large clump of tussock grass and sitting on an earth mound about a foot high, was a beautiful white albatross preening itself. We realised that we were now standing at the edge of a colony of black browed albatrosses. While not as big as the giant wandering albatross, the black browed is still a large and beautiful bird. The mounds of earth that formed the bird's nests, were well down in the grass tussocks and only visible when we got close to them. The marked path for humans took us right along the edge of the colony with birds on their nests no more than two or 3 feet away from us.

We slowly worked our way down the hillside, through the tall grass, towards the sea. We could then stop and see the vast extent of the colony. It stretched across the valley to the opposite hillside and dropped steeply down towards some cliffs and a windy sea. The wind funnelled up the valley, giving the birds ideal conditions for take-off and landing. At first we could not see that many birds, but as we watched, we realised that most were well hidden and sheltered by the tussock grass. When they moved or took off we could see that there were probably thousands of birds here, covering a wide area of the valley and hill and the steeper areas towards the cliff that we could not properly see. As we watched, returning birds fluttered and wobbled in the air, wings extended and balanced on the gusty wind as they tried to hover. Then, when they were over their own nest, they folded their wings and fell out of the sky onto the mound, in a form of controlled, feathery crash.

As we looked more closely, we realised that there were other birds there too, almost totally hidden down in the tussock grass. These were cheeky looking, red-eyed, rock-hopper penguins and they shared the colony with the albatrosses. No more that eighteen inches tall, they barely came up to the height

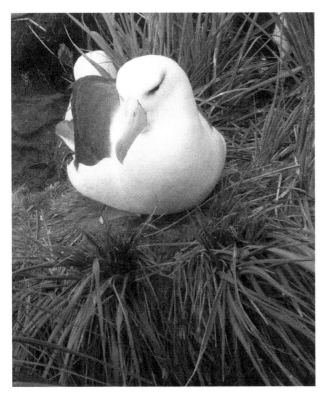

Blacked Browed Altatross.

of the albatross's nest mounds. However, both families of bird seemed happy to share the colony; the penguins busied their way about their narrow tracks and rocks, and the albatrosses slept on their nests. The rock-hoppers, with their red eyes, looked like hung-over, black-suited teddy boys, with fancy souvenir plumes stuck into their caps as they 'strut their stuff' around the colony. While the albatrosses flew up here the rock-hoppers would have to walk all the way. The albatrosses appeared dignified and refined and above it all. Their plumage looked like soft velvet, and their black brows gave them a superior and disapproving look as the tourists and penguins shuffled by their nests.

We returned to the ship via the Napiers' house above the jetty where, as at Carcass Island, afternoon tea was offered to all.

Port Stanley

It was a dull morning with low cloud as the *Fram* sailed into the outer harbour of Port Stanley. We could see beautiful, deserted sand dunes and golden sandy beaches – we later learnt that were they all still full of land mines! Having passed the beaches, the ship swung to port and passed through a narrow rocky gap into the wonderfully sheltered inner harbour. As we entered the bay we could see Stanley stretching along the shore line. A town of what looked like two parallel streets. The houses were mostly single storey and new ones were being built at one end of the town. Stanley grew up as a watering, provisions and repair stop for sailing ships in the 1840s. Its location near to Cape Horn meant that many ships, having survived the Cape, were able to seek refuge there and repair any damage before sailing on up the Atlantic. The opening of the Panama Canal and the arrival of steam ships meant that Stanley was much less visited and the locals turned to sheep farming for their livelihood.

We went ashore and were met by Gerald. Gerald had been introduced to us by a friend who had visited the Falklands a couple of years before. He was a seventy-year-old Falkland Islander and is the fifth generation here. One of his ancestors was sent to Australia on a convict ship for theft, but the ship only got as far as the Falklands, where it was wrecked. Gerald occasionally takes visitors on small tours of the islands. *Fram* was only in port for a few hours so Gerald took us first to Pleasant Cove, which we knew better from the TV news as Fitzroy. This is where the RFAs Sir Galahad and Sir Tristram were bombed in the war by Argentinian aircraft. Fitzroy is the name of the local settlement but the area of water, where the ships were bombed, is called Pleasant Cove.

We looked at the memorials that have been built on the shore: one to the Welsh Guards, and the one to the RFA crew members who lost their lives in the disaster. The memorials have been built overlooking the stretch of water where the ships were hit. They are by a small cove which has a gently shelving beach,

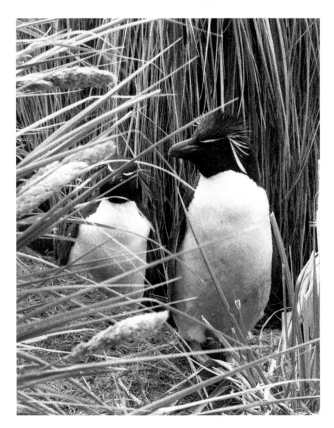
Rockhopper penguin.

and is where a lot of the survivors came ashore in lifeboats or life rafts. If this cove had not been here there does not appear to be anywhere else they could have easily got ashore as the inlet is bounded by low cliffs and rock. That the disaster should have happened at all is still a contentious issue. Why were two fully loaded troop ships sent to this enclosed area of water in broad daylight and without any air cover? The Argentinian soldiers saw the ships masts above a hill as they sailed along the coast and raised the alarm. It was quite moving to try and replay the newsreel films of the disaster and overlay it on the calm, sunlit, pleasant stretch of water we saw before us.

Gerald showed us the mountains around Stanley where the Argentinian troops had dug in to defend the town. He drove us up to Mt Tumbledown, a desolate and empty place, and we saw the remains of a wrecked Chinook helicopter from the war. We were shown the hills that we had heard and read about at the time as the battle moved ever closer to Stanley. We stopped at the foot of Mt Harriet, where the Royal Marines of 42 Commando staged a night attack on the 350 Argentinians guarding the top. The temperature was -5 degrees Celsius and the marines had walked over about five miles of peat cuttings before they were able to start the attack. They captured the hill after five hours of fighting, with the loss of two lives and twenty-four men injured. They took over 300 prisoners. We drove up onto Wireless Ridge, for a view over Stanley. Gerald also mentioned that the radio reporter on Wireless Ridge who famously said 'There are white flags flying over Stanley!' was wrong, and it was actually someone's sheets on the washing line.

As well as the distances between where they landed at San Carlos and Stanley, the ground itself was totally non-user-friendly. Vast swathes of loose jagged rocks covered the whole area and stretched across the hillsides in great swathes. Where there was no rock, then there was tussock grass which, when trying to move across it rapidly as the British soldiers were, would easily snap an ankle or leg if a soldier put a foot wrong. Yomping across this stuff with 50 or 60 pound bergens on their backs, various ammunition belts and pouches as well as carrying a rifle must have been an awesome task.

The lasting impression of the Falklands was one of the vast size of the place. It all sounded so 'local' on the television, but the distances between these hills and Stanley were huge. I had always imagined that Mount Pleasant, the new airport and main UK base, was situated just above Stanley. In fact it is forty miles away. Most of the tarmac roads on the Islands today were just rough, unmade tracks at the time of the war. It is only the army's presence that has generated the money to build proper tarmac roads.

The day had started out cloudy, with low mist and drizzle. As the day wore on the weather improved and the sun eventually came out. Seeing it in sunshine or cloud made no difference – it was an inhospitable, barren and tough terrain. Visualising how the soldiers managed to fight their way across the open ground and then climb up these mountains at night to attack the Argentinian positions made us appreciate their toughness and bravery even more. Overall, while the principles of defending your own territory against invaders must be upheld, regret for the waste of young and brave lives, on both sides, is the natural reaction.

South Georgia

We left the Falklands and headed for South Georgia, a two-day sail away to the south east. Again the wind was astern and a following sea made for a pleasant passage. One afternoon, as we were sitting watching the ocean slide by the window, we were lucky enough to see two fin whales swim side-by-side close to the ship. Their backs broke through the top of a wave as they blew and we could clearly see their size and the small fin on their backs. One of the naturalists had seen them too, and confirmed that they were fin whales. Fin whales are the second largest whales after the blue whale.

After a couple of days sailing we arrived at South Georgia, probably the most beautiful sub-Antarctic island in the world. First sighted in 1675 by an English sailor, it was 1775 before Capt. James Cook was the first person to land here and he claimed it for Britain in the king's name (King George). It was Cook's reports of the vast fur seal colonies that started the rush south by hunters after their pelts. When the fur seal population had been decimated, the hunters turned to whales. There were, at a peak, a total of six whaling stations on South Georgia. By the time the last ones left in 1964, the Southern Ocean whale population had been reduced to an estimated 4 per cent of its original size.

We arrived at the remote Fortuna Bay on the north east coast. Fortuna was a British whaling ship that was wrecked here. As we entered the bay the weather was dull and cloudy, but by the time *Fram* had dropped anchor at the head of the bay, the sun was out. High, snow-covered mountains surrounded us, steep cliffs rose from the water and sea birds wheeled around the ship. In the distance, at the foot of a glacier, we could see a colony of penguins.

The Shackleton Hike

I had volunteered to go on a hike, organised by the ship's expedition staff, called the Shackleton Hike. This hike followed the final few miles of Shackleton's famous, desperate trek across South Georgia in 1916 to seek help and rescue for his men still stranded on Elephant Island, down in the Antarctic. Shackleton and his two companions had already sailed, with three others, in a small open boat from Elephant Island to King Haakon Bay on the west side of South

Arrival in South Georgia.

Georgia. However, Shackleton recognised that neither the boat, nor the rest of the crew, could survive any more days at sea trying to sail round the treacherous northern tip of the island to the east side, which was where the whaling stations were. The nearest whaling station to where Shackleton landed was Stromness, and so he and two companions climbed, walked and slid, nonstop, for thirty-six hours over the Allardyce Mountains, which until then had never been crossed let alone mapped, to reach Stromness whaling station and safety.

We were to attempt to walk the last ten or so miles from Fortuna Bay, over the hills and down into Stromness. For me this was an emotional event. Shackleton has always been my lifetime hero and I had read his account of the trek many times. To be able to follow his footsteps, when he was literally on his last legs and near to death, and to see exactly the sights he saw as he neared his final destination, was awesome.

There were twenty-six volunteers for the hike and six expedition staff. We were taken ashore to the starting point for the hike. It was stressed to us that once we were ashore and moving, there was no going back, as the ship was sailing as soon as we had set off so that it could sail round to Stromness to pick us up. Once we had started, we had to finish.

The shore of Fortuna Bay was home to a big colony of king penguins, and quite a few elephant seals and fur seals dotted the shore around the colony. The king penguins had many brown fluffy chicks with them, which had already had grown to the same size as their parents.

After safety briefings and again being told that this was it, if we wanted to go back, now was the time, we set off. The first part of the walk was a stiff climb up the wet and slippery grassy hillside at the back of the beach, which we had to climb in zigzags, with occasional stops to get our breath back. Shackleton described it as a 'steep snow and ice slope'. We stopped at the top and looked around to take in the scenery. Way down below us we saw the *Fram* slowly sailing out of the bay. To the west, across a rocky plateau, we could now see the grey, black and jagged pointed forms of the Allardyce Range as it stretched across the skyline. The peaks were covered in cloud, but the snowy lower slopes and glaciers were clear of cloud and gleamed in the sunshine. In front of us and stretching away to the mountains was the vast Fortuna Glacier. Shackleton, and his team of Frank Worsley and Tom Crean, had come over these mountains and worked their way around the glaciers until they had emerged at the Fortuna Glacier. It was while they were on this section that Shackleton thought he heard a steam whistle going off. He looked at his watch. It was 6:30 a.m. If he was right and the whistle was from Stromness whale factory, then there would be another whistle at 7 a.m. to get the men to work. The three of them listened intently. Then at 7 a.m. they heard it. A second whistle. The whistle's sound carried up and over the mountains. They were almost there and there were people in Stromness to rescue them. It was the first outside man-made sound they had heard since they had left South Georgia eighteen months ago. They skirted round the north side of the glacier and came down off the mountains into Fortuna Bay. They then walked round the end of the bay to the point where we had just landed and began the final section of their hike.

On the top the ground had turned from grass to loose, broken shale stones, like large pieces of slate, so care was needed to avoid slipping on loose pieces. Where we could, it was easier to walk in the snow-covered areas than on the open ground. Gradually we climbed higher up to a plateau. Here, a halt was called and we sheltered just below the crest of the ridge for a five minute break while everyone caught up and a short rest. From here, the mountains seemed even more impressive and presented a daunting sight. The idea of trying to set off to cross them without a map, or any survival gear was not an attractive idea. Yet Shackleton and his men did it in just the clothes they stood up in and had been wearing for months already!

The extent of the König Glacier and the huge Fortuna Glacier could be seen. It seemed that the whole of the area between us and the mountains was one vast and treacherous glacier. We could see that the route ahead took us down into a small, snow-filled valley, at the bottom of which was a frozen tarn covered in snow. On the other side, our route climbed up again to a high ridge. We could only discern that it was a frozen tarn, as on its flat surface the ice had a blue

Crean Lake on the Shackleton Hike.

tint and darker patches that looked different from the snow on the ground. This was Crean Lake, named after Tom Crean. As Shackleton and his men walked, they were not aware it was a lake until they started to sink through the snow covering the ice and felt it giving way. They hastily retreated to the slopes.

On the other side, the ground climbed again up a shale hillside with large areas covered in snow. We spread out to find the easiest route for ourselves. We crossed the ridge and, like Shackleton, imagined that from the top we would see Stromness. However there was yet another ridge a few hundred yards further on. At the top of this next slope, also a mass of shale pieces, we stopped. There, 2,500 feet below us but still far off, was Stromness Bay, basking in glorious sunshine with the mountains of South Georgia stretching away to the south. To the right we could see the buildings and sheds of Stromness whaling station, probably largely unchanged since Shackleton saw them in 1916. To complete the scene, coming into the bay was the *Fram*.

Shackleton described this last part of their hike as 'extraordinarily difficult'. It was mid-winter when he crossed the island and late spring/early summer when we did the hike. Shackleton, and ourselves, were now in a high pass between two jagged, snow-covered mountains, which dominated the pass. A wall of ice and snow wrapped the lower levels of the mountain and sloped straight down to us. The icy wind whistled up from the sea. From here they descended a steep, snow-covered, shale-scree slope to a small plateau that ended in a sheer cliff. Once at this place they searched for a safe and quick way down to the coast. We found the same slopes covered in snow and descended hundreds of feet through deep, ice-crusted snow to the last ridge and cliff. It was tiring work, stepping sideways so as to keep our balance on the steep slope, moving a step at a time, knowing that if we fell we would roll, or slide, all the way down. The idea of sliding down on our backsides occurred to some of us, but the risk of slamming into a snow covered boulder, or totally losing control and flying off the cliff at the bottom, persuaded most of us to try and stay upright.

At the bottom we stopped on the top of the steep cliff, high above the coastal plain. The whaling station was away to our right, with a flat river plain separating us from it. Once on that it would be a simple walk down the river to the station. Shackleton had the same view, but there was no obvious route down this last cliff. Across to the left they found a river running in the same direction; they followed it, wading through it waist deep at times, to keep moving on downwards. Having come down the steep river course, they found themselves at the top of the waterfall. The first part was over 30 feet high. They could not go back up to find a route round and the rocks beside the falls were all covered in solid ice, so they decided that the only way down was to go down through the falls themselves.

They tied a rope to a boulder and lowered each other down, until the three of them stood, frozen and soaked, at the bottom. This was their last hurdle. They

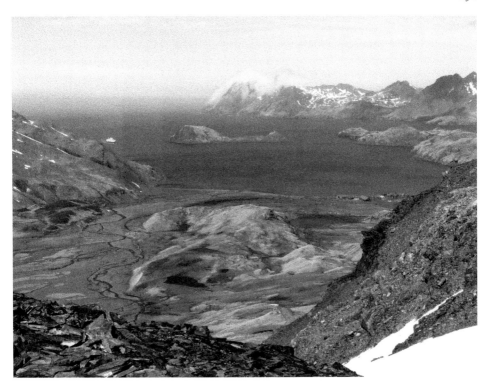

Stromness whaling station from the hills.

then walked, exhausted but exhilarated to have made it, the last 1½ miles to the whaling station and safety. From where we were we could hear the stream and the waterfall across to our left. We were led by the guide across to the left, then we scrambled and slipped down a steep, rocky slope at the end of the cliff until we emerged onto the river plain right at the bottom of the waterfalls. We stood and looked. It was really three waterfalls, the highest one being the biggest, but at over 50 feet high in total, it was a significant obstacle to descend for fit men, properly dressed. For Shackleton's exhausted and starved team it must have been the final kick in the stomach.

We walked and splashed our way through the water, across the wide river bed and its plain, and arrived at the now deserted whaling station just as the first of the other passengers were getting ashore from the ship. No-one lives at Stromness now and our 'rescue' depended totally on the ship's arrival. Unfortunately, the whaling station was abandoned long ago and is now totally off limits due to the vast amount of asbestos that it contains. The nearest we could get was 200 yards. However, the structures and buildings would not have changed much since the day Shackleton arrived here. It would have been good to finish the walk at the factory manager's house, as Shackleton had done. However, it was one walk I will never forget.

The waterfall.

The following morning we anchored right on the middle of Grytviken Harbour, further down the coast. It is a beautiful bay with land on three sides. In front of us the old Norwegian whaling station stood on the shore with the bright, white-painted managers house, now a museum, gleaming in the sun. Derelict whale catchers lay grounded by the factory and the whale meat and blubber reduction plants spread along the shore. Behind the museum we could see the spire of the whalers' chapel. Behind this and on two sides of the bay, the mountains rose up towards the higher peaks and the blue sky beyond. On the third side beyond the shore, we could see the small whalers' graveyard where Sir Ernest Shackleton is buried; low hills led the eye away to the far mountains. Shackleton began his Trans–Antarctic Expedition from Grytviken in 1916. He returned again in 1922 with another expedition but died of a heart attack on board his ship. His wife asked that he be buried here, in the whalers' graveyard, as he loved the place so much.

Grytviken Harbour

Grytviken appeared to have changed a bit since our last visit twenty years before. Along with the wooden store sheds, the old corrugated iron buildings that housed the whale processing factories had all been removed. However, the government had then preserved the huge iron machinery so that visitors could see what the processing plants themselves looked like, without the worry of maintaining a lot of old and decaying buildings. Engraved metal plaques at each site told the visitor what the area was used for and led them onto the next part of the process.

We sailed at lunch time, out across Cumberland Bay and into the Southern Ocean. The captain came on the ship's tannoy and warned us of a windy night ahead. As we headed south along the east coast, the wind gradually picked up from the south west. The scenery was still spectacular and the sun was still shining. However, as the evening wore on, the sun disappeared and the clouds took over. The last rays of sunlight filtered down through gaps in the clouds and illuminated parts of the snow clad valleys and glaciers as we left South Georgia. In the gloomy twilight we saw out first large iceberg of the trip out in the murk and realised we were really now in the Antarctic. Once we had passed Cooper Island, at the south eastern end of South Georgia, and Cape Disappointment, the southernmost tip, we lost the shelter of the island and felt the full force of the wind and sea. The wind grew and reached severe gale force nine as we headed south-west into the wind and sea. It was a rough, bouncy, crashy, night. We were woken throughout the night by crashes and bangs, as loose items in other cabins let go and flew from shelves and desks to crash to the deck. The ship eased her way south-west and the seas let us know who was the boss. *Fram* rolled and pitched but without slamming her bows too much so things did not get too uncomfortable. Our cabin was forward and we heard the anchor cables banging and rattling in their pipes. It was still rough the next morning, but the wind started to ease in the afternoon. By 2 p.m. a wet and weak sun broke through and the seas started to moderate, although the odd wave still gave us a smack. The ship was had only been doing 9 or 10 knots all night, so as not to get damaged by the seas, so we were now well behind schedule.

The Antarctic Peninsula

Our first call was to the South Shetland Islands, first sighted in 1819 by Capt. William Smith, a British skipper who had been blown off course while trying to round Cape Horn. They were named South Shetlands, as they lie on a similar southern line of latitude to the northern line of the Shetland Islands off the north of Scotland.

Icy coast of the South Shetlands.

Southern tip of South Georgia.

Our first call in the Antarctic was Half Moon Island in the South Shetland group. It is a small island, about a mile long, in a large bay off Livingstone Island and it is home to thousands of Chinstrap penguins. The day was beautiful, all blue skies and sunshine. We had already enjoyed the fabulous icy scenery of the other islands as we approached Half Moon. The last time we had been here it had been cloudy, cold and dull, but today was perfect. The island was totally snow covered, so the penguins stood out in their smart black suits and white shirts. We walked across the island, up the hills and round the rocky outcrops, following the penguins' paths as they went about their business. These little fellows, no more than 18 inches high, were totally fearless of humans and regarded us with looks of curiosity rather than fear. They are well named, as the chinstrap marking under their chins make them look exactly as is they are wearing a hat held on by the strap. Having studied us they then got on with nest repairs, or headed back down to the sea. Others waddled their way up the steep and icy slopes back to the colony, carrying small pebbles for nest building.

That evening we entered the amazing bay of Deception Island. It is an active, but flooded, volcano. It last erupted in 1969. From seaward it looks like any other small island, but on the eastern side of the rim of the volcano there is a narrow gap where the ring is broken and the sea is able to flood the volcano. The *Fram* passed through a gap between high rocky cliffs that form the narrow 200-yard-wide entrance, called Neptune's Bellows. Once through, the whole bowl of the volcano opened out before us. We saw that the island was no more than a huge ring of rock around a totally flooded volcano. The warm volcanic water meant it remains ice free and the sheltered location made it an ideal harbour. It was used as a whaling station from 1904 to 1931.

Fram now headed south down the Gerlache Straight, but poor weather dogged us. Snow storms and strong winds broke up the local pack ice and drove the loose ice into bays and beaches, which in turn prevented us getting ashore. We could barely see the entrance to the narrow, ice-choked Le Maire Channel, never mind sail through it. A call at Paradise Bay was postponed and alternative places such a Cuverville Island were also eliminated from the plans. However, we did manage a visit to Port Lockroy, a former British research station during the Second World War. It is on Goudier Island, just off Wiencke Island. Even here, *Fram* had to anchor close to the shore for shelter so that the polar cirkel boats could be used.

The snow and ice on the island was still thick and the expedition crew had to cut steps up over the ice from the sea to enable us to get ashore. The station is perched at the top of a small rise and has its flagstaff with the Union Flag flying. It has now been restored and is a fascinating insight into the living conditions and life as an Antarctic scientist of yesteryear. There were the bunk rooms, a workshop and a galley, still with old food tins, sauce bottles and everyday items on the shelves. Today it is open in the summer months as a post office,

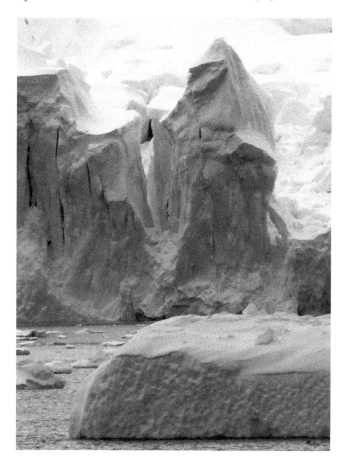

Glacier front in Paradise Bay.

souvenir shop and museum and run by four charming and enthusiastic young ladies, who are all passionate about the Antarctic and friendly towards visitors. Port Lockroy is also home to a colony of gentoo penguins, who cluster around the station buildings as if waiting for an invitation to come in for a warming cup of tea. When we visited, however, a full gale was blowing and the penguins remained hunkered down in the snow. Life in Antarctica carries on regardless though, and we watched one pair of busy penguins mating as the snow flurries whirled around them in a gale of wind.

The following day, our last in the peninsula, we tried again to land at Paradise Bay, supposedly one of the most beautiful bays on the peninsula. However, loose ice along the shore prevented any landings and the frequent snow storms howling down the bay cut the visibility to zero. The ship waited to see if things would improve. They did, but only a bit – just enough for the captain to say that we could launch the boats. So instead of a landing, those of us that wanted to put on big, bright-red, one-piece polar suits and took rides around the bay in the polarcirkel boats. As we motored through the snow, between the bergy bits,

Fram in Niko Harbour.

Fram in Antarctica.

'Sooty' (light-mantled sooty albatross).

the *Fram* often vanished behind ice floes or was lost in snow showers, only to re-emerge, solid and safe across the bay. We motored close to the glacier front and felt the silent majesty of the place. Even in a snow storm the light shone through the ice of the glacier and threw out beautiful blues and greens from deep within. This was as close as we had been this trip to mainland Antarctica and unless the weather improved it would be as close as we ever got.

Once we were all safely back on board the captain decided to have one more try to get us ashore and we headed for Neko Harbour, a short sail through a narrow passage from Paradise Bay. Neko Harbour is a deep inlet that cuts across the peninsula to within about 25 miles of the Weddell Sea on the East side. Neko Harbour is also named after a whaling ship that was moored here in the early 1900s. As we entered the bay, the weather changed. The wind died and we found ourselves in the most beautiful, silent and calm Antarctic scene. The clouds eased away, blue sky appeared, the sun emerged and we were treated to the most beautiful Antarctic views that we had seen all trip. White mountains stretched away into the distance, glistening glaciers and shimmering snowfields stretched right around the bay and loose, broken ice sparkled on the surface of the sea. *Fram* stopped just off a small gentoo colony and we finally got ashore onto mainland Antarctica.

Congratulations were in order as this was a highlight of the trip, standing on the Antarctic mainland. We spent the afternoon enjoying snow, the scenery and watching the gentoos.

Then it was time to go. The ship had to leave for Ushuaia or we would all miss our flights home. It was a beautiful evening as we sailed out of Neko Harbour. Glorious sunshine, a few clouds, bergy bits floating and glistening in the sun and the ice clad mountains, some shaded by the clouds, others spot lit

Entrance to Niko Harbour.

by the sun. A couple of whales were blowing not far off the ship's port side. Our second visit to this fantastic place was almost over and it blessed us with a lovely evening as we sailed up the Gerlache Strait. As *Fram* headed north for Drake's Passage, we spent the evening sitting in the observation lounge watching the sun set on the mountains of the Antarctic Peninsula. It was a sad evening as we realised that it was unlikely that we would ever be back here again.

Our final day at sea was flat, calm and sunny. Sooty albatrosses flew around the ship and we could see Cape Horn in the far distance to the west. Later, a brisk breeze brought a short snow shower, which covered the decks in snow – surely it was King Neptune's farewell to us before we disembarked the next day in Ushuaia.

CHAPTER 13

Akademic Ioffe and the Northwest Passage

Early Exploration – A brief history.

In John Collier's painting, *The Last Voyage of Henry Hudson*, the heavily bearded Hudson sits in the stern seat of an open boat, his staring eyes tired, desperate and searching. His young son sits at his feet looking up for help as Hudson holds his hand. A sailor lies alongside his son and stares blankly at the bottom of the boat as he clutches an animal skin to his chest for warmth. In the background is a desolate snow-clad mountain and floating icebergs; the icy emptiness of the Arctic surrounds them in a situation from which there is no escape. The painting, in the Victorian Romantic mood, portrays Hudson just after he had been cast adrift by his mutinous crew in June 1611, in the bay which now bears his name. He was on an expedition to search for the Northwest Passage. Together with seven loyal crewmen and his son, they were left for dead and were never seen again.

They would not be the last to vanish in the search for the Northwest Passage. Over the centuries many men lost their lives through starvation, disease and scurvy while either looking for the passage, or looking for those that had gone before and vanished. Such tales of horror add to the mystery and fascination of the polar regions and the Northwest Passage has more such tales than its due. Many of these tales, from both sea and land expeditions, tell of shipwreck and survival, of murder, starvation and even cannibalism. It is a region that has attracted brave men searching for glory and the Orient, and even braver men risking their lives searching for compatriots who have been lost in the white wilderness. It was here, in the Canadian Arctic, that Hudson, Frobisher, Davis, Baffin, John Ross, John Franklin, William Edward Parry and James Clark Ross, all found fame.

An early attempt to find a sea route round the top of America was made by John Cabot in 1497, under the orders of King Henry VII. However, the first real attempt at discovering a northern sea route to the orient was made in 1576 by Martin Frobisher, a Yorkshire man and contemporary of Sir Francis Drake.

With Spain and Portugal ruling the seas and the route to the Orient around Africa in those days, another route was needed. Frobisher sailed in a tiny 30-ton bark called the *Gabriel* with two other ships. His voyages, to what is now Baffin Island and Newfoundland, were an attempt to find a route around the top of America, which in those days was thought to be a thin island and not a broad continent.

In 1588 John Davis set out on the first of three voyages with two 35-ton ships, the *Sunneshine* and the *Mooneshine*, with crews of thirty-five and nineteen. They managed to sail up the west coast of Greenland and along the south east coast of Baffin Island, but found no evidence of any route to the west.

The defeat of the Spanish Armada in 1588 meant that Britain ruled the sea routes – this enabled the British to sail around the Cape of Good Hope to India and the Orient and so, for the moment, exploration for the Northwest Passage was no longer relevant. However, the commercial pressures between rival trading companies soon reignited the need for a faster route to the Far East and the search for the Northwest Passage resumed. The Muscovy Company, founded to trade with Russia, employed a Capt. Henry Hudson. Hudson and his 80-ton ship *Half Moon* set out in 1609 and explored the areas now known as Maine, Virginia and New York, discovering the Hudson River. In his next voyage in the *Discovery*, Hudson discovered Hudson's Bay and sailed to the southernmost part where they overwintered. After some strange decision-making and questionable leadership by Hudson, the *Discovery* found herself beset for the winter in James Bay, at the very southern tip of Hudson Bay. By the following spring, once the ice had released them, the crew had had enough and mutinied. Hudson was cast adrift and left. Further voyages in 1610–1616 by Button and Baffin all explored the eastern approaches and Baffin Bay, but all failed to find the Northwest Passage.

Over the next two hundred years others tried and failed either by sea or by land to find the mythical Northwest Passage. By the 1800 some openly doubted the existence of the passage and that if it existed, then it had no viable use as ships had to over winter in the Arctic and consequently lost any time advantage that the shorter route might offer. One such doubter was William Scoresby, a whaling captain from Whitby who had extensively surveyed the northern seas. He advised the Admiralty of his views but was ignored as they did not tie in with the Admiralty's ideas or aspirations. However, when in 1815 the whalers reported that the ice had receded in the polar seas, the First Secretary of the Admiralty, John Barrow, seized on the news, as he had a need to find useful work for the Royal Navy after the defeat of Napoleon. He planned and sent numerous expeditions north and west all with an aim of finding a sea route to the Orient. Increasingly though this was combined with scientific work, mainly in the field of electromagnetics and the earth's magnetic field.

In the early 1800s one expedition, led by John Ross, sailed into Lancaster Sound, but when he saw his route ahead blocked by what he decided was a chain of mountains, he decided that Lancaster Sound was just an inlet and turned for home. At the time a number of his officers disagreed with him, believing that the mountains were a polar mirage. They also disagreed with his decision to turn for home and felt that he should have pressed on to the west.

One of Ross's officers was William Edward Parry, and it was he who later proved that the mountains were a polar mirage and Lancaster Sound continued on through the Arctic. This discovery brought lasting shame on Ross. Parry sailed west through Lancaster Sound to reach Melville Island at 112-degrees-west before being stopped by the ice and forced to overwinter there in Winter Harbour. At about the same time John Franklin had been sent out overland by Barrow to explore the northern tracts of Canada, with the aim of sailing down the rivers to the Arctic Ocean and to discover the Northwest Passage. He led two such expeditions even though the first one nearly killed them all, but he mapped large tracts of the Arctic coast line.

Parry sailed again in 1824, exploring an offshoot to Lancaster Sound, the Prince Regent Inlet. Although not successful in discovering the passage, he did leave a large stock of supplies at Fury Beach which was to save the lives of many who followed later. John Ross returned to the area in 1829 in the *Victory*, a small 185-ton paddle steamer.

The Franklin expedition of 1845 is perhaps the climax of the search for the Northwest Passage. It was the biggest polar expedition ever mounted, with stores to last five years, but it vanished, along with two ships, *Erebus* and *Terror*, and all 129 men, into the icy depths of the Arctic (the wreck of one of the ships was later discovered by a Canadian expedition on 7 September 2014). Franklin's expedition was mounted by the Admiralty to further the science of magnetism, which at that time was a major science, as well as to find the Northwest Passage. The North Magnetic Pole had been found by James Clark Ross in 1831 at 70 N 96 W, and there was a strong scientific need to map, measure and better understand how the earth's magnetic fields and poles worked, as it was vital to navigation at that time. After Franklin's expedition vanished a number of search expeditions were mounted. Those who searched for Franklin also discovered and mapped vast tracts of the arctic seas and islands. They found fame and their names are repeated as place names throughout the Arctic; names like John Rae, Robert McClure and Francis Leopold McClintock.

The final piece of the jigsaw, the Northwest Passage, was actually found during the search for Franklin in the 1850s. It was found by a Shetlander, John Rae, a doctor who was working for the Hudson Bay Company. He spent ten years working as a doctor there and learnt much about survival and arctic travel from the Inuit. Through these skills and his natural stamina, he became involved in surveying the arctic coast to help try and complete the map. In 1854 he had travelled west over the Boothia Peninsula and after cresting a hill, he found himself looking down on what was then known as King William Land. Rae realised that it was actually an island and not part of the mainland, which would allow the passage of a ship round the east and south side of it and so complete the passage. Previously it had been thought that King William Land was joined to the mainland. It was the ice-choked waters down the west side of it that had stopped Franklin and others, but now Rae had found a way past. In fact, it is just one of a number of Northwest Passages, as other routes have since been found further north around the top of Victoria Island. It was John Rae who, through his contact with the Inuit, listening to their stories and examining the relics they had found, was able to report back to Britain on the last days of the Franklin expedition's survivors, and the tales of cannibalism that shook Victorian Britain at the time.

In 1851, McClure in the HMS *Investigator* approached from the west through the Bering Straits to search for Franklin. He had sailed from the United Kingdom with Richard Collinson of HMS *Enterprise*, but after leaving Hawaii they had become separated and did not see each other again, although they did both spend winters off Banks Island. The *Investigator* became frozen-in off Banks Island and they were stuck there for three winters. During that time McClure went out with sledges from Banks Island and realised that he could see Melville Island, where Parry had reached, and as a result knew that he had found the Northwest Passage, or in truth, one of them. In 1854, having given up hope that his ship would be freed from the ice and to avoid starvation, he finally led out his crew by sledge and headed east. They met men from Capt. Kellet's HMS *Resolute*, which was part of Belcher's fleet that was sent to look for Franklin and McClure. Kellet had found messages that McClure had left at Winter Harbour on Melville Island and had come from Beechey Island by sledge searching for him. Consequently McClure claimed to be the first man to pass through the passage, albeit by different ships and sledging.

The Northwest Passage was not finally conquered until Roald Amundsen sailed through in 1903–6 in the small 45-ton herring sloop *Gjoa*. It took Amundsen and his six-man crew three years to make the journey as they overwintered at Gjoa Havn, on the south side of King William Island, to learn all they could about polar survival from the local Inuit. Amundsen was fascinated that a people could flourish in such a wasteland. He studied their food, clothing, sledges, dog-handling and hunting techniques and realised that they were actually highly skilled, given the small amount of raw materials they were able to use to survive well in the Arctic.

It was not until 1940 that another successful attempt was made to transit the Northwest Passage. That was by the Royal Canadian Mounted Police schooner *St Roch*. She was captained by the Norwegian-born Henry Larsen. *St Roch* sailed from the west coast of Canada, and over two winters sailed through from west to east. She then turned round and sailed back again, arriving in Vancouver in 1944; she was the first ship ever to complete a two way crossing.

2014: Our Expedition

I was to join the Russian ship *Akademic Ioffe*. An ice-strengthened ship, but not an icebreaker, she had been chartered by One Ocean Expeditions of Canada. To commemorate Henry Larsen's voyage on board the *St Roch* in 1940–2, we were to attempt a west to east passage from Cambridge Bay, on the south side of Victoria Island in the far north of Canada, to Baffin Island. As part of the commemoration, Henry Larsen's daughter, Doreen, was on board with us and entertained us one evening with a slide show from her father's time in the Arctic.

Bad News

The plan was to fly by charter flight from Edmonton, Alberta, to Cambridge Bay on the southern end of Victoria Island. There we would join the ship and sail east, up past King William Island, through the Bellot Straights and into Prince Regent Inlet. From there we would sail to Lancaster Sound and out into Baffin Bay, finally finishing the voyage at Iqaluit at the southern end of Baffin Island.

Our joining instructions were to stay overnight at the Fairmont Hotel in Edmonton, so that all the passengers would be together and ready for the early morning charter flight up to Cambridge Bay the next day. That evening the expedition organisers, One Ocean, called us all to an unscheduled meeting in the hotel at 7 p.m. As this meeting had not been part of the programme I felt uneasy about its purpose. The news was not good. The operations director, Aaron Lawton, told us that ice conditions near Victoria Island in the southern part of the Northwest Passage, and especially Victoria Straight and Franklin Straight, were so bad that the ship had not been able to get down to Cambridge Bay from Peel Sound, up in the north. Also, McClintock Channel, to the northwest of King William Island, was choked with ice. Getting the ship to Cambridge Bay would require the use of an icebreaker and take almost a week, a week that we did not have. Lawton explained that the ice conditions were nine-tenths pack and made up of old second-year and multi-year ice. This was almost 2½ metres thick.

Had it been first-year ice, about 1 metre thick and not so densely packed, then the ship could probably have got through. In consultation with the ship, they had decided that the ship should make for Resolute, a small Inuit settlement which had a landing strip, on Cornwallis Island, some 400 miles north of Cambridge Bay. Our charter flight would fly us there to join the ship instead, but it meant that we would miss the first part of the voyage. He did, however, say that Prince Regent Inlet was pretty much free of ice and he was sure that the ship would take us down there instead, to see the Bellow Straights and Fort Ross. We obviously had little choice in the matter and we all left the meeting feeling disappointed but still hopeful of having a good trip.

So, before we had even left the hotel, our expedition through the Northwest Passage had failed. We would still be going *to* the Northwest Passage, but not *through* it. It also meant that we would not see the bare and barren wasteland that is King William Island, where Franklin's desperate men came ashore after they abandoned their ships, *Erebus* and *Terror*, and started their doomed haul to the south in the hope of finding help. Nor would we sail through the Bellot Straits, the narrow stretch of water used by Henry Larsen in 1942. It was a big disappointment at such an early stage, but that is the essence of the Northwest Passage. Its history is one of ice preventing ships sailing through and this had added to its fascination and attraction over centuries. For us to assume that we had any 'right of passage' to sail happily through would have been impertinent and naïve, even at the end of the summer season. We were bound by the same laws of nature as everyone else since the 1600s and 1700s. In 2013 the ice was bad as well and ships could not get through, even in high summer. That year's ice did not melt, and only increased with the winter freeze. So much for global warming! There was more ice in parts of the Arctic in 2014 than there had been for many years.

Joining the ship

The Boeing 737 of First Air took off from Edmonton. We refuelled at Yellowknife, then flew out across the Tundra and over the southern part of the Northwest Passage. We could see from the plane the vast sheets of pack ice that choked the main passages. We could see that both McClinton Sound and Victoria Straight had a lot of ice; both looked choked solid. Only a full icebreaker could get through. Looking down at all the ice it seemed obvious that One Ocean had been right to divert the ship to Resolute. We flew on to Resolute, on Cornwallis Island. Resolute is named after HMS *Resolute*, one of Edward Belcher's ships sent to look for Franklin. Resolute is recorded as one of the coldest inhabited places on earth.

Resolute was all we expected it to be. A wind blasted airfield and a small terminal building sitting on a level area of rock, dirt and gravel. A few old trucks sat outside and most looked as if they would never move again. There were large fuel oil drums lying around and a few rusty sheds. This was high summer

Northwest Passage choked by pack ice.

and it looked terrible. It was desolate, bleak and appeared devoid of any life or vegetation. Ice and wind had scoured every living particle from the landscape and it was now just rounded grey–brown hillocks. An old bus took us down to the shore where we gathered prior to clambering into the Zodiacs, trying hard to keep our feet dry, to go out to the ship. Our luggage was put in cargo nets and sent on by zodiac, to be craned aboard the ship. From where we were standing we could see the settlement itself, about a mile away from the airstrip, just a lonely collection of a few wooden huts, nestling down in a shallow valley as if trying to keep out of the wind.

There was no sign of the ship, just a few small ice floes drifting on the current. A flock of Arctic terns sat on one of them, but flew off as we approached. A zodiac ride later, we rounded a low headland and we soon found ourselves on board the *Akademic Ioffe*.

The Ship

Akademic Ioffe (Capt. Poskonny Gennadi), was built in Finland in 1988 as one of two identical, sophisticated ocean research vessels for the Russian Institute of Oceanography. She is 117 m long with a gross tonnage of 6,450. She is powered

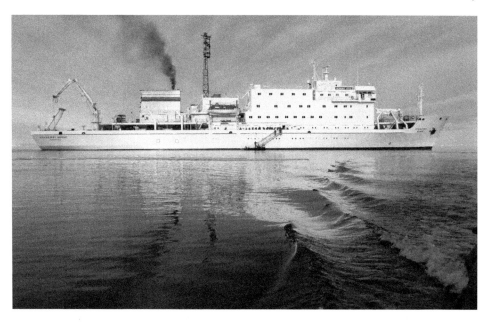

Akademic Ioffe.

by twin-diesel engines, twin-controllable pitch propellers and has a bow and stern thruster. Although not an ice breaker, she is classed as ice strengthened, so is able to sail through ice floes and loose pack ice. She can carry 110 passengers and has a crew of forty. One Ocean staff on board totalled twenty.

I was sharing a three-berth cabin with two other single males. When I got there one of the other two guys had already arrived and claimed a settee birth under the porthole as his. This was Harold, a Canadian who now lived in Arizona; a tall seventy-eight-year old, but still very active. In his working life he had been a field geologist.

We both looked around and smiled. The cabin was tiny. It had two bunks, one over the other athwartships and Harold's settee-birth fore and aft under the port hole. This was already made up as a bed and stayed folded out all the time, despite the tiny size of the cabin. There were some wardrobes, drawers and a small desk, which already had Harold's battery charger and a book on it. I decided to quickly claim the bottom bunk before the third person arrived and so I put my bags on it. I did not fancy trying to clamber down ladders from the top bunk, at night and in the dark, if I needed to go to the loo!

I had no sooner claimed the bunk than the door opened and the third member squeezed into the now, very crowded, cabin. Luckily, like Harold and I, he was also a slim man. This was Dominique, a sixty-year old French man, full of Gallic charm. He accepted the top bunk with a shrug of the shoulders and a 'It will be OK'. Dominique had been a police forensic investigator in his working life. He told us he was here just to see the wildlife, but mainly the birds. We had to use a communal bathroom and showers on the other side of the ship, which only had two loos and showers. We discovered that this was also used by about fourteen or fifteen other guys, all members of the expedition staff, who had cabins on the same deck – it got a bit busy in the mornings. The three of us agreed that the cabin was too small for us all at any one time and only one person could be in the cabin at a time, apart from sleeping at night, of course. So in the mornings I would get up, take my clothes to the shower room and get dressed there after my shower. Then Dominique could get up, and then Harold, who always seemed to sleep better and longer than Dominique and I. At night it was the same routine in reverse with Harold often being first to bed. We decided that unpacking would have to wait and that a coffee was the priority, so we went to find the lounge. The bar/lounge was a cosy and comfortable area towards the stern and had a well-stocked bar and a constant supply of hot coffee. This was the main social meeting point on the ship.

The meals on board were fine, and as good as we could expect on an expedition ship. They were served at single sittings in the large canteen-style dining room. Breakfast and lunch were both self-service buffet style while dinner was a waiter service. A lecture room was one deck down, where all the talks and slide shows were given. In addition, the ship had an open bridge policy, which meant anyone could go up to the bridges at any time. The bridge was large, with large open bridge wings, so there was always plenty of space to stand and watch the polar world go by.

The ship, being Russian, had a sauna, so later that day I went to find it. It was up on six deck (near the posh cabins!). In addition to a large sauna, there were also three shower cubicles, a large changing area with a table and mirrors and shelves full of fresh towels. For the rest of the trip this was where I went up for my morning shower, and as no-one used the sauna at 6:30 a.m. I always had the place to myself. Harold and Dominique must have wondered where I had got to as I was never in the bathroom when they got there and as I never revealed my secret and private bathroom.

First Ice

The first morning on board was icy. I don't mean that the sea was full of ice, but the wet outside upper-steel decks of the ship had turned to ice overnight. It was a bit like black ice on the road. It just looks like a wet deck, but is in fact sheer ice. I had gone outside up on the top deck to take a photo, and the next thing I knew I was flat on my back. Luckily I was unhurt. Others were not so lucky. About ten minutes later Harold did exactly the same thing but badly hurt his leg. He had it strapped by the doctor, but it became swollen and caused him some pain for a few days. When he got home, although the pain had gone, some of the swelling had not and his doctor told him he had a spiral fracture (whatever that is?). Elaine, a lady on her own on the trip, was also caught out. She had decided to go out on deck, slipped on the ice and broke her wrist in the process. She spent the rest of the trip armed with a plaster cast, after having it x-rayed in the Pond Inlet Medical Centre.

Beechey Island

Our first destination was Beechey Island, named after one of William Parry's lieutenants. This is where Franklin overwintered during his first year in the Arctic. *Erebus* and *Terror* anchored in the well-sheltered bay and the crews set up scientific huts ashore. It is also the burial site of three men from Franklin's crew who died that first winter in 1845/6. The three were petty officer John Torrington, royal marine William Braine and able seaman John Hartnell. The graves were found in 1850 by Scottish whaling skipper William Penny, who had been on over thirty whaling trips to the Davis Strait and knew the area well. He was sent to find Franklin by the Admiralty. There was mystery over what they had died of for many years and to some extent that has not been fully resolved, but their bodies were exhumed and post mortems were carried out by John Geiger and Owen Beattie in the 1980s. That evening, Owen Geiger,

Beechey Island graves.

who was in the area on board our sister ship the *Akademic Vasilov*, came on board and gave a lecture. The *Akademic Vasilov* was about to take part in a survey to discover the wrecks of Franklin's ships, *Erebus* and *Terror*. Geiger's book, *Frozen in Time*, is about the exhumation of these bodies and what he and Beattie discovered about the Franklin expedition from what they found at Beechey. He talked about how well-preserved the bodies were after 150 years in the ground, and how it had made it much easier to carry out the tests to see how they died. They found large quantities of lead in their bones, but concluded this alone was not the cause of death. They thought that they had actually died of pneumonia. There is a fourth grave there, just a little further up the beach from Franklin's men's graves. It is the grave of Thomas Morgan, a sailor from HMS *Investigator*, who, having survived three winters frozen-in off Banks Island, managed to get to Beechey Island with McClure, but sadly died on board his rescue ship. His shipmates buried him with the three others.

Beechey Island is a bare lump of rock about 1000 feet high and sits at the south–west corner of Devon Island and joined to it by a thin, low, gravel isthmus. It forms a fine sheltered harbour. The seaward end is high and sheer, although the rock itself is much eroded, leaving it looking like an unpainted and decaying Hindu temple. It tails off to the north and ends as the thin, low strip which links it to the main island. It is totally devoid of vegetation and is greyish brown in colour. The few remnants of Franklin's building, including Northumberland House among other buildings, as well as a small monument put there by his widow, sit on a raised area on the north–east side. The graves of his three men lie to the north, about 500 yards along the beach. The graves are midway up the beach, near to where it starts to sweep round towards the isthmus to Devon Island. The headstones stand alone in the flat, featureless, grey-brown landscape, without so much as a cemetery wall for shelter. Beechey Island is a gloomy, spiritual place, a place where sad history still lives. Perhaps the men who died here died a less painful, or less drawn out and miserable death, than their shipmates who sailed on in such hope, but died of starvation and cold.

Unfortunately, when he sailed from here, Franklin failed to leave any letters or reports, as he was supposed to, to tell others of his plans and his likely course after leaving Beechey Island. In fact, Franklin's orders were that if he discovered that there was no clear passage to the north up through the Wellington Channel, he was to sail south. That is what he did. He sailed north up the Wellington Channel and right around Cornwallis Island, then headed south, down Peel Inlet. Unfortunately, the rescue ships that came later always found Peel Sound full of ice, so they assumed that Franklin could not have gone that way and turned their searches to the north. And so Franklin vanished into history.

After Beechey Island, our ship headed for the Lancaster Sound, but we stopped for a while after two polar bears were spotted on some large ice flows.

Three polar bears in the sunset.

The bears paid little heed to us until they felt the ship was encroaching on their area and then they just got up and wandered off, glancing suspiciously backwards at the ship as they went. These two bears seemed to be either a mother and a large two-year-old cub, or two males together. Soon they were lost from sight behind the ice ridges on the floes.

We stopped briefly at Prince Leopold Island, at the very top of the Prince Regent Inlet, to see a guillemots nesting site on a series of vertical cliffs that rose straight up, hundreds of feet out of the sea. It was a beautiful and calm evening with a dramatic sunset on a flat calm sea. The plan had been to go down Prince Regent Inlet to the Bellot Strait, a narrow tidal channel that runs between Somerset Island and the Boothia Peninsula. We also hoped to go to Fort Ross, a historic site from the Ross expeditions of the early 1800s. However, the satellite ice forecast showed that there was a possibility of the ice cover increasing to three-tenths or four-tenths in the next twenty-four hours. So even though there was still plenty of open water and the forecast ice was thin with only three-tenth ice cover, the expedition leader, Steve, and the captain decided not to proceed. After missing King William Island, with its Franklin connections, due to ice, this was another disappointment. I tried to press Steve as to why we did not spend half a day going to see if the ice forecast was right and his answer

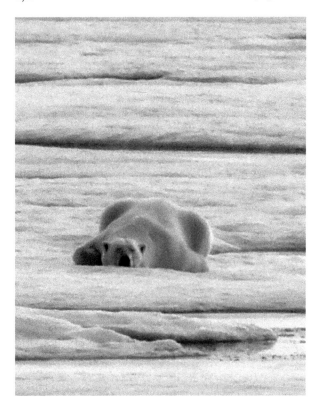

One chilled-out polar bear.

was that it was more important to get us ashore for a walk somewhere than try and get to Bellot Strait. I disagreed as we had come to see the arctic sights, not go for walks. He told us we will not see any more ice and I half wondered whether they were reluctant to take the ship into any form of ice.

That night was beautifully calm and as we stood on deck and watched the sunset; the rich brown colours of the bare hills drained to grey and black, and three bears were spotted on an ice flow. They were a few hundred yards away but the low evening sun turned their coats pure gold and tinged with pink. As they ambled along on the edge of the ice their reflections were mirror-like in the opening of sea beside them. They seemed to be happy to have us near, but not too close and the mother kept a close eye on the cubs as she led them along. One of the cubs spotted a gull sitting on the edge of the ice and made a run and a jump for it. The gull rose gracefully from the ice and watched from the air as the cub missed its footing and tumbled straight into the water. At the sound of the splash its mother looked back in disgust then wandered on, leaving the cub to drag itself out of the sea. Once it was on the ice the mother moved away and the cubs followed, off into the ridges of the floe.

Dundas Harbour

Instead of heading south down Prince Regent Inlet, we sailed north across the Lancaster Sound to Dundas Harbour on Devon Island. Devon Island has the distinction of being the largest totally uninhabited island in the world. Here, a zodiac ride and a short walk took us to some old Thule (pronounced – *Toola*) culture ruins. The Thule people were the indigenous race here before the Inuit and were at their peak about 1000 years ago. We also went to a ruined hut used by the Royal Canadian Mounted Police (RCMP). The RCMP based small patrols up here and patrolled the whole region by dog sledge during the winter and by boat in the summer. This is a similar activity to that carried out by Denmark's larger marine detachment, 'The Sirius Patrol', at Danehaven on the north–east coast of Greenland.

The ship later sailed into the Croker Fjord, named after Ross's Croker Mountains, and everyone gathered on the foredeck while we looked at the face of the Croker Glacier, a large glacier coming down from the interior of Devon Island. Its broad front was silent and still, we all enjoyed a beer on the fore deck in the flat, calm weather while we watched the glacier. In the far distance muskox grazed near the water's edge. During the trip the *Akademic Ioffe* worked her way south down the east coast of Baffin Island with daily landings and a couple of calls to Inuit settlements.

Calm seas at sunset.

Whales and Aurora

The ship then headed east for Navy Board Inlet, a long fjord between Baffin Island and Bylot Island on the north–eastern tip of Baffin Island. The whole area at the northern end of Baffin Island and all of Bylot Island is part of the Sirmilik National Park. Sirmilik means 'the place of glaciers'. After an afternoon ashore at the northern end of the inlet, called Low Point, where we stalked a snowy owl to about 100 yards, we continued sailing up the inlet. It was a favourite spot to see narwhal and the ship steamed to the head of the fjord and anchored to await the morning.

At the very head of the fjord we found the elusive and rare narwhal. A pod of about fifty were swimming in the shallows with a single bowhead whale. Narwhal are one of the most shy and timid of the smaller whales, growing to about 15 feet in length, while the bowhead is one of the largest, reaching up to 80 feet in length, so it was interesting to see them together. We were able to watch them blowing and rolling in the shallows, but as the ship slowly approached, they fled. We spent the best part of the day waiting for them to return on the tide but they had found a quieter corner in another part of the fjord and we only saw them as we sailed out in the late afternoon. This was a great day, as not only had I never seem them before but they are one of the Arctic's most rare creatures. The long tusk of the male has been prized since Viking times and was hailed as the mythical unicorns tusk in Elizabethan England. In fact, the tusk is one of the male narwhal's two teeth and can grow to lengths of about 6 feet. While we were in Baffin Island a local Inuit caught one with two tusks, an even rarer event.

Two separate pods of orca, or killer whales, were spotted over the next two days. The first pod of about a dozen orcas included a couple of big males with tall dorsal fins. Two female whales from the pod came across to investigate the ship and swam round it for some minutes. Then these sleek, black monsters swam fast towards the ship's side and when they were about twenty yards away suddenly dived underneath, causing a volley of shrieks from the women on deck watching it happen. They appeared on the other side and obviously content that we posed no threat swam back to the rest of the pod. The second pod was more reserved but we were able to watch them as we slowly passed them. As they fell astern they formed black silhouettes against a golden sunset. There was one iceberg between us and the sun and this gave the whole scene a golden aurora, while the orcas swam between us and the iceberg showing off their tall dorsal fins. It is always a great thrill to see such beasts and even though they rarely attack man, they are a fearsome sight. They have no natural enemies in the ocean and are known to be highly intelligent.

We had just fallen asleep one night when the ship's sound-system crackled into life. 'Aurora to starboard!' 'Aurora to starboard!' Dominique and I

Orca with iceberg in the sunset.

struggled to get up together and grab some clothes. Not easy in the tiny, dark cabin. We bumped into each other as we hopped into trousers and tried to pull on thick jerseys and boots. Harold remained unmoved and stayed in bed having seen aurora many times in the past. It was a fine aurora show and worth getting up for. Several of us stood out on the bridge wing and watched in awe as we gradually got colder and colder. The aurora stretched right across the sky in a thick ribbon of white light from the southern horizon to directly above the ships mast, shimmering in whites and tinges of green, shot silk swirled and twisted in the heavens for over twenty minutes, widening then thinning, fading then blooming again, before suddenly fading away to nothing and leaving the sky dark again. It was in the south as the ship was well north of the aurora line which runs around the globe at about 70 degrees north.

On the east side of Baffin Island are some majestic fjords. We entered one of these, Scott Inlet, which led us through a narrow gap in the mountains into Gibbs Fjord. This fjord was magnificent. It was another clear, calm, sunny day and the sun imbued the bare mountains with a sandy golden colour. The fjord ran inland for 50 miles, but was only 2 miles wide at the seaward end. We spent the whole morning gently motoring up to the head. The sheer sides of the fjord rose straight up with no shoreline at all, up to peaks of 5,500- and 6,000-feet high. Beneath us the water was 1,500 feet deep. These fjords, which, geologically, are flooded U-shaped valleys, will give the Norwegian ones a good run for their money! Harold was in his element here, giving impromptu passionate talks on the history of the rocks we were looking at and how they were formed, what they were made of and how old they all were. A polar bear was spotted swimming along the shore line, undoubtedly looking for seal or birds.

On the way down the coast the ship stopped at a couple of Inuit communities, first at Pond Inlet opposite Bylot Island, and later at Pangnirtung on Cumberland Sound at the southern end of Baffin Island. Both communities had interesting museums and escorted us round their settlements. At both of these they gave us culture shows covering dancing, throat singing and games for cold nights in an igloo. It was fascinating to see that the games tended to involve inflicting pain on your partner until he submitted. The games needed extreme physical and dextrous exertion, based on one-handed hand stands or press ups! The local folk dancing at Pangnirtung on Cumberland Sound comes from a time when Scottish whalers were regular visitors here and we were treated to a thirty-minute dance. This display was danced to accordion music on a looped, non-stop tape of Jimmy Shand music and was easily recognised as a medley of Scottish country dances. After half-an-hour the Inuits, sticking pretty well to the Scottish dance moves, were all sweating freely and decided that we had seen enough. We were then invited to sample some local food. They served us with whale stew and fish soup, or was it whale soup and fish stew? Anyway I took a bowl of the whale broth. I could not discern any large lumps of whale meat, just some vegetables and some white and grey pieces of something. I asked one of the cooks which bits were whale meat. He said that the white bits were. It was beluga stew made from white beluga whale skin and blubber.

Inuit

In Pangnirtung they showed us a traditional Inuit house. This was not an igloo, but a small, low, single-storey, single-room house of the type they built for themselves before modern, section-built houses arrived. As we arrived, a black and white dog was dozing by the door in the sun. He grudgingly moved to let us in. The roof was low and the only natural light came from a sky light. There were no windows at all. There was a sleeping area, a cooking and eating area and an area for taking off wet, outside clothes. The houses seemed to be made of pieces of packing cases and any spare materials they could find. The roof was covered in heavy plastic sheeting and lashed on with ropes. They used heather as insulation between the wall panels and decorated the walls with pages from magazines! In the house we visited all the walls and ceiling was covered in pages from ladies fashion magazines.

The Inuit learnt how to live and survive well in the Arctic over the centuries. Their food might not have been to European taste, but that was driven by what was available. They avoided scurvy as they ate fresh meat, albeit mainly seals

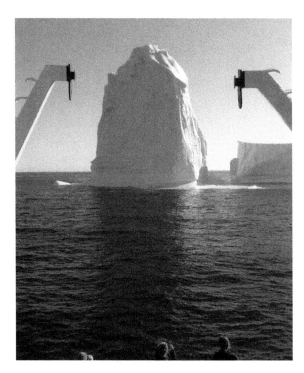

Ice tower iceberg.

or the occasional small whales or polar bear. Scurvy was always the biggest threat to European sailors in the Arctic and certainly badly affected Franklin's men, but fresh meat prevents it, as well as other sources of vitamin C. The Inuit could travel and navigate easily in small groups, with light flexible sledges and dog teams as well as kayaks; they could hunt successfully and live off the sea, land and the ice. They clothed themselves in native animal skins, like seal and caribou, which provided better warmth and insulation than European wool based clothes of the time.

After the remains from the Franklin expedition were found and it had been reported back to the Admiralty by John Rae, a lot of people tried to blame the Inuit for the deaths and the cannibalism. It was probably a reaction to the shock of the discovery, but to me it makes no sense. Why would the Inuit, who at that time did not have guns but could happily hunt and fend for themselves twelve months of the year in the Arctic, decide to kill and eat a crowd of filthy, starved, scurvy-ridden, dying men who even had guns with which the could defend themselves? Why would they then tell the story to John Rae, and others that came afterwards, if they themselves were the perpetrators? If the Inuit were as violent as the Establishment claimed them to be, then there would surely be many sorry tales of battles and killings over the years. The Inuit acted as guides for the white man, provided food for the starving, and shelter when needed. Many Inuit stories, repeated and passed down by Inuit over the years, as well as their tales about sightings of Franklin's ships and men, were borne out to be true. At the time though, the tales were regarded as fiction in the United Kingdom, as they were not what the Establishment wanted to hear. The Establishment's view in the 1850s, simply put, was that 'British sailors could never resort to cannibalism and the Inuit are savages'.

If only some of the European explorers had followed the Inuit example and learnt some of their skills, then polar exploration would have been different. Those who did learn from the Inuit succeeded. Nansen was a believer of their skills and their use of dogs. So too was Amundsen, who beat Scott to the South Pole by three weeks thanks to his dogs and light sledges. John Rae had also learnt their skills and spent years in the high Arctic.

Icebergs

As we sailed down Baffin Bay into Davis Straight we passed many icebergs, some stranded, some sailing free, some tabular, some angular and ornate. One tabular berg was estimated by the captain as over 2 kms long. These had all come from the Greenland side of the Straight, swept around the bay on the circular current.

Icebergs always fascinate people. Every iceberg is unique and every time one sees them, the shapes are different, the light is different and the colours are different. I am always amazed at the variety of colours and textures that make up a berg. The colours run from pure white through to pale blues and deep brilliant blues, and from greens through to soft greys. Their textures range from a solid, white, concrete look to soft ice-cream textures, then to almost transparent glass. One of those we saw was the tallest berg that anyone on board had ever seen. We diverted to look at it and sailed slowly round it. It was a pinnacle of ice standing alone and must have been well over 100 feet high, as it was easily twice to three times the height of the ships bridge and that was 45 feet above the sea. When we got near we could see that the berg consisted of an eroded, but large, tabular base, and from one side of it this huge tower of ice stood tall and erect. Its sides were sheer and its top was pointed, like a pitched roof. It was visible for miles. It was resembled a modern office tower-block made of white granite.

Cumberland Bay found fame, or infamy, during the 1840s and 1860s when it became the centre for bowhead whaling. Previously whalers had operated from their ships out at on the open sea. This was often a dangerous and risky business due to weather, ice, being wrecked on rocks etc. However, in 1840 skipper William Penny and other Scottish whalers entered Cumberland Bay and found not only a new stock of whales, but also that the bay remained ice free up to January most years. About thirty ships a year visited the area and in 1857 a shore station was set up. Some ships deliberately overwintered here, mixing with the local Inuit population. One bowhead whale could produce about 150 barrels of oil and a ton of whalebone which equated to a total of over 15 million over thirty years in Cumberland Sound area alone. The bowhead whale population is now recovering and a whale sanctuary has been set up at Isabella Bay, a huge bay north of Cumberland Sound. We spent a forenoon in Isabella Bay watching these huge whales. Bowheads are the second heaviest whale after the blue whale but are still shy creatures. They can live to over 200 years old so it was incredible to think that some of these whales could have seen Franklin sail by on his way to meet his fate. They swam around the shores of the bay, gently surfacing, blowing then arching their backs as they dived again. Occasionally one would go deeper and put its tail flukes into the air as it went.

I spent some time that evening chatting to Harold. He had spent his working life as a geologist out in the field. He was a cheery guy, easy to get along with and had made friends with most people on board. Among other places that he had been were the Antarctic, where he had spent many months doing seismic work out on the Ross Ice Shelf. He had spent most of his time out on the Canadian Shield, mostly living in tents, and had even discovered a gold mine in the Yukon. He was a widower who had lost his wife to cancer at the age of forty-two, after fighting it for five years. He now spends his winters in Arizona, near Phoenix, and his summers in Vancouver. He is currently writing a book about his life.

By now we had reached the southern end of Baffin Island, having sailed the full 1000 mile length of it from Prince Regent Inlet and Lancaster Sound. We had sailed the northern and eastern part of the Northwest Passage, but just not the southern leg around Victoria Island and past King William Island.

We anchored off the town of Iqaluit, capital of Nunavut province. It lies at the top of Frobisher Bay. Martin Frobisher discovered this area and thought that this was a sound that would lead to the Orient. He thought it was the Northwest Passage itself. However, before he could prove it he was distracted from investigating the area properly by the discovery of gold further south by some of his party. They returned to England with the gold ore and believed they were now rich beyond their dreams. Money was naturally forthcoming to mount further trips to get more gold ore, but unfortunately, after two years work and ferrying large quantities of the ore back to the England, it was found not to be gold at all, but a relatively worthless form of iron pyrites.

We had heard that the town had a problem with a refuse tip that was on fire and the local fire brigade had been called in to sort it out. They decided to pump sea water into the tip to put out the fire. There was no jetty or pier at Iqaluit that we could use to get ashore with cases, so on earlier visits the ship had found a suitable beach landing that was close to a road so that buses could collect passengers and cases.

The first Zodiac to go in discovered that we could not use this landing spot as the fire brigade had closed the road and run their hoses from the sea across the road to the dump. The only alternative was to attempt to land nearer to the town by the small bay used by local craft.

This was fine, except that it was low tide. Due to airline schedules we could not wait for high tide, so we all donned our boots and waterproofs again and paddled from the Zodiacs for 400 yards up the muddy bottom of the small boat haven. However, all went well and they managed to get all the bags ashore too. Somehow we all made it without falling face first into the mud and eventually, our cases all arrived at the airport.

So ended our voyage to try and transit the Northwest Passage in the footsteps of Henry Larsen. 'To but not through' is my definition of the trip, but it is a trip remembered for the great wild life, an impressive display of the awesome Aurora, amazing icebergs and fantastic fjords, which was made all the more enjoyable with two good guys as cabin mates.

CHAPTER 14

Three Key Elements – Ships, the Sea and Ice

Ships

Since the day when I was handed out of the Mail Steamer to the waiting boatman, I have always found ships fascinating. If there are ships to look at, climb on board, or sail in, then I am happy. Why? It's hard to say exactly. There is no one single factor, but a combination of things. Their size is one thing: ships are always big especially when they are in port and you are close to them; even small harbour tugs have a solid, impregnable look and feel to them. Ships all seem to have their own character according to their role and they are living things and traditionally called 'She'. As ladies of the sea, their graceful and elegant lines make them a pleasure to look at. Some are more graceful looking and ladylike than others but, an elegant ship is a beautiful sight while a scruffy coaster can exhibit a tough no nonsense attitude.

In many ways ships are a contradiction. They are designed to do a job of work as cheaply as possible; to carry cargoes and make money. That they can also be attractive to look at is a great bonus. It is hard to believe that the graceful, sculptured hull forms of ships that have evolved in design over the centuries to better meet the elements; are made up from cold, hard, flat steel plates and that they are not created by an artist or sculptor. They could have evolved looking like square railway trucks which essentially do the same job! The wooden ships of old all started out as flat planks on the shipyard floor that were bent and steamed, carved and turned into the right shapes to do the job in the best way they could. Traditionally, steel ships were built from sheets of steel that were cut and bent, in to ribs and frames, and riveted together out on the open slipway. Today ships are assembled as kits, complete hull sections in covered assembly halls. Ships are made up of hundreds of thousands of individual components, sub assemblies, assemblies and even whole hull sections are now built separately and completed with all the internal equipments, fixtures and fittings before they are placed next to their neighbours in the building dock. These are then welded together to form the complete ship.

While ships can have a romantic aura about them, shipbuilding itself is not a romantic occupation. Ask any shipyard worker about working conditions in the shipyards, especially in the old days. Summer or winter they were outside in the wind and the wet, handling huge pieces of hard cold, sharp edged steel; climbing high in the unfinished frames of ships' hulls or working deep inside the machinery spaces. There was the endless noise of the riveting hammers and while modern welding is quieter, shipyards are still noisy and dangerous places to work. However, the workers have the pleasure of watching a new ship being created and most workers develop a strong attachment to her. From the laying of the keel block through to her launch they are a part of her and put part of themselves into her.

Launch Day is the highlight. It is the day they have all worked for. All the yard workers and their families, as well as local VIPs and other guests, gather to watch the launch. Local school children are given the day off and local businesses shut on launch day. The ship herself sits waiting, high and proud, her hull and superstructure freshly painted and gleaming; dominating the surrounding area until the final release from the land so she can slide down the ways and float free at last.

The shipyard directors and VIPs make their way to the special viewing platform at the bows. The smooth lines of the bow tower up, directly above the platform and dwarf them all. The ship's sponsor names and blesses the ship; the champagne bottle swings through an arc and smashes against the bow. The champagne fizzes down the hull and everyone cheers. All eyes watch for the ship to move, but she doesn't. She is still there. What has gone wrong? Then, when the triggers are released and the sliding cradle is free to move, gravity slowly exerts itself on the ship and then she moves. Imperceptibly at first, did it move? Yes it did and now it is definitely moving. The crowd cheers again as this steel monster of a fixed structure that has grown on this spot over many months and now dwarfs all the buildings around her, starts to move. Slowly, silently, she gathers speed. Faster and faster she goes and remorselessly heads for the water. A feeling of awe at the sheer scale of this moving mass grips all who watch and hushes the crowd. A lump rises in the throat as the ship is born but at the same time a fear grows in your heart that she is now going too fast. Nothing can stop her now. She is totally out of control. How can something so big move so fast? She is rushing towards the water, eager to be free of the land. As her stern reaches the river she pushes the waters out of her way sending great waves across to the other bank. She races past the crowds and then the huge drag chains start to work and clouds of rust dust rise from the masses of heavy chains that are attached to her sides. They scream and rattle as they are dragged down the ways behind her, slowing her and restraining her from careering into the opposite bank. Pieces of timber from her launch cradles pitch out from underneath her as she hurls herself into the sea like a child at the sea side on the first day of the holidays. As her bow clears the end of the slipway and reaches the water it dips and bobs up in a little curtsey of thanks to the shipyard and those who have built her. The ship is now afloat for the first time. After the excitement of her headstrong rush into the water she now lies at peace and benignly lets the tugs gather round her and gently take her to the fitting out basin for her final completion.

The other factor common in all ships is the feeling of power: either they have engine power or sail power with which to drive themselves through the seas, no matter what the weather. Whether it is a square rigger, an America's Cup racing yacht, a tug butting its way into a fresh gale or a destroyer at speed, there is a sense of power. Maybe it is the QE2 racing to New York at 29.5 knots through a Force 8 gale no matter what, or a Second World War battleship charging through rising seas, there always is a strong sense of power and supreme confidence. When a ship is at sea, moving under its own power and responding to the forces of the wind and waves, it is a living thing, a warm, vibrant creature and home to the crew that live and work aboard her. But, when it is tied up alongside without her crew, with no generators or engines throbbing away then it becomes a cold, damp and dead object.

Every ship is a unique capsule of life, a world to itself separated from and independent of life on the shore. Ships come in all different shapes and sizes, different nationalities and different cultures. All the ethnic and cultural differences between countries are apparent in their ships. Watching ships lights at night, as they silently creep across the horizon, I wonder not only 'What ship, where bound?' but, what language are they speaking and where is their home, when will they see their families again?

Some types of ship may be of no interest to you until you sail in them and then as you become a part of the ship a relationship develops. Like a human relationship, you get to know and trust a ship. You get used to her motion and learn to live in her. She in turn protects you from the elements and takes you to your destination. Attachments are formed as they become your place of work and your home and they carry you to wherever in the world they might be going.

Just as the launch of a ship is a cause for celebration so the death of a ship is a time for mourning. In Hull I was involved in de-equipping a number of the older trawlers before they went to the breakers yard and it was always a sad experience to see these fine old ships, which had sailed many tens of thousands of miles to and from the Arctic, safely carrying their crews outward and homeward hundreds of times, being towed away to be ripped apart by the oxyacetylene cutters of the breakers. Taking out the radars and radios, was a final confirmation of their fate. This was the point of no return for them. We would watch silently from the manager's window as the once proud and defiant ships, now stripped out and empty and forlorn, were towed out of the fish dock and down to the breakers, never to return. Most of us had memories of each of the ships and their crews and we all felt real pangs of sadness.

The Sea

What is it about the sea that gets into our blood and minds? After all, it is cold, wet and inhospitable; if we fall into it we can drown. The sea can make us seasick and feel like dying. The sea can be rough and it can destroy and kill ships and men. So why on earth should we like it? Perhaps, it is because the sea is a constantly moving, living thing; like the ships that sail across it. It has a life and moods of its own that forces an emotional response from us. The sea's moods directly affect our own and we tend to mirror the moods of the sea. If it is a cold, grey miserable day with white horse and a rising wind, we tend to feel gloomy and depressed. However, if it is a bright, sunny day with a sparkling sea then all feels right with the world.

On a fine day, the gentle waves roll slowly under a boat causing a soft, rocking motion that calms and relaxes us. The wooden thwarts creak quietly, loose ropes slap idly against a mast, or the engine trobs steadily on. The motion is therapeutic and eases our tensions and stress. We feel relaxed and, given a chance, we will nod off into a pleasent nap. The sea gives us the isolation from the land that we often need, the chance to get away from our shore life. The sea is a barrier across which shore side troubles cannot pass. There is always a lurch in the heart when, on departure, the gangway is removed and the last connection with shore life and loved ones is broken. Equally, there is a thill of excitement as we are now on our own. Now we are free! But also, now we and those left behind are alone: we are powerless to help those left behind, just as they are powerless to help us. They are on their own, just as much as we are. For that, we love or hate the sea.

The sea demands 100 per cent attention. Forget it, or take it for granted and it will punish you. It makes those who go to sea appreciate that the day to day events of life ashore are relatively trivial when compared with keeping your ship and shipmates safe at sea. The sea gives us total freedom and perhaps that is why, more than anything, we love it.

The sea is timeless. It is the same today as it was thousands or even a million years ago. It looks the same, it behaves in the same ways that it always has. What we see today is what our forefathers saw when they went to sea. The grey rollers of the Atlantic are the same now as when the Vikings sailed them. It is the same for all men of all nations of all times and we all have to learn to respect it or it will catch us out. But it is also our route to the rest of the world. From any piece of beach in any reasonably well built boat and an infinite supply of food and fuel, we can go, quite literally, to the ends of the earth.

Nothing and no one can stop us. No passport controls, no security checks; nothing but total freedom.

The Polar Regions

The polar regions are remote, and the fact that so few people have ever been there makes them interesting. Hot places with their dust, dirt, sweat and biting insects have never really appealed to me; but I have always wanted to visit cold ones. I love the clean, freshness of the polar regions, the crackling of the crystal clear frozen air, the deep silence and the clear, almost endless, visibility.

I am not saying I like being cold! Liking the cold of the Arctic is not the same as saying I like being cold, in just the same way that liking being alone is not the same as saying you like being lonely. The cold when it gets hold of you is not a good feeling. When the temperature drops to -20 °C and -30 °C then the cold takes on a stronger character. One moment you are feeling warm in your multi layers and down parkas but then, without warming the cold will quite literally grab you. Maybe it is a hand or it will creep down your neck but the next thing you know is that you have this thing attacking you like a vice. The cold presses into your body. You can feel it enter your clothes, sneaking between your gloves and your sleeve. You feel that your clothes are invisible to the cold as it goes straight through them, as if it was penetrating the stitch holes. In a matter of seconds it has got you. It squeezes and goes on squeezing until your bones feel it. Your clothes feel useless, you may as well be naked! Then there is only one thing to do. Get warm somehow! Jump, walk, run, go inside anything to escape this vice like grip that has attached itself to you. Once your circulation goes, in cold like this, it is very hard to get it back by normal rubbing or blowing onto your hands. The secret, I think, is never to stand around and let yourself get cold in those low temperatures. Dress fully inside then go out and keep moving, doing whatever, but do not stand around! At the same time you should not work so hard that you sweat as the sweat will freeze on your skin the minute you stop working. The coldest that I have been in was -34 °C on a flat calm and sunny January day in Finnish Lapland. This would be almost tropical for the real hard men of the Arctic Commandos or real polar explorers. One minute I was warm and standing enjoying the view, the next the vice had grabbed me. With -40 °C, even -50 °C and below with gales force winds and chill factors, what must the cold in the polar winter really be like? A good idea can be found in Apsley Cherry Garrard's *The Worst Journey in the World*. This describes Scott's last expedition to the South but during the expedition three members of Scott's expedition, including Cherry Garrard, made a trip took from Cape Evans on the west side of Ross island to Cape Crozier on the east side, a round trip of over 200 miles, in the Antarctic winter, to search for emperor penguin eggs.

Gales blasted them almost from the start and a storm blew their tent away with temperatures of -50 °C to -60°C. But they survived. How is a mystery to me.

The earliest books I read were often about the polar regions. In the golden days of polar exploration to get to the polar regions could only be done by long sea voyages whereas today it is possible to fly there, so the explorers of the early days had to be both explorers and mariners and often came from the Royal or Merchant Navies. To me those books conjured up a world far beyond our own. To see the sights that they first saw, the icebergs, the glaciers, the endless ice pack: and to experience some of the risks that they took, such as their ships getting frozen into the ice and having to overwinter in it, these were the feats that I daydreamed about when I should have been listening to school masters.

While most of my recent voyages have been as a passenger rather than as a crew member, for me that does not diminish the atmosphere or the excitement that a ship, or a voyage, can generate. It is true that as a passenger you are not a part of the crew and will always be one step removed from the decision making aspects of maritime life. In many cases you will not even be aware of what dramas may be unfolding on the bridge or down in the engine room. Even if you are aware of them then you will probably play no part in their resolution. But never the less, being a passenger is far, far better than not being on a ship at all. You share the same seas and weather; see the same ports and events as anybody else on board and you all share the experience of the voyage and the character of the vessel regardless of your role in it. Whatever happens to the ship happens to everyone on board not just the crew or just the passengers. Being a passenger gives you the luxury of deciding where you want to go and selecting a ship to get you there. As crew you can only sail on ships you are appointed to and can only go to the places the ship is sent.

People sometimes have fixed ideas about the size of ships and will say 'Oh I wouldn't go on anything that small'. Equally some say 'Oh you wouldn't get me on anything that big'. However, whatever the size or type of vessel, once you are on it and it is taking you where you want to go then it becomes your world and your home. You accept it and adjust to it as you do to living in a small flat or a large house. From trawlers to the QM2, from small minehunters to giant Russian icebreakers, they are all ships and were 'home' for a short time and I enjoyed the experience of being there and grew attached to the ship.

Ships that Pass with Time

Time passes and ships pass on due to the changing needs of man and the types of ship he needs. In the Antarctic in the nineteenth century it was sealers in small wooden sailing ships from America, the UK and other northern countries who first ventured south in search of the famed fur seals. The Antarctic continent itself had not even been sighted then and sealing was carried out on the many sub-Antarctic islands. Antarctica was first sighted by a British sealing captain, William Smith, in 1819 when he sighted snow covered land. Reports spread and in January 1820 the Russian explorer Bellingshausen sighted land and three days later land was sighted by the RN's Capt Brantsfield. He had been sent by the Admiralty, with Capt Smith, to investigate Smith's claims. The land seen by Smith was the South Shetlands but Brantsfield sailed on further and found the Antarctic Peninsula. Once the fur seals had been killed almost to extinction and the sealers left, it was the great explorers who held centre stage. They went south in old sealing or whaling ships or specially built vessels like the Amundsen's *Fram*. Men like Shackleton and Scott, Amundsen, Mawson, Biscoe and Ross and many other brave men from many countries who fought their way in, tried to survive the cold and the winds, achieve something for science or exploration and then fought their way out.

With the South Pole attained by Amundsen in 1911, and confirmation that the great southern continent was covered in a mass of ice, interest dwindled; so with the explorers passing another commercial prey was found, the baleen whale. In first half of the twentieth century the only ships that went to the Antarctic were the whaling fleets with catcher vessels and large factory ships, where whole whales were hauled on board up the stern ramp. Now, the whalers have gone and thanks to them most of the whales too. All that remains of those times can be seen at places like Grytviken, and Stromness in south Georgia.

Now fifty years on and it is the specialised ice strengthened expedition ships that pass down through the Roaring Forties into the great Southern Ocean. Ships are now carrying a new breed of crew and for the first time, passengers. Naturalists, ornithologists, lecturers, marine biologists and passengers keen to see and learn about these fantastic and remote regions and the wild life that lives there, rather than working men who joined a whaling expedition for the simple reason that it was good money.

In the Arctic it is a similar story, the first ships to explore the region were the fur sealers from Norway and Russia. Then came the whalers from Europe and Arctic whale camps such as Smeersburg and whaling captains such as the Scoresbys. When Arctic whaling passed its peak in the nineteenth century it was replaced by trawl fishing in the twentieth century. In the UK the old whaling ports such as Hull, Whitby, Dundee Aberdeen and many others became the centres for trawl fishing. Ships from the UK, France, Germany as well as Russia and East Germany, France, Poland and Portugal all sailed to the northern seas from the Grand Banks to Novoya Zemlya in search of cod and haddock and Greenland Halibut.

Again time and industries have passed. During the Cold War submarines and warships patrolled the northern seas. The Cold War is over, so we are told, but some think it is just a lull while Russia rebuilds her powerful submarine fleet.

However, for the moment at least, it is big cruise ships and small expedition ships that sail across North Cape Bank in the Barents Sea past Bear Island to Spitsbergen. Very few trawlers are now seen in these once rich grounds. One wonders what sort of ships will be sailing these waters a hundred years from now. Perhaps the cod will have returned and large scale fishing will resume? Perhaps oil exploration will send drilling rigs and supply ships into these regions, who can say?

There are still many places I still want to visit, and some places I want to visit again. We are very fortunate as we now live by the sea and we can see ships passing by every day. From the VLCCs arriving at the oil terminal with tugs busying around to get them onto the berth, to product tankers and small container ships going up and down the estuary, to the occasional RN ship and large cruise ships that drop anchor nearby. I am a bit of a dreamer and often look at magazines and travel brochures and say to Doreen, 'Ah, now there's a voyage I would love to do'.